Michele Haapamaki was educated at the University of British Columbia and McMaster University in Hamilton, Canada. She holds a PhD in modern British history and writes on contemporary and historical aspects of war and society.

THE COMING
OF THE AERIAL
WAR

Culture and the Fear of Airborne Attack
in Inter-War Britain

MICHELE HAAPAMAKI

I.B. TAURIS

LONDON · NEW YORK

Published in 2014 by I.B.Tauris & Co Ltd
6 Salem Road, London W2 4BU
175 Fifth Avenue, New York NY 10010
www.ibtauris.com

Distributed in the United States and Canada
Exclusively by Palgrave Macmillan
175 Fifth Avenue, New York NY 10010

International Library of Twentieth Century History 65

ISBN 978 1 78076 418 4

A full CIP record for this book is available from the British Library
A full CIP record for this book is available from the Library of Congress

Library of Congress catalog card: available

Typeset in Garamond Three by OKS Prepress Services, Chennai, India
Printed and bound by CPI Group (UK) Ltd, Croydon, CRO 4YY

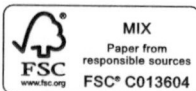

For my parents

CONTENTS

ACKNOWLEDGEMENTS

The process of researching and writing this book has been an absorbing multi-year journey, and along the way I have incurred many debts. I would like to express my appreciation to the staff of all the libraries and archives where research for this book was undertaken: McMaster University, the British Library, the British Architectural Library at the Victoria and Albert Museum, Cambridge University Library, the Centre for Military Archives at King's College, the Islington Local History Centre, the London School of Economics, University College London, and the National Archives at Kew.

I am also grateful for the rich intellectual life I experienced at the McMaster University History Department where this study first began, and the encouragement of colleagues and many friends now scattered around the world. I have benefited from scholarly exchange at the Center for British Studies at the University of California, Berkeley, the Northeast Conference on British Studies, and the Institute of Historical Research, London. My research has been supported by funding from the Social Sciences and Humanities Research Council of Canada. I would like to thank Stephen Heathorn, Pamela Swett, Martin Horn, Stephanie Olsen, and Brett Holman for reading this work at different stages of its development. Tomasz Hoskins at I.B.Tauris provided helpful editorial guidance and I am grateful for his enthusiasm for this project. I thank Tricia Edgar for her careful editing of the text. Any errors that remain are my own. My parents, my mother Idinha Haapamaki and my late father Taisto Haapamaki, inspired and encouraged me in all that I have undertaken, and this book is dedicated to them.

LIST OF ABBREVIATIONS

AASTA	Association of Architects, Surveyors and Technical Assistants
AIR	Air Ministry Documents (National Archives)
ARP	Air Raid Precautions
ATO	Architects' and Technicians' Organisation
CAB	Cabinet Papers (National Archives)
CID	Committee of Imperial Defence
CPGB	Communist Party of Great Britain
CSAWG	Cambridge Scientists' Anti-War Group
DORA	Defence of the Realm Act
HO	Home Office Papers (National Archives)
ILP	Independent Labour Party
LBC	Left Book Club
LCC	London County Council
MARS	Modern Architectural Research Group
MBSJC	Metropolitan Boroughs Standing Joint Committee
MP	Member of Parliament
NA	National Archives (Kew, London)
RAF	Royal Air Force
RIBA	Royal Institute of British Architects
UDC	Union of Democratic Control

INTRODUCTION

Air power may either end war or end civilization.
>   — Winston Churchill, House of Commons,
>   14 March 1933[1]

It is the tendency of every generation to imagine that their circumstances are particularly novel, or that their terrors are newer or more immediate. The fear of sudden destruction, either natural or man-made, has found particular resonance in the industrialized age. It is the thin layer of murky film that lightly covers our collective subconscious, manifesting itself in particular fears at different junctures. In our current young and troubled century the fear of weapons of mass destruction, enabled through science and the devious capacities of the human mind, floats perpetually as a nightmare scenario. Yet our present preoccupation with terror and the possibility of a devastating attack being visited upon Western civilization has long antecedents.

As shattered Europeans were coming to terms with the effects of trench warfare and institutionalized slaughter in the First World War and preparing for the next international conflict, the locus of the threat moved upwards. The capability of aerial bombers to deliver deadly payloads of high explosive, gas, or chemical weapons gripped the consciousness of military men, international commentators, and the public at large. In the words of one historian, 'visionaries, enthusiasts, disarmers, civil defence, and pulp fiction' all contributed to the fear of aerial attack and debate over how the civilian population could be protected from these dangers.[2] In a series of speeches on the subject of peace, the pacifist and philosopher Bertrand Russell gravely advised his audiences that Paris and London could be destroyed in two days during a coming war. Many others echoed this prognosis, and although it rings as hyperbole to the contemporary mind, it was accepted as a near-universal certainty. In a now famous speech to the House of Commons in 1932, Prime Minister Stanley Baldwin summed up Britain's air peril with the memorable phrase 'the bomber will always get through'. This image of doom echoed popular theories of air warfare from the inter-war years, and Baldwin merely reflected these accepted precepts in stating, 'the only defence is in offence, which means that you have to kill more women and children more quickly than the enemy if you want to save yourselves'.[3] Such dire predictions were little questioned by writers, commentators, and politicians of all stripes.

This book serves as a composite portrait of fear of the next war in interwar Britain. Each of its chapters speaks to a different aspect of the 'landscape of fear',[4] to use the phrase recently posited by Amy Bell to describe how emotions were regulated during World War II. The primitive, biological survival instinct inherent in expressions of fear manifests itself in contradictory ways and is contingent on social conventions. As one psychologist wrote about expressions of fear in 1940:

> The whole atmosphere of modern war is likely to revive those unreasonable fears that the human race has inherited [. . .] gas masks that make us look like strange animals; underground shelters [. . .]. Small wonder, then, that we are afraid lest in the face of real danger our first impulse should be to behave like little children [. . .]. We are afraid of being afraid.[5]

These fears collectively impacted how preparations for civilian protection were envisioned. The anxieties of the 1930s, which intensified as the political events of the decade progressed, were intertwined with theories about war and annihilation. As Richard Overy has described it, these omnipresent fears held an 'almost independent existence, external to human affairs'.[6] This study seeks to demonstrate how fear of future war translated into lived historical experience and how it impacted planning for a war in which there would be little distinction in the vulnerability of combatants and civilians.

The complex amalgam of attitudes towards war and the anticipation of aerial attack sheds light on politics and social change throughout the interwar years and into World War II. Fear worked in two directions; first it was created and mobilized for specific purposes by a variety of agents. Interwar accounts of the aerial threat were rarely crafted without some sort of agenda at the forefront – the fear of catastrophic destruction was emphasized for reasons ranging from political expediency to the commercial imperative to sell books or newspapers. Second, commonly accepted fears took on a life of their own, in turn influencing culture, military policy, and domestic politics. The interwar period was characterized by doomsday scenarios of the next war, and the fact that the most drastic predictions failed to materialize in Britain, even during the worst of the Blitz, does nothing to lessen the central importance of these notions to war preparations. The Home Office, simply unable to truly plan for a scale of devastation that might obliterate the capital or cause mass panic throughout the nation, instituted measures that, at their root, were designed primarily to maintain order and prevent a fatal breakdown of morale. This book is about fear, war, preparation for air raids, and citizenship in interwar Britain as demonstrated through the planning for national air raid precautions (ARP). It is particularly concerned with the critics of government plans and how their arguments interacted with expressed fears of aerial destruction; this singular issue offers insight into much of the interwar political sphere.

I will borrow from the notion of a 'culture of anticipation', explored by Roxanne Panchasi in her history of interwar France, *Future Tense*. She insists that 'The Future' is a useful category of historical analysis. The act of anticipating the future can become a sort of collective practice of pre-mourning for a culture that has not yet disappeared, but that is imagined to be quickly dissipating.[7] Though British anxieties differed from the French context, similar themes underlie this study of the threat of aerial attack. Panchasi centres fears of the next war on the new vulnerability of the national *'frontière'* from aerial technology and the protection of the national and individual body through preparation for air raids. The conclusion that nostalgia is generated in advance of, as well as after, a great loss, serves as an important insight into the psychological world of interwar citizens. There was a palpable sense in 1930s Britain of an impending loss of culture, sovereignty, Imperial greatness, and even Britishness itself.

Fear is a complex, intangible, but perpetually intriguing subject of enquiry that mixes the irrational and primal with societal notions of appropriate expressions of emotion. It involves a series of emotional engagements, judgements, and instincts that we can only vaguely begin to understand. Low-level fear is now accepted as an ever-present part of our society – colour-coded terror warnings, health panics, war, crime, natural disasters, nuclear accidents, and weapons of mass destruction dominate the news and our mental space. Our amygdala, the emotional and fear-sensitive centre of the brain, has evolved to respond involuntarily to any possible threat. Fear is clearly a more powerful motivating factor than pleasure, a concept well-understood by politicians, speechwriters, advertisers, and the creators of political attack advertisements.[8] Dan Gardner has pointed out that the modern perception of the probability of an attack by weapons of mass destruction or the chance of being killed by a terrorist are wildly overblown, and ultimately this inflated perception of risk serves the interests of politicians, the media, and the 'terrorism industry'.[9] One academic writer has concluded that terror today is not just of the attacks themselves, but the 'terror of the next attack'.[10] These observations acknowledge the difference between immediate fear and anxiety, and that many citizens find the anticipation of attack more terrifying than attacks themselves.[11] The ways in which terror takes on a life of its own is an important story of the interwar years.

Fear must be understood in both individual and societal contexts, reflecting the customary values and accepted 'emotional regimes'. William Reddy has minted this useful phrase in describing how individuals manage their emotions within specific cultural circumstances. For example, historians of the eighteenth and nineteenth centuries have focused on 'sentimentalism', and the cult of sensibility, as one framework to delineate these vague concepts. Others have used the language of 'emotional community' and 'emotional navigation'.[12] Reddy has pointed out the pitfalls of contextualizing the emotional regimes of past subjects, pointing out that the 'reality' of emotions to the historical subject remains difficult to access. Important studies by Joanna Bourke have also highlighted the problems of analysing this emotion in an historical context.[13] We have no accurate way of understanding how expressed fears were felt at the time and whether recorded fears can be regarded as proportionally reflective of the feelings of the population at large. In addition, the boundaries between fear and other emotions are not always clear-cut – anger, disgust, hatred and horror are also intertwined. And, paradoxically, fear can also temporarily exhilarate. For example, while it is easy enough to imagine the fear that gripped many who endured bombing raids in London, there is also ample evidence of individuals feeling excitement and even euphoria. Most importantly, we cannot assume that 'fear' was experienced in the same way as we would understand it. Bourke, like other historians of emotion, cautions against using contemporary psychology to analyse the feelings of historical subjects.[14]

While we acknowledge the complexity of fear, and its frequent dilution with other emotions, there are many aspects of culture and fear that we can assess. Fear and war, for example, are bound up with culturally appropriate expressions of masculinity as national belonging, as outlined in the work of Michael Roper and Martin Francis.[15] We can also trace the influence of fear in more mundane contexts. Panchasi divides cultures of 'anticipation' into two modes: activity and expectation. While humans acknowledge that the future comes of its own accord, there is a psychological need to balance it with 'activity' to attempt to mitigate anxieties.[16] This

study ties activity into the narrative of interwar fears. The fear of
the future is most often referenced through cultural sources such as
film and fiction, but war preparations, political debate, and physical
planning are part of this narrative as well. As Bourke phrases it,
historians need to ask: 'what is fear *doing?*'[17] The answers reveal the
dynamic of power relations in a society and the mediation between
the individual and the social. This study brings fear and emotions
into the power dynamic of class-based political dissent in interwar
Britain, which translated directly into wartime experience. Fear
does not exist in isolation from other factors such as government
policy. Official structures have an influence on expressions of fear
and *vice-versa*.

The questions of bombing attacks against civilians, and the
attempt to protect the public from such dangers, became much more
immediate than I had imagined when I began research for this book
in London during the summer of 2005. History and contemporary
events collided with the Underground and bus bomb attacks of 7
July 2005. Only a day before the bombings the city had been
celebrating the awarding of the 2012 Summer Olympic Games.
Along with shock, horror, and grief, the most palpable change was an
undercurrent of fear. The people of London did respond with their
characteristic *sang-froid* and I was to witness this as the tense days
of July wore on; yet fear was certainly always present. The
Commissioner of the Metropolitan Police, Sir Ian Blair, warned that
subsequent attacks could not be ruled out, and might even be
expected given the 'clean' background of the attackers – none of
whom was previously known to the police. Security checks appeared
at public places; Underground and train journeys to central London
on weekends, representing casual and voluntary travel, dropped off
dramatically.

With this strained atmosphere outside, I continued my research at
the British Library on preparations for air war in the 1930s. Within
its walls, seated at my softly-lit desk with hundreds of other readers
in quiet contemplation, I read about the fears of bombing that
another generation had faced. There were certainly stark differences
between the two eras. The fears of our predecessors were of a defined

enemy, a nation-state that might bomb cities as part of a conventional, declared war – even if some also suspected that a stealth knock-out blow could occur. Our fears are of a more mysterious and nebulous nature – fears of a terror that derives its power from randomness. An attack almost did occur once again that summer with the failed copycat bombings of 21 July when four explosive devices failed to detonate. The hunt for the four suspects, who had all managed to flee the scenes of their attempted attacks, consumed speculation for weeks. One day later, police mistakenly shot an innocent Brazilian worker, Jean Charles de Menezes, 11 times at Stockwell station, believing him to be one of the bombers. The attempts by the Metropolitan Police to cover up the incident – and initially blame the shooting on de Menezes' own actions, which proved unfounded – created a public uproar and focused civilian libertarians' attention on the powers of the authorities to act against perceived threats. On 28 July, another Thursday, the day of the week on which the two earlier attacks had occurred, the police presence at Underground stations was visibly heightened, a thick tension blanketing the city. The fugitive bombers were soon in custody, arrested in Birmingham, London and Rome. The perception of danger abated considerably for the moment, reassuring an anxious public that this particular threat had been halted.

These dramatic incidents prompt difficult and intractable questions of the extent to which governments may proceed in the name of public safety, and to what extent we can truly be kept safe. The demands of industrialized warfare and the increasing inability to fully assure civilian safety have forced an ongoing re-evaluation of how we view the role of government and the functioning of democracy. Government and police forces in Western democracies may tackle terrorist threats in an overzealous and authoritarian manner. Yet citizens also wish to be assured, as did interwar Britons, that their government is doing *enough* to protect their safety. The balance between security, liberty, and governmental power – the subject of countless newspaper columns, books, and television debates – is an extremely fine one. We now find ourselves at the opposite end of the spectrum as our interwar forebears whose main concern, detailed in this study, might have been too *little* government intervention and too *much* 'self-help'.

*

This book is a contribution towards the growing scholarly literature about civilian defence, which has begun linking it to broader cultural, social and political developments. Earlier studies have tended to focus either on government policy and military preparedness before the war, or else on subjects such as the experience of aerial bombardment by civilians during World War II itself, most particularly the Blitz. The official British government histories of ARP, published in the 1950s, were *Problems of Social Policy* by Richard Titmuss and Terence O'Brien's *Civil Defence*.[18] These accounts set out themes that would be followed by military historians for several decades, depicting ARP as an adjunct to strategic policy and a function of 'top down' bureaucracy. Literature about interwar military planning has thus largely treated the subject of ARP as a minor facet of national war preparedness. One historian has noted that the dearth of literature, especially official literature, on the interwar formation of ARP may be due to the fact that the subject was viewed as an 'embarrassment for central government'.[19]

Public reaction to ARP in the 1930s was extremely complex, with a mixture of fear, indifference and resigned acceptance. It has therefore been difficult to access public feeling and to craft coherent narratives of how government policies were received. In an influential article on the critics of government plans, Joseph Meisel has suggested new directions for the study of ARP through the consideration of critics and ideological differences with central government.[20] His narrative is a step towards placing the critics of ARP within a wider perspective, considering the debate as a clash between the fundamentally different views of civil society held by the government on the one hand and progressive scientists and ARP activists on the other. Another means of assessing public reaction to ARP has been to consider the role of the local authorities and activists in the administration of ARP, a subject explored in the articles of

Robin Woolven. The provision of most services was highly localized, producing problems and opportunities for local councils.[21] I will pick up on these themes in this narrative, demonstrating that criticism often devolved to the local level, further expanding on the activism of the Borough of Finsbury referenced by Meisel.

Other approaches have placed the provision of shelters and civil defence within the broadly defined issue of 'morale'. As one historian on the subject has described it, civilian morale is one of the 'woolliest' concepts to explore.[22] Yet we have been able to assess, for example, the importance of community and the strength of social structures in how people perceived the threat of air raids.[23] Morale functioned in both a negative sense – fear of civilian breakdown – but also in a positive sense, denoting the necessity to inspire sacrificial public effort. A recent important intervention into the field has been Susan Grayzel's *At Home and Under Fire*. She emphasizes continuities between World War I and II and makes an important contribution towards understanding the importance of gender in 'domesticating the air raid' and providing a universal model of wartime civil identity and citizenship. She views interwar developments as contributing to a non-gender-specific type of civil behaviour denoted primarily as 'stoicism'.[24] My book echoes Grayzel's insistence on the need to consider wartime in a larger timeframe. It will also pick up on other important strands of the civilian–state relationship in the interwar years. My contribution to the literature is twofold: first, a deeper study of the critics of government ARP, particularly regarding the evolution of their arguments, than has been done in previous work. Second, it explores fear as more than a question of scaremongering literature or government worries over civilian morale by following Bourke's question: 'what is fear *doing*?' 'Fearmongering' consisted of a two-sided dialogue between critics and government with an aim to provoking action, and it provided the grounds for contesting views of citizenship and the role of civilians in wartime.

The exploration of this 'culture of fear' serves as the background for the main concern of this book: the multiple meanings of the 'People's War', the creation of wartime narratives and myth-making, and citizenship. The overriding argument suggests that debates over air raids, fear, and the planning for war presaged the notion of the People's War. These ideas, and the building of popular wartime mythology, have provided a seemingly endless wealth of material for historians to analyse and deconstruct. The latter movement has been led by Angus Calder's landmark book *The Myth of the Blitz*, which explored the extent to which wartime social relations were still bound by old constraints, including that of class.[25] Historians such as Stephen Fielding have taken issue with the previous narratives of the People's War as the sole, be-all-end-all driver of social change that led towards the postwar welfare state.[26] The phrase, however, did reflect how many *wished* to view the war, and we are concerned with how the term was defined by different constituencies. Some historians, such as Robert Mackay, have proffered a 'counter-revisionist' perspective, highlighting that civilian morale and social cohesion were far stronger than 'elites' had imagined, and operated at a level far above 'propaganda'.[27]

My study contributes to this area of historical enquiry in two ways. First, it casts the People's War in a much longer time frame than simply the events of the war itself. It is important for historians to integrate the events of the 1930s, particularly regarding domestic politics, substantively into their narratives of the wartime psyche. This book reflects the view that a longer continuum must be taken into account, extending at least from the end of the First World War. It brings various meanings of the People's War forward to include politics and culture in the 1930s. Wartime issues, including class divisions and integration of civilians into the total war, were related directly to the fear of aerial warfare, the debates of the interwar years and the degree of protection that civilians could expect from their government. These subjects reflect a vast-ranging area of study, and this book is representative of only several core debates regarding ARP. There are many other elements beyond its scope; I touch only lightly on concurrent discussions, including deep-seated pacifist protest, feminist arguments, the material culture of publicity and supplies such as gas masks, and the structure of ARP administration at both local and national levels. Second, this work expands on conceptions of citizenship and belonging from the perspective of

ARP critics. It reflects on what it meant to be part of the moral community that they espoused; critics emphasized the responsibilities of *government* in return for patriotic service. Studies of the national community have emphasized the performance aspects of wartime identity. Sonya Rose explains that during World War II, citizenship was predominantly understood to be a moral and ethical practice to enable the nation to survive the extremes of the war. This patriotic discourse focused on the self-sacrifice of citizens in the national community, but furthermore presented the notion of a 'moral community' that would build a 'new Britain' following the war.[28] Historians such as Lucy Noakes and Susan Grayzel have contributed to an understanding of what it meant to belong to the national community, particularly as it related to gender.[29] These ideas were based on a long-standing concept of the British nation, but with a new popular twist that promised material reward for patriotism. The experience of the First World War proved that government could intervene in the economy, having a positive impact on employment, standards of living, and social welfare. The critics of government ARP were keen to capitalize on this notion.

Differing political factions used the narrative of the People's War to derive the ideological capital they desired. For some, the results of the 1945 election were the communitarian fruits of socialism. Many of the subjects of this study, who constituted the core of ARP critics, belonged to various hues of the left. However, the ARP debate is not merely a political story of the hard left, though many of the prominent critics were unofficially aligned with radical politics. I argue that the significance of these discussions belongs equally to the moderate, mainstream debate over the role of the state – arguments that were at the core of the People's War and which originated in the Labour movement of the late Victorian and Edwardian eras. The critics spoke as professionals, academics and scientists who were wholly integrated into professional and public life, and they fall within the tradition of reform and dissent rather than revolutionary impulse. Consequently, this study will explore the attempts by these critics to combine their progressive visions within the existing liberal tradition. Voluntary institutions and the Victorian way of 'self-help' still dominated British life, and were equated with a 'British way' of ARP that bolstered arm's-length government plans for dispersed shelters. The critics looked to the experience of civilians in the Spanish Civil War for evoking a new model of cooperation and solidarity. Their vision of the People's War involved active citizenship, not merely passive obedience to authority. Many factors contributed to how citizens responded to demands by the central state. There was no radical break with the status quo towards socialism or a consolidated state; nor were volunteerism and 'liberal' ideals jettisoned. At the same time, the role the civilian and individual citizen was permanently altered in numerous ways.

The chronological scope of this study encompasses the years 1918–39. In the interwar period, the Committee of Imperial Defence and later the Home Office were tasked with instituting 'passive defence,' including shelters, air raid drills and ensuring civil order in the case of future war. Informal planning for aerial defence lasted until the institution of the ARP Department of the Home Office in 1935. Official suggestions were publicized with circulars to the public, and the force of orders and regulations were formalized through parliament with the ARP Acts of 1937 and 1939. Following the Munich Crisis of September 1938, and the lack of preparedness that was brought to light, planning speeded up considerably. This period is particularly important as a greater sense of urgency did not occur until Britons were confronted with the example of aerial bombing from Guernica and other cities in Spain, featured in dramatic headlines in British newspapers. It is this period that is the main focus here, concentrating on the quickly shifting political terrain and the nature of preparation for air raids immediately prior to the war.

*

The opening half of this book sets up theories of attack, expressions of fear, and the personalities who typified opposing perspectives on the issue. The first two chapters will pair literary and cultural expressions of aviation and fear with military theories about aerial attack and its effects on civilians. It first explores dueling attitudes towards aviation in interwar Britain: enthusiasm and fear. Understanding these competing impulses is vital in exploring how Britons viewed the threat from the air. Enthusiasm was derived from the dashing, romantic image of the flying 'Aces' of the First World War, and from early hopes that aviation would usher in an age of international cooperation. On the converse was the specter of future destruction, a preoccupation that became more pronounced in the latter part of the decade. Having established these moods, the Chapter 2 looks at predictions of the lethality of air warfare, its effect on morale and the impact that such notions had on government policy. It concludes with the establishment of the basic tenets of household-centered ARP by the Home Office in the late 1930s.

The Chapter 3 raises the question of poison gas, considering both the preoccupation with sensationalistic predictions of mass death, as well as counterviews which presented the threat of gas warfare as relatively minor. The contrarian point of view on poison gas is now almost forgotten, and consequently has been little-analysed, but it represents an important facet of interwar military thinking. In the early 1920s, some military men and professionals felt that gas had proved less deadly than conventional weapons and therefore was a more humane means of warfare. Their arguments, accepting that civilians would have to submit to 'gas discipline' just like soldiers, contrasted with those of anti-gas campaigners who emphasized the sanctity of civilians and the need for disarmament and international cooperation. While they were unable to overcome the taboo on gas warfare, contrarians did contribute significantly to discussions of governmental advice.

Chapter 4 details the work of two critics of the far left and far right – respectively C.G. Grey of *Aeroplane* magazine and J.B.S. Haldane, who embodied interwar 'leftist science'. Haldane and Grey were on opposite sides of the political spectrum, and they represent key elements of lobbying and political agitation during these years. Grey was a renowned voice of professional aviation and was prominent in civilian lobbying for aerial armament. Haldane, on the other hand, advocated deep shelters and increased civilian air raid protection at the expense of business interests, armament contracts, and military budgets. This section serves to demonstrate how the right and left responded in characteristic ways to the fear of air warfare.

The following chapter considers the psychology of terror during the Spanish Civil War, and how British observers crafted images of civilian fortitude and defiance. This is a pivotal section, the hinge between the two parts of the book, since it was the morale of the individual under the duress of attack that most concerned interwar planners and led to policies meant to contain and carefully manage fear. Aerial warfare in Spain served as a propaganda tool for critics of government policy. This section focuses on 'lessons' of aerial warfare that observers gathered from the Spanish experience and that they attempted to translate to the British context: the stoicism of ordinary citizens under conditions of attack, the necessity of purpose-built deep shelters, and the role of local communities in providing shelters. The experience of Spanish civilians was used as a model in constructing a narrative of active citizenship necessary for the People's War.

The balance of the book concentrates on the controversies over how best to prepare for aerial attack in interwar Britain, controversies which were deeply imbedded in politics and idealized British behaviour. The translation of theory and predictions into actual policy for civilians exposed and emphasized societal divisions. Chapters 6 and 7 consider the wide-ranging critique of government preparations for air raids that was mounted by a broad coalition of the left and directed towards practical provisions and rooted in fear of the loss of civil liberties. They believed that preparations should include a mass, communitarian approach to sheltering, based on technical observations from Spain. The tenor of these debates over gas-proof rooms and deep shelters will be explored along with issues of class and finance. Cognizant that they might be unable to prevent war itself, critics were at least certain that the institution of a military state through ARP provisions should be prevented. A prominent theme in leftist critiques was the allegation that ARP was not intended to protect the population but to keep the public disciplined and dutiful. These commentators were particularly concerned with ill-defined authority to 'prevent public panic' that would be accorded to air raid wardens. Ultimately, critics sought to replace coercive measures with their idea, partly derived from Spain, of the 'democratic defence' of communities.

Chapter 8 will look at the 'stiff upper lip,' stoicism, and how ideas based on proper British behaviour formed the basis of government policies. Accepted clichés about the national character formed an inherent part of government policies. The difficulty in differentiating between Englishness and Britishness is well acknowledged by historians of Britain. The subjects of this study were mostly English and speaking on behalf of English cities. And, naturally, many of the supposed national characteristics that they attributed as being British were more particularly of a stereotypical English type. Yet for the most part, they utilized Britain and Britishness in their literature as inclusive terms. Marjorie Morgan has noted that well into the twentieth century British and English travellers often used these terms interchangeably.[30] Following this lead, as well as the current convention of using Britishness as an inclusive (if complicated) term, this study will do so except in cases where the primary source explicitly refers to Englishness.[31] A central idea in the British way of ARP was the ethic of volunteerism, rather than compulsion, and it formed the basis of organizational policy – contrasting with the 'compulsion' of the authoritarian regimes. The chapter looks particularly at individual responsibility, 'self-help' and the reception towards the idea of sheltering at home, considering the wartime evidence of the large sociological project Mass Observation. It also explores the contrasts that were made with air raid planning in the continental nations of France, Germany, and Spain, and how depictions of national character(s) were infused into these discussions.

The final two chapters delve into the most significant attempt to prepare for air raids through the construction of mass shelters to accommodate thousands of residents, planned by the Borough of Finsbury and the Tecton architectural firm. The critics' aspirations for deep shelters remained theoretical until 1939, when this project provoked the government to reject alternative deep shelter plans completely. Chapter 9 considers the origins of progressive architecture in the interwar period, the background of the Finsbury project, how the plans were drafted, and the press reception that the project received. Chapter 10 reflects on how dissent and patriotism co-existed within the new 'regime of fear' that was constructed in anticipation of war. The Home Office, under Sir John Anderson, convened the Hailey Commission to respond in particular to the Finsbury plan, but also to address the general agitation for deep shelters. Finsbury's plan may have served as the trigger, but the work of the commission was about much larger issues than the proposal of a relatively poor and powerless borough of Northeast London. The Hailey Commission officially forbade the construction of purpose-built deep shelters, enforcing the policy of dispersal and home sheltering.

The conclusion brings together the impact of air raids, psychology, citizenship, and public reception of ARP during wartime itself, demonstrating how theory was translated into practice. The issues and questions proposed within this work are of ongoing relevance to societies at war: the book examines the nature of terror and the ideas of mechanical destruction, national belonging, duties of citizenship, and the problem of public morale.

PART I

CHAPTER 1

SITUATING MOODS –
AVIATION ENTHUSIASTS
AND FEAR

A new mould of men has been cast. Their feats of bravery
haunt us, baffle us, and satisfy completely the spirit of romantic
daring inherent in our island race.

[The pilot] has just triumphed over time and space; defied
gravity; and soaring into the blue empyrean has attained a
means of expression that gives him an elasticity denied to all of
us bound to the ground [...]. He has acquired the ecstasy that
only a pilot knows.[1]

—Cecil Beaton, *Winged Squadrons*

England is no longer an island. There will be no sleeping
behind the wooden walls of Old England with the Channel our
safety moat. It means the aerial chariots of a foe descending on
British soil if war comes.[2]

—Lord Northcliffe

At the southern end of Park Lane and Mayfair, tucked in behind
Hyde Park Corner, stands the building occupied by the Royal
Aeronautical Society. Its impressive façade denotes the importance

that its founders attached to the conquest of the air, and the depth of resources that the Society has commanded since its inception in 1866 – many years before the first aeroplanes took to the air. Even with the mere existence of hot air ballooning to signal the future, its early members believed it was their destiny to conquer the skies. The Society's stately interior evokes the atmosphere of the storied gentleman's clubs that populate nearby Mayfair, St James, and Pall Mall, looking out to the broad greens of Hyde Park and adjacent landmarks, such as the Dorchester Hotel. But while most legendary clubs catered to the aristocracy, gentlemen of leisure and governing elites, the members of the Society saw themselves as parallel elite – a self-appointed aristocracy of aviation. The early history of aviation is intimately connected with the biographies of flyers, journalists, and aeronautical entrepreneurs. The allure of the air was as much involved with the 'magnificent men' (and women) as it was with the wonder of their fantastical 'flying machines'. This book will feature a great deal of mini-biography, highlighting how devoted admirers of aviation and those who feared its destructive power both contributed to the landscape of optimism and fear in 1930s Britain.

The Aeronautical Society took up residence at its present building in Hamilton Place just prior to the outbreak of World War II, following a period during which national interest in both civilian and military aviation had reached ever-higher levels. Flying was also embedded in competition and nationalism. Early in the 1900s, the newspaper baron Lord Northcliffe enthusiastically supported British aviation, realizing the civilian and military potential of flight. Somewhat dismayed that the Germans and French had sent military observers to speak with the Wright brothers in the United States but that Britain had not, he annoyed officials with his 'impertinence' in attempting to interfere with military matters.[3] The Edwardian era featured sensational air races and contests that were followed with great anticipation by broad segments of the population. The *Daily Mail* sponsored several contests, including a £1,000 prize for the first cross-channel flight, which Frenchman Louis Bleriot won with his legendary 1909 flight. In 1906 the paper had first offered a staggering £10,000 prize for anyone who achieved a London–Manchester flight. The prize remained unclaimed until 1910, when it too was won by an aviator from across the Channel, Louis Paulhan. The French were enthusiastic aviators, deeming themselves 'the winged nation'. J.T.C. Moore-Brabazon, later Minister of Aircraft Production in the War Cabinet, took the *Daily Mail* prize of £1,000 as the first Englishman to fly a mile.[4]

The wide circulation of magazines such as the *Aeroplane, Popular Aviation* and *Popular Flying*, which published the Biggles short stories by W.E. Johns, attests to the allure of flying in the public mind. The journal *Flying*, also edited by Johns, published thrilling tales of heroes of aviation, including a series on war aces from the Great War.[5] Aviation was a new frontier where *Boys Own* fantasies of wartime courage and adventure could be realized in a space equal to the edge of empire in an age when earthbound adventurism seemed to have been done before. Imported Hollywood films emphasized the inherent glamour of flying – from the famed silent picture *Wings* (1927) to *Hell's Angels* (1930), which was the most expensive film made to that date. It almost bankrupted producer Howard Hughes, and reflected his lifelong obsession with flying. Box-office successes from the 1930s include *Ceiling Zero* (1936), *Test Pilot* (1938), *Dawn Patrol* (1938) and *Only Angels Have Wings* (1939) – the latter directed by the legendary Howard Hawks and starring Cary Grant and Jean Arthur.

Flying was imbued with romance but also was a domain to display individual courage and heroism. The fame of the flying 'aces' of the First World War – including Billy Bishop, Edward 'Mick' Mannock, Albert Ball, and the 'Red Baron' Manfred von Richthofen – provided one chivalric footnote in an otherwise ungentlemanly war and fuelled many fictional tales for young boys. The notion of the 'Lone Wolf' tied into many levels of masculinity, and the mythology of the gentleman aviators provided an enduring image of romance and bravery, and served a model for a dynamic military culture. The idea of the gentlemanly aviator was viewed as the equivalent of the man-to-man medieval duel, though the result for the loser was more deadly. Americans found the idea particularly intriguing, and it formed a lasting basis for an obsession, or 'mesmerizing vision', with air power and the building of the US Air Force.[6] Henry Newbolt's *Tales of the Great War* (1916) propagated this image, and as a wartime work it was part of an attempt to appeal to volunteers on a remodelled notion of chivalric ideals. Newbolt declared that:

> Our airmen are singularly like the knights of the old romances; they go out day by day, singly or in twos and threes, to hold the field against all comers [. . .]. There is something especially chivalrous about these champions of the air; even the Huns, whose military principles are against chivalry, have shown themselves affected by it.[7]

The Royal Air Force (RAF), established in 1918, its motto *Per ardua ad astra* ('Through adversity to the stars'), provides an illuminating summary of how aviators viewed themselves. In the interwar years, the 'aristocratic' elements of flying were downplayed, and it was viewed as a more democratic arena, even if officers and enlisted ranks in the Royal Air Force (RAF) continued to largely be divided along class lines. Without a private income, the barriers to entry for flyers were substantial.[8] This democratic sentiment perhaps had its epitome in the spectacle of the great T.E. Lawrence (of Arabia) enlisting in the RAF simply as 'Private Shaw'. His startling decision prompted scores of theories about his motivation, and it continues to do so to this day. Whether it was some bizarre sort of inverted vanity,[9] or a simple desire to escape from fame, his tenure as Private Shaw before his premature death in a motorcycle accident in 1935 represents the democratic ideals of interwar aviation – participation was determined by passion, ability, and work rather than pedigree.

The art of flying also made international celebrities of civilian aviators such as Louis Bleriot, Charles Lindberg, Antoine de Saint-Exupéry, Alan Cobham, Jim and Amy Mollison, and the tragic Amelia Earhart. The fame of female aviators, and their not uncommon presence in aerodromes throughout North America and Europe, highlights the full democratizing aspects of the aeroplane, although flying was often equated with masculinity. Heroism, military or otherwise, could now be disassociated from pure muscular brawn. The aircraft itself performed the heavy lifting; the individual provided the courage, dexterity, powers of judgment and technical acumen required to fly successful missions. At this time, of course, there was really no such thing as a routine flight. Weather, mechanical failure, and other difficulties could spell instant peril. The omnipresent element of danger, added to the image, mythology and adventure of flying. The aviator's devil-may-care approach to danger and the possibility of death provide an interesting angle on the question of air power and fear.[10]

The Converse of Awe and Power: Fear

These effusive depictions of interwar aviation may seem a rather strange selection with which to introduce a book purportedly about air warfare and fear. Yet, on the other hand, they also highlight the important range of emotional responses to aviation and aerial warfare that will be explored in the first few chapters. The undercurrent of fear was omnipresent. Hope that aviation would usher in a new age of international understanding, scientific progress, and educational and leisure travel[11] co-existed alongside fears that new technologies would disrupt international relations and the fabric of daily life. Commentators in the interwar period also vacillated between enthusiasm and despair regarding the prospects of British military aviation, particularly its defensive capabilities.

The early 1920s were characterized by increasing optimism regarding the possibilities of the RAF in policing the far-flung empire. British engineering and innovation cemented national pride and martial supremacy. However, by the mid-1930s, the fear that the nation had fallen irretrievably behind in aircraft manufacturing led to a dispirited tone evident in the aviation press. There was pessimism over the preparations against air raids. In the sphere of civilian aviation, enthusiasts such as C.G. Grey, whose controversial writings as the editor of the *Aeroplane* magazine are explored in Chapter 4, tirelessly touted British aviation. At the same time, they worried that competitors from the continent and the United States would surpass British manufacturing.

If the late nineteenth century was characterized by lighthearted and fanciful visions of the future and technological change – Jules Verne, undersea vehicles, hot air balloons, and similar contraptions – the twentieth century was quite unmistakably of a darker and gloomier outlook.[12] By the late 1930s, the optimistic views that air technology would engender an era of international cooperation appeared rather outdated and naive, and narratives of fear dominated public discourse. To quote Ian Patterson from his study of Guernica and its implications for future aerial bombardment:

> The catastrophe predictions suited the arguments of the RAF because they strengthened its case for more money, men and machines. They suited the pacifists because the worse the threat, the more powerful their case for strategies of disarmament. And they suited the novelists because people really wanted to read about the apocalyptic collapse of civilization.[13]

Basil Liddell Hart suggested in the *Daily Telegraph* that in the event of a severe gas attack, 40 per cent of London's 7 million inhabitants would flee in 48 hours and 80 per cent within the week.[14] J.F.C. Fuller was another prominent commentator on mechanized warfare who similarly predicted doom following the first enemy air raids of 500 planes carrying 500 ten-pound bombs: 'London for several days will be one vast raving Bedlam [...]. What of the Government of Westminster? It will be swept away by an avalanche of terror.'[15] The foremost Marxist military commentator T.H. Wintringham believed that massive fires would render London uninhabitable and result in the deaths of several hundred thousand citizens.[16]

Fears of the next war influenced art, literature, politics, and political decisions, including the now-maligned appeasement of Hitler through the British and French unwillingness to come to the assistance of Czechoslovakia in 1938. Neville Chamberlain is almost universally blamed for the Munich Agreement and for the 'peace for our time' speech delivered on 30 September 1938, but it is important to remember that the majority of the populace strongly backed his policy and were in fact relieved at the halt or postponement of the outbreak of war. The dread of aerial warfare was not limited to the civilian population – right up until 1939 military leaders seriously overestimated the power of the Luftwaffe to inflict bomb damage on British cities. Consequently they had their own role to play in advocating the costly and short-lived 'peace' struck in 1938.

At the outbreak of war in 1939, military planners assumed that a bombing campaign against London would be imminent and that such a campaign would result in the collapse of civil society and government. These fears were so omnipresent that actual attack seemed anticlimactic. It is almost banal to note that aerial destruction was not as complete as the most pessimistic had predicted, as terrible as it was with the loss of over 60,000 civilian lives. As the founders of the nationwide sociological survey 'Mass Observation' noted:

Had not statesmen and thinkers said that [war] would be "the end of civilization?" It was mixed in people's minds with the end of the world, in the supernatural as well as in political events, and the ultimate chaos of the Shape of Things to Come.[17]

Winston Churchill complained that all concerned had been 'greatly mislead by the pictures that they [the Air Staff] painted of the destruction that would be wrought by Air Raids'.[18] Yet Churchill himself had made liberal use of these predictions, demonstrating that the use of fear as a political tool was powerful, even if these individuals sincerely believed in the veracity of the claims they were making.

The 1930s has been viewed as a decade of extremes: the 'Red Decade', the 'Hungry Thirties', or in the words of W.H. Auden, a 'low dishonest decade'. Others have viewed these years in sad, regretful terms, such as Robert Graves and Alan Hodge's account of the period, The Long Weekend, written in 1940. The book ends with the metaphorical chapter 'Rain Stops Play, 1939', depicting politics and war interrupting a languid, gentlemanly cricket match, a foreign imposition on the bucolic shores of a peaceable Britain.[19] The popular memory of the decade tends towards the polarized ends of the political scale, even though both the far left and far right claimed a tiny minority of committed adherents. On the political left, the images that predominate are of hunger marchers, communists on street corners distributing copies of the *Daily Worker*, the Trades Union Congress and the miners' strikes, and the ill-fated general strike of 1926. On the opposing political extreme, the powerful image of Oswald Mosley's blackshirts, the British Union of Fascists (BUF) rallies at Olympia, and the 'battle of Cable Street' in the East End of London hold similar sway. Yet others have viewed the 1930s as an era of national and individual stagnation, marked by uncertainty and timidity, dominated by the fundamentally conservative 'little man in the suburbs'.[20] This middle-middle and lower-middle class constituency was the suburban *Daily Mail*-reading Briton, inhabiting a third space distinct from the 'green and pleasant land' mythology of traditional Englishness and the hard-edged urban existence of the working classes in the great industrial cities.

Despite the varied experience of the 1930s, predictions of the end of civilization were one cultural motif that permeated common experience. The reasons for and historical explanations of interwar pessimism are manifold. T.S. Eliot was possibly extreme, but likely not alone, in expressing the view soon after the First World War that 'Whatever happens will be another step toward the destruction of Europe. The whole of contemporary politics [oppresses] me with a continuous physical horror like the feeling of a growing madness in one's brain.'[21] The very titles of many historical surveys of the interwar period capture the *zeitgeist* well. Roy Hattersley has offered *Borrowed Time*, evoking the sense of war's inevitability.[22] Richard Overy in his recent book, *The Morbid Age*, expounds on the fears of many contemporary observers that Europe was threatened by a general crisis and decay of civilization. Many national leaders, writers, scientists, and intellectuals expressed an acute sense of despair.[23] They spoke to debates that would continue long afterwards, up until the present day.

'Feeding the Beast' – Popular Fiction and the Nature of Fear

In 1908, H.G. Wells made the spectre of aerial invasion popular through his novel *War in the Air*, which emphasized the destructive power of aerial technology and the fear that England had lost its position of international superiority and ingenuity.[24] Popular fiction such as *The Invasion of 1910* (1906) by William Le Queux reflected the invasion scares of the early century and fears of new weaponry. The depiction of air raids and enemy invasion in science fiction prior to the First World War were rooted in fears of mechanical modernity.[25] The fear of tanks and machine guns translated into a general fear of the 'war machine' itself and the belief that war had become rationalized and industrialized.[26] Following the war, the straightforward invasion scares represented in literature widened to encompass all manner of doomsday scenarios. Historians of science fiction have noted that such novels proliferated most particularly following the rise of Fascism. Martin Ceadel has pegged an increase in pessimistic writings beginning from 1933 onwards, and explains that even novels devoid of literary merit shed light on public and governmental attitudes towards war and aerial bombardment. The fiction-publishing world was replete with melodramatic predictions of war and the end of civilization, most making for turgid and appalling reading. Taken together, these novels highlight the fear of aerial warfare and public attitudes towards the new technological realities of modern warfare.[27] It was non-military commentators, including novelists, who foresaw that aerial warfare would not only be used piecemeal against specific military targets, but also indiscriminately to break the will of the enemy.[28] Novels such as Hugh Addison's *The Battle of London* (1923) popularized concepts such as the 'one-day war' that would suffice to destroy civilization. Such notions also dominated strategic air force thinking.

Aviation continued to fuel many apocalyptic visions, evident in an almost obsessive reference point for many writers. Virginia Woolf was acutely obsessed with aeroplanes and air crashes, and flying featured prominently in four pieces of her writing. George Orwell's work was particularly indicative of the atmosphere of fear regarding air power, and his 1930s fiction almost deserves its own category for its repeated references to the inevitability of air warfare. In *Coming Up for Air* and *Keep the Aspidistra Flying*,[29] his greatest novels highlighting disgust for and dissatisfaction with the suburban bourgeois life, the protagonists regarded the prospect of bombs falling with something approaching relish and anticipation. The inhabitants of 1930s Britain were depicted as sleepwalking towards disaster – already spiritually dead and merely awaiting the final *coup de grace* of physical death at the hands of enemy attackers.

Novels involving the destruction of civilization through poison gas were particularly popular in the 1930s, becoming darker during the rise of Fascism in Europe. The prospect of gas warfare being deployed against civilians was described with 'a host of half-accurate, but pejorative, descriptions and adjectives, [provoking] vivid images of human suffering and agony'.[30] The first of these major novels was published in 1926. The second Earl of Halsbury's novel, *1944*, reflected his deep conviction that chemical weapons would supersede conventional weapons, and it was particularly influential in military circles.[31] A member of the establishment, he had ties to the RAF and the Admiralty, hence reflecting that hyperbolic fears held some resonance even in the official and semi-official sphere. Although Halsbury's novel was both speculative and sensationalistic, his arguments had a profound influence on political thinking, given that he held the status of an expert commentator on the subject. He was widely quoted as predicting that one gas bomb dropped at Piccadilly Circus could kill every resident from Regent's Park to the Thames.[32] Following in these themes, some of the best-selling apocalyptic novels included *The Gas War of 1940* (1931) by 'Miles', a pseudonym of the novelist Stephen Southwold, which sold 100,000 copies,[33] and *The Poison War* (1933) by Ladbroke Black. One of the best known of the 1930s war scare novels, along with Harold Nicolson's *Public Faces* (1932), was H.G Wells' *The Shape of Things to Come* (1933). This widely publicised book reflected darker themes of poison gas attack and the collapse of civilization. Adapted into film by the famed director Alexander Korda in 1936, it depicted a world in which strategic bombing and chemical warfare reduced humankind to a new Dark Age. Yet it was a remarkably bifurcated film in which the second half brightened considerably, promising hope through the development of a super-cadre of young scientists and aviators. However, the society that replaced the old one was a regimented, cold and unfeeling technocracy. The subtext was that destruction of the old civilization was both inevitable and in some senses necessary for a new one to arise. A type of 'superman' would save mankind, although this might denote the end of the grace and civility of civilization. It was a vision that coincidentally echoed the ideology of the far-right and fascist sympathizers.

The Far-Right and Aviation: The Full Circle of Ideology and Machine

As destruction and salvation featured as dual components in many visions of aerial power and the future, it seems *apropos* to end this chapter with the enthusiasms of the British right-wing and the effect they had on national aviation. As Robert Wohl writes, although there is 'nothing inherently fascist about flying, [in] the atmosphere of the 1930s it is easy to see how people could make the connection'.[34] Of course, enthusiasm for aviation surpassed class and political boundaries. As has been stated, liberals strongly believed that transnational aviation and an international air force could serve as a catalyst for a new age of cooperation rather than competition. Individuals across political boundaries also viewed aviation as a military panacea that might help avoid the type of combat experienced on the Western Front. Christopher Caudwell (born Christopher St John Sprigg), a Marxist writer who was killed fighting for the Republican cause in Spain in 1937, extolled the power of flight, editing a book entitled *Great Flights*. He viewed flying as a 'feasible form of heroism and individual self-assertion' that could persist despite the horrors of infantry warfare.[35] His analysis of T.E. Lawrence and his tenure in the RAF was that the hero of Arabia believed 'in the machine as mere machine, but in the machine consciously controlled by man, by whose use he could regain the freedom and quality of primitive relations without losing rich consciousness of the ages of European culture'.[36]

Most proponents of aviation, however, were politically inclined towards the right. The obsession with aviation is identified as a motif of Fascism, particularly that of Nazi Germany, although Italian fascists were more ardent aviators. For the British right wing, aviation and ideology provided a custom-made expression of the values of their new model society. The totalitarian qualities of aviation appealed to those who sought to purge the perceived weakness and decadence of contemporary civilization. Just as the aviator dominated the landscape he surveyed, so the totalitarian imagined the complete refashioning of society. Even liberal modernist architects and designers such as Le Corbusier celebrated aviation as a means to re-engineer cities.[37] His book, *Aircraft* (1935), was a bold hymn to the intersection of modernist design, planning, and the stark mechanical aesthetic of aircraft. His book fits within the aesthetic legacy of the Futurist movement, with its focus on 'Aeropainting' – aviation as a dynamic art form. Lyricists of the fascist movement identified themselves as bold and daring, the perfect representations of the aristocracy of the air and the 'new man.'

Fascist Italy stands out as the prime example of the fusion of modernist aviation with this ethos. Under the Air Minister Italo Balbo, the promotion of Italian flying feats prompted both elite and popular adulation. The poet Gabriele D'Annunzio's narrative of the heroic flyer from the First World War symbolized the new culture of the air. It was characterized by the elements that Italian Fascism prized: elemental masculinity, a love of a state of war, willingness to court death in pursuit of glory, personal sacrifice on behalf of the state, technological advance, and national honour. Italian journalist Guido Mattioli decreed that 'Every aviator is a born fascist'.[38] Italian aviators fostered the dynamic image of fascists as 'heroic figure[s] who had realized the oldest dream of humankind – the conquest of the skies'.[39] Balbo himself declared that it was 'infinitely more difficult to create a pilot than build an airplane'.[40] Airmen, in this formulation, were a cut above the regular citizen – a fact that the general population should acknowledge and appreciate. As Mussolini stated in a 1923 speech: 'Not everyone can fly [. . .]. Flying must remain the privilege of an aristocracy; but everyone must want to fly, everyone must regard flying with longing [. . .] all devoted citizens must follow with profound feeling the development of Italian wings.'[41]

In a slightly different way, Nazi Germany also invested in the glamour associated with aeroplanes, air forces, and most particularly doomed airships such as the Hindenburg. Their endeavours in this field were particularly nationalistic, given the resented prohibition on flying imposed by the Treaty of Versailles. Peter Fritzsche's book *A Nation of Fliers* documents the intertwining of German nationalism and aviation from the imperial dreams of the Kaiser's Second Reich to national 'redemption' through rearmament in Hitler's Third Reich.[42] During the Weimar Republic Ernst Jünger, speaking for the radical German right, wrote *Luftfahrt ist Not!* (*Flight is Necessary!*). In it he praised the 'soaring flights' of hardy young gliders as a sign that the Germanic race retained its innate strength and was not in decline.[43] The Nazis also used 'gliding clubs' as a means of circumventing restrictions on aircraft imposed by the Treaty of Versailles. An emphasis on aerial strength served as part of the National Socialists' propaganda narrative of strength and national rebirth. Leni Rifenstahl's infamous film *Triumph of the Will* (1935) depicted Hitler descending through the clouds in a plane.[44] The 'saviour' of the nation would come with the accoutrements of the future age, shedding the image of the past and, by proxy, shedding German failure and the shame from the First World War.

The influence of continental movements within England was fragmented and indirect. In many ways England continued to remain culturally conservative in the interwar years, although recently scholars have moved away from rural, bucolic, traditionalist views of Britain, acknowledging that it was a highly urbanized society in rapid flux.[45] New interpretations for this fundamental 'conservatism' have moved beyond the self-congratulatory explanation that extremist movements held little or no purchase in a liberal and democratic Britain. Historians have pointed instead to particular factors both within and without the fascist movement that hindered its spread. Martin Pugh points to economic circumstances and the limited nature of the depression of the 1930s. The majority of the population did not experience a substantial change in their standard of living, thereby forcing the fascist movement to focus on a narrowly-defined disenfranchised constituency. The apex of national crisis occurred in 1931, but the leader of the BUF, Oswald Mosley was not able to organize his first solid challenge until 1932, too late to profit from the vulnerabilities of the British parliamentary system.[46] There was, however, something to be said for the abhorrence of the British public for violence. As soon as Mosley's followers demonstrated their thuggish side they lost much support. However, the fact that British fascists never emerged as a serious political movement does not mean that there were not significant cultural expressions of fascist ideology, the cult of the aviator among them.

There were many links between aviation bodies and rightist organizations. For example, connections of personnel or funding can be traced to the Air League of the Empire, the Royal Aeronautical Society, the National League of Airmen, and the BUF, along with the smaller, elite Anglo-German Fellowship and the January Club, which was at times facilitated by well known and influential individuals such as Lord Londonderry. As Secretary of State for Air from 1931 to 1935, he was perhaps the most important of the pro-German politicians. Lord Rothermere, publisher of the *Daily Mail*, was an ardent fascist sympathizer and supporter of appeasement. He had been President of the Air Council from 1917 to 1918 and later became a fierce critic of the Ministry in the 1930s, calling for an 'Air Dictator' to bolster the standing of the RAF. He purchased his own private aeroplane and was an advocate on behalf of British aviation. Along with other radical, attention-getting pronouncements, he attempted to embarrass the Ministry on various occasions, just as his brother and fellow newspaper baron, Lord Northcliffe, had done in an earlier era. Rothermere provided early support for the BUF, though he later withdrew it due to the violence of the blackshirts.

Other vocal supporters of aviation who were right-wing or overtly partial to Fascism included the reactionary William Joynson-Hicks ('Jix'), Home Secretary from 1924 to 1929, best known for hunting 'Reds' and involving himself in Prayer Book reform debates. He was a major proponent of air power, as was Rear Admiral Murray Sueter, who belonged to Rothermere's Anti-Waste League.[47] Sir Alliott Verdon Roe, designer of the Avro aircraft and the first Englishman to fly in 1908, was also an eminent Mosley supporter.[48] The Scottish landowner Lord Sempill was yet another example of an aristocratic flyer who gravitated towards fascist organizations in the 1930s.

It should be noted that it was possible to be an ardent supporter of aviation without being rightist or pro-German. Winston Churchill was, of course, the primary example of such a politician, as were other Conservative MPs, including J.T.C. Moore-Brabazon the pioneering aviator who later served in the War Cabinet. The Air League cultivated backbench enthusiasts who sat on the Parliamentary Air Committee, such as Moore-Brabazon, Harold Balfour, and Lindsay Everard. In fact, as David Edgerton points out, the mere fact of being pro-German did not necessarily entail being opposed to British rearmament, and these views were often much more complex than imagined.[49]

It does not come as a great surprise that many fascist sympathizers were current or former military men, both officers and enlisted ranks. Richard Griffiths has explained the links between fascist groups and Air Force men, and ex-servicemen in general.[50] Prominent military commentator Major-General J.F.C. 'Boney' Fuller and self-proclaimed Middle East expert Captain Robert Gordon-Canning served on the Policy Directorate of the BUF as Mosley's advisors. A number of RAF officers and amateur airmen were regular attendees at the meetings. Wing-Commander Sir Louis Grieg was Gentleman Usher to the King and identified as a member of the elite January Club.[51] Many of the links might be deemed tenuous, but there were discernable ties between respected associations that existed to further the cause of British aviation, and fascist groups. Airmen were especially predisposed to pro-German feeling, believing that Germany had been unfairly punished by being forbidden to have an air force at all. In addition, romantic ideas associated with aerial warfare from the First World War persisted, and many British aviators were likely to remember their old foes with a degree of kindness.[52] For many, the air duels provided the only theatre in which the tradition of the heroic individual warrior continued to hold true. Bernhard Rieger has suggested that this image of chivalry and heroism in the First World War was peculiarly English. Germans, in contrast, actually emphasized the independence and ruthlessness of its renowned pilots rather than their supposed gentlemanly qualities.[53] Consequently, at least for British ex-airmen, notions of the 'international brotherhood of aviators' cannot be discounted. The chivalric myth and the sense that aviators owed their primary loyalty to each other was difficult to overcome. These ideals were expressed in Rex Warner's novel *The Aerodrome*. The protagonist of the piece serves in the Air Force at the whim of a dictatorial Air Vice-Marshall who encourages aviators to see themselves as a brave 'new race of men', to whom life outside the aerodrome is distant and inconsequential. Consequently they become disdainful of civilians, viewing themselves as a new aristocracy – superior, daring, and a breed apart. The myth of the dynamic, ideal airman connected strongly with political leanings that one historian has termed British 'generic Fascism'.[54]

The elements of enthusiasm and fear evident in this chapter existed in the imagination, almost a dream-like parallel world to the more pedestrian one of aircraft construction, the training of civilian and RAF pilots, the building of aerodromes across the nation, and the formation of commercial aviation routes. There are, naturally, limits to how far we can take contemporary hand-wringing about the end of civilization. There were certainly many such predictions before 1914, and they have continued little abated since. There is, however, something unique about hopes and fears expressed in the superlative language of the interwar years, particularly the latter 1930s. This chapter has highlighted some of the predominant moods concerning aviation. Fear was only one emotion in a complex set of reactions towards this new and revolutionary technology. In the following chapter we turn to the concrete ways in which the lessons of fear and civilian morale were derived from the First World War, and the notions that underpinned planning for aerial bombardment in the next war.

CHAPTER 2

ANTICIPATING NEW WEAPONS AND THEORIZING AERIAL WARFARE

The first air attack targeting civilians in London occurred on 31 May 1915, killing seven people, injuring 35, and causing £19,000 in damages. The spectre of Zeppelins darkening London's skies, hurtling bombs indiscriminately to the ground and sending residents fleeing to the shelter of Tube stations was startling enough to shatter even strong nerves. D.H. Lawrence was unlikely to have been alone in envisioning the Zeppelin as an apocalyptic symbol.[1] The most successful air raid occurred on 8 September 1915, causing almost half of the damage of the combined Zeppelin raids. By the end of the war, raiding aircraft had dropped 6,000 bombs on Britain, causing 556 fatalities and 1,357 injuries. Gotha attacks proved more destructive than those carried out by 'Zepps'. On 8 March 1918 a one-ton bomb fell in Warrington Crescent W9, north of Paddington – it was one of the largest bombs dropped during the war and the most materially destructive. Twelve people were killed, and nearly 30 houses on the street were either totally or partially destroyed. The creation of the Royal Air Force (RAF) on 1 April 1918, an independent military branch to replace the more *ad hoc* RFC, was a response to the heightened role of airpower in warfare and reflected in part the need to defend Britain from aerial marauders.

As with any novel attack, the lessons derived in the immediate aftermath have long-standing consequences. In modern times, we can think of the shock of the simple tactics employed by the 9/11 terrorists. The sporadic bombing raids of the First World War had a direct effect on attempts to control fear and maintain civilian morale in a future war, and they provided a starting point for theorizing new weapons and the tactics of aerial warfare. Historians Tami Davis Biddle, Uri Bialer, and Barry Powers have emphasized how the First World War set events in motion that almost inevitably emphasized the perils of failing civilian morale and the importance of offensive striking capabilities. Their accounts construct a portrait of the Air Ministry building, constructed on precedent and fear in order to craft a central role for the RAF. This chapter will demonstrate the process by which the anxiety regarding the threat from the air and its likely impact on popular morale had a direct impact on the drafting of air raid precautions (ARP) plans. Consequently, government planners drew on the long tradition of self-help and individual sheltering in order to disperse the population and lessen the probability of mob actions or mass casualty events. These Air Ministry precepts ultimately ensured that conflict would ensue as critics demanded full equality and communally provided ARP accommodations.

Attack and the Fear of the 'Knock-Out Blow': The Legacy of the First World War

Initial reports on the domestic effects of bombing by the Committee of Imperial Defence (CID) following the war set the tone for all future civil defence measures, emphasizing the disproportionate negative impact on morale compared with material damage. During the war, the CID had noted that 'there is little doubt that in certain parts of the country the zeppelin is now dreaded out of all proportion to what is justified by its past achievements on land'.[2] Offensive conclusions followed similar lines. The earliest reports by the Air Ministry regarding the impact of offensive bombing raids on German targets during the First World War mirrored those that had been made in reference to civilian morale in Britain. The psychological effect induced by constant stoppages in production could be highly detrimental. Although raids caused comparatively little damage to infrastructure, the impact on the discipline of employees at German factories was disproportionately severe. The very unpredictability of such raids and the sounding of constant air warnings led to critical delays in the production of munitions, and in total war the shutdown of railways or factories is 'tantamount to defeat'.[3] In 1924 the CID concluded: 'It has been borne in upon us, that in the next war it may well be that that nation [sic], whose people can endure aerial bombardment the longer and with the greater stoicism, will ultimately prove victorious.'[4] The possibilities of precision targeting were consequently woven into RAF doctrine, re-configuring the way the future battlefield was imagined and shifting the emphasis from conventional ground and naval tactics to the air.

The specific findings of postwar planners combined strongly with continental and home grown ideas about the 'knock-out blow' – a sudden strike, possibly even preceding any formal declaration of war, which could leave the capital in ruin, the nation defenceless, and the population in chaos. In this vein, Hugh Trenchard left the most influential legacy of any senior officer involved in the Great War and exerted 'total influence' on strategic RAF thinking.[5] He presented himself as a saviour of the RAF, arguing that the aircraft should be viewed primarily as an offensive and not a defensive weapon. 'Trenchardian' thinking dominated strategic plans for interwar defence and his statement to the Parliamentary Committee on Air Power in 1923 remained the guiding principle throughout the interwar years: 'It is on the bomber that we must rely for defence. It is on the destruction of enemy industries and above all on the lowering of [enemy] morale caused by bombing that the ultimate victory rests.'[6] It was viewed as 'heresy' to question these tenets of offensive doctrine. Trenchard's ideas fused well with the musings of foreign military theorists such as the Italian proponent of air war, Giulio Douhet. As an enthusiast and proto-fascist who commanded military aviation during the First World War, Douhet 'waxed poetic' about the glories of air warfare.[7] He summarized his grandiose visions in his 1921 book, *The Command of the Air*, outlining ideas that would become the standard doctrine of bombing theory. He argued that civilians were now more vulnerable to attack and that industrial societies could be obliterated with relative ease, perhaps within days. Populations would be unable to withstand such bombardment and would force their governments to sue for peace. Douhet was not the only proponent of these ideas, and he may have served as more of a manifestation of the conventional wisdom than as its cause. His ideas were developed in tandem with other influential commentators; in Britain, J.F.C. Fuller and Liddell Hart forwarded similar notions which affected RAF doctrine. The idea of the 'knock-out blow' soon permeated strategic thinking and had a discernable impact on policies such as the decision to invest heavily in strategic bombing capabilities.[8]

Even though mass disaffection did not occur during the First World War, the public did exert pressure on war strategy, a development that critics perceived as a dangerous precedent akin to 'mob rule'. In March 1916 the *Manchester Guardian*, questioning the state of British air defences, proposed a British fleet of Zeppelins to counter German planes.[9] In the aftermath of Gotha attacks in June 1917, there were calls for retaliatory raids on Germany. The *Daily Mail* published photographs of child victims of an air raid along with a 'Reprisal Map' of German towns.[10] There were also demands that existing military aircraft be deployed primarily for home defence, rather than in support of land forces on the continent. Such examples prompted concern in conservative circles that public fears might completely overtake the prosecution of the war. The *Spectator*, a newspaper catering to conservative and upper middle-class readers, argued that policy should not be based on public emotion and anger.[11] Defence measures were nevertheless largely aimed at satisfying the demands of the civilian population, and aircraft that had hitherto been imagined in offensive terms were brought into use for civilian defence.[12]

The literature on British air policy and civilian defence during the First World War lends credence to the argument that government policy on public safety was in fact reactionary and based on acquiescence to public demands. One historian has deemed the reaction to 'light bombing' to be rather extraordinary. The Royal Flying Corps (RFC) virtually doubled from 108 to 200 squadrons.[13] Central authorities initially refused to provide air raid warnings or to advise the public of air raid casualties due to the fear of panic or defeatism. From the First World War through the interwar years, the narrative of ARP is largely one of government unwillingness trumped only by absolute necessity or overwhelming public pressure. Many of these measures were eventually instituted, perhaps because of a greater concern that the lack of their provision would cause more, rather than less, panic. However reluctantly implemented, these official responses established the precedent of popular action leading to improved civil defence. No doubt aware of the role public pressure played in instituting rudimentary ARP during the First World War, the critics of the 1930s attempted to muster a similar sense of public outrage in the years preceding World War II. As strategic bombing theory came into its own in the interwar years, fears of public unruliness in the face of air attack were also foremost in the minds of ARP planners, as was the determination to keep individuals under cover in their own homes, rather than in mass public shelters.

The reaction to air raids immediately brought to the fore questions about class and race regarding the behaviour of the working-class residents of London. For the most part, it was residents of the East End who utilized Tube stations as shelters, due to the fact that these densely populated and industrial areas were targeted by German planes, as they would also be during World War II. As Gotha raids commenced in September 1917, up to 300,000 Londoners, mostly from these eastern boroughs, sought shelter in Tube stations. Race was an important part of these official conversations, since there were many Jewish immigrants and refugees living in the area. Amy Bell has pointed to the fears, rampant during both wars, of the 'cowardice' of the population who would remain in London in wartime – 'working classes, Jews, and children'.[14] Officials feared that these individuals sheltering in Tube stations would pose a problem for the maintenance of order, as they were assumed to be more susceptible to general panic. Noel Pemberton Billing, an aviator and independent MP known for his extreme right-wing views, called in the House of

Commons for the police to ensure that British women and children were guaranteed primary access to these shelters before they were filled by foreigners.

Yet there was contradictory evidence to support claims of either panic or stoic acceptance of air raids. The supposed 'lessons of morale' were foremost in the minds of interwar planners; the official historian of ARP, Richard Titmuss, certainly bears this out. His account traced an arc between the First World War, the lack of decisive new information on aerial warfare, and the obsessive power that the question of civilian morale exercised over policy makers.[15] Government planners in the 1920s were so concerned about morale that Cabinet records reflect a vague notion that the civilian population should be militarized, and that those fleeing civilian posts due to bombardment should be considered 'deserters'.[16] Though nothing came of these plans, not least because of the impossibility of organizing and enforcing such measures in a democratic society, the fact that they were considered shows the impact that the aerial threat had on all such discussions.

Based on these assumptions, planning for the next war continued apace, commencing almost immediately after the 'war to end all wars'. Naturally, the fear of aerial attack was rather one-sided, centring on the possibility of London and British cities being annihilated. The CID concluded in 1922 that an enemy air force could drop almost 300 tons of bombs on London within 48 hours. Only two years later Sir John Anderson – then Permanent Under-Secretary for the Home Department, and the future head of governmental civil defence as Lord Privy Seal and Home Secretary – had revised this figure to 350 tons in the first 48 hours in the event of a major attack, with 100 tons per day for a month to follow.[17] These figures rose further still for the rest of the decade and into the 1930s. In 1934 Winston Churchill suggested in the House of Commons that 30,000–40,000 casualties could be expected in a week to ten days of aerial attack.[18] The official historian Terence O'Brien concluded in the years following World War II that 'casualty inflation' was endemic in the interwar period, beginning with the first ARP meetings in the mid-1920s when authorities revised casualty estimates upwards. The 'beast' of public anxiety reflected in fear-mongering literature came full circle, impacting official belief and government policy. As Juliet Gardiner notes in *The Blitz*, these developments also meant that the government was better prepared for dead citizens and immense physical destruction but was less equipped to deal with the psychological trauma and physical displacement of the survivors and the bereaved and the bombed-out citizens of British cities. The threat had been imagined in an abstract way: panicked citizens or annihilated ones. Little thought was given to displaced, shocked, but ultimately forbearing civilians.

The 1920s: Early RAF Years and the Fantasy of War Without Warriors

While concerns over civilian morale at home were paramount in the immediate aftermath of the First World War, the 1920s quickly became a decade of enthusiasm about the offensive capabilities of air warfare abroad, particularly in British colonies. This excitement, highlighted in Chapter 1, also led to the notion that military intervention might be undertaken purely through the use of aerial bombardment. Ideas about air warfare in the interwar period were, as one historian has noted, largely 'imagined' before they were actually invented.[19] This fantasy remains a besetting sin of Western politicians and military strategy to this day, as evidenced in instances of military strategies recently pursued in both Iraq and Afghanistan. Not only was air power viewed as budgetary panacea, but from the British perspective it was envisioned as a means of achieving war objectives with as few warriors as possible, and those far removed from their targets. At least in theory it promised to be a cleaner option than 'putting boots on the ground' in modern parlance, though very rarely has any mission proved entirely achievable by air power alone. Nevertheless, it seemed the ideal solution for the prodigious military requirements of a nation still shocked by the infantry losses of the First World War.

Recent historiography has shed some intriguing light on the origins of air control within the British Empire, most particularly in

'Arabia' and Iraq. Priya Satia in particular has explored how the decision to employ air control in Arabia was partially a function of its inexpensive nature, but was also an artefact of the British cultural imagination. The desert was portrayed as a primitive, unknowable locale and its people governed by a mystical mindset incomprehensible to Western rationalism. By consequence, air warfare was *not* inhumane or barbaric when employed against a fatalistic warrior people who, to use a more recent construct, 'only understand force'. In fact, bombing could actually be construed as the most humane method of policing due to the grave terrorizing of civilian populations. Following such demonstrations of British strength, further opposition to Imperial rule would be unlikely.[20] No less a romantic figure than T.E. Lawrence ('Aircraftsman Shaw') encouraged Hugh Trenchard, Chief of the Air Staff and the 'Father of the Royal Air Force' in this aim. He advised sending British airships to explore the area.[21] While air control was initially viewed as *only* applicable to Arabia, enthusiasts were certain of its paradigm-changing capabilities throughout the Empire.

Airpower was soon thereafter deployed against recalcitrant rebels in Iraq, Somaliland, Mesopotamia, and Afghanistan. Politicians such as Winston Churchill, short-lived Secretary for Air, heralded these efforts as a novel means to police an empire on the cheap.[22] The new service was considered to be a panacea for imperial governance, and the hyperbolic billing was contagious. Churchill, of course, was never one to resist the lure of a good adventure, whether through his personal involvement (the 'Siege of Sidney Street', to name but one example), or by proxy through the aegis of empire. The campaign in Somaliland against Mullah Muhammed's Dervishes seemed particularly impressive, coming in at a total cost of £77,000.[23] As David Omissi has observed, 'The *correct* explanation of the Dervish defeat in Somaliland became irrelevant, as both the War Office and the Air Ministry interpreted the campaign in different ways to advance their own political strategies'. He argues that the survival of the RAF was also tied to its policing successes in Iraq.[24]

Due to these triumphs, the RAF carved out an important imperial role and was rewarded with appropriate consideration in the military budget. The generally accepted cost-effectiveness of aerial warfare ensured that the RAF was viewed as a cure-all for Britain's daunting strategic commitments. The newly-formed RAF ended the First World War very well equipped, with over 25,000 serviceable aircraft and another 40,000 planes on order. The need for defensive aircraft was also recognized, in acknowledgement that such aeroplanes would be forced to scramble quickly and effectively during a possible first-strike attack.[25] The RAF was completely re-outfitted several times in the interwar years with the newest aircraft, as David Edgerton has persuasively argued in his revisionist accounts of interwar British investment in science, technology and armaments.[26] Yet high-ranking officers were never entirely satisfied with their allotments and were convinced of the tenuousness of their position as the newest of the armed services.

The promoters of the air force felt they urgently needed to justify a continued flow of resources and 'manipulated the quest for an offensive doctrine in its crusade for independent status'.[27] The service did not lack prominent supporters, including P.R.C. Groves, a senior officer with the Air Ministry during the First World War and a well-known military strategist. He served as British air representative at the Geneva disarmament conference of 1932. As Honorary Secretary-General of the Air League of the British Empire and editor of the magazine *Air* from 1927–9, his ideas were widely disseminated to both popular and specialist audiences. He called for greater attention to be paid to the RAF, including his occasional commentary in *The Times*.[28] In his most important book, *Behind the Smoke Screen*, he argued that Britain had sacrificed its air power to budgetary constraints and feared that it was falling victim to a 'progressive danger' by failing to keep pace with advances in aviation.[29] J.M. Spaight, an influential civil servant at the Air Ministry, was one of the most prolific writers on the subject of aerial warfare and published books with titles such as *Air Power and the Next War*.[30] L.E.O. Charlton, air force officer and aerial strategist, published three books also outlining themes of neglect and decline.[31] These individuals were all intimately connected with the RAF and contributed to its propaganda effort by emphasizing the decisive role that an air force would play in future warfare.

There was no shortage of 'evidence' to summon in order to demonstrate the supposed weaknesses of British air defence. H. Montgomery Hyde, aide to Lord Londonderry, Secretary of State for Air 1931–5, believed that there were hardly enough squadrons to meet Imperial defence requirements for the Middle East and India alone.[32] Internal Air Staff documents from 1937 reflected the official position that the RAF was in no condition to go to war and would not be ready for at least two years. Using the threat of German air armament to prod the treasury for increased funding, the Air Staff pessimistically stated: 'There is no chance of their reaching equality with Germany in first-line strength [...] indeed we also stand in grave risk of falling seriously behind that country in the quality of our aircraft actually.' This information was, in truth, based on an intelligence misapprehension of the strength of the Luftwaffe. Nevertheless, the Air Staff summarized their position as one of 'shocking weakness,' a situation that could be only remedied by an infusion of additional resources.[33]

The 1930s: The Public Face of Civilian Defence

The official phase of civil defence began with the creation of the ARP Department of the Home Office in 1935 to provide an official basis to hitherto vague policies. This stage of preparation involved the detailing of 'active defence' plans, including the consultation of experts, the issuing of ARP circulars to local authorities and the passing of the ARP Acts of 1937 and 1939. The passage of these Bills in parliament gave the weight of law to the precepts of ARP, including the funding scheme through local authorities. As we will see, the economic implications of this structure provoked dissent, especially among Labour MPs, but their concerns did little to prevent the ideas of the 1920s CID from being realized.

Wing Commander E.J. Hodsoll had been involved with policy planning since 1929. He was appointed Secretary of the Department. Hodsoll had gained the confidence of the CID in the 1920s, and his

RAF background enabled him to understand the aerial threat. He was also said to possess a 'hide like a rhinoceros' in pursuit of his goal of publicizing ARP and attaining the cooperation of local authorities.[34] The year 1935 was one of increased concern within both the Air Ministry and the Home Office regarding civil defence. As one official government publication noted, Germany's reintroduction of conscription in 1935 forced a panicked British government to work towards increasing the home defence air force to 1,500 aircraft.[35] The Home Office in particular was aware that policies would need to be implemented and standardized, and that the public would need to be made aware of recommendations for ARP. Only then could the tasks of organizing local volunteers and air raid wardens begin – the very wardens whose 'put out that light!' injunctions would provoke the resentment and ire of their fellow citizens.

Little imaginative thinking on ARP took place between the early 1920s and the late 1930s, a period that otherwise included many strategic and technological developments. The Air Ministry was so pleased with the original report that it remained the doctrinal document on the subject until 1937.[36] These ideas required radical re-thinking when the more imminent threat of war forced the Home Office to formulate specific polices and put the force of law behind ARP measures. The shortcomings of the ARP Department and confusion over policy provided many areas of contestation for government critics. It is true that the ARP guides left many policy voids, sometimes intentionally so, in order to leave room for flexibility and alteration. During the writing of the official history, former civil servants objected to implications of inadequate planning by their departments and were keen that the record should make clear that these plans needed to be formulated under duress in a short period of time.[37] Yet incompleteness and flexibility was also held to be the British way of planning, the ideological basis of which will be explored in greater detail in Chapter 8.

ARP involved several intertwined areas of concern. While the public focused most on anti-gas provisions, gas masks, and directions for preparing their home shelters, ARP also consisted of measures to deflect or prevent bombardment, such as the much-despised blackout provisions. These requirements would ultimately place a large labour burden on householders throughout wartime. In addition, there were preparations to consider, such as decontamination stations (in the case of gas attack), first aid, wardens, fire watching posts, and supply centres. Much of the advice was predicated on the policy of dispersal that had been followed throughout World War I and endorsed in the 1920s. The idea of dispersal subtly underlined the concern over civilian morale and mandated that individuals should remain in their own homes or workplaces in the event of an air raid and avoid large groups. This policy partially served as a convenient means for the government to abrogate the costly option of building mass shelters along the lines being proposed for continental cities. However, there was a far more crucial reason for the policy of dispersal, and this was the avoidance of the potential devastation of public morale by a mass casualty event.

One way that the subject of ARP was introduced to the public was through the publication of circulars that were delivered to individual householders. Between 1935 and 1939, eight volumes of these were published on subjects ranging from *Personal Protection Against Gas* to *The Duties of Air Raid Wardens*.[38] Some were distributed free to householders and others made available at a charge of 2*d*. The first ARP circular was published in 1935, when E.J. Hodsoll issued *Anti-Gas Precautions and First Aid for Air Raid Casualties* to local authorities. It was to sell the most copies of any of the circulars.[39] As suggested by its title, it placed a disproportionate emphasis on gas, despite suggestions that high explosive bombs posed a far greater threat. This reflected the collective memory of gas warfare from the First World War and its prominence in the public imagination. The Chemical Warfare Research department of the Home Office undertook experiments and instituted plans to distribute 38 million gas masks, which were being manufactured at a rate of up to 150,000 per week by early 1937.[40] Anti-gas measures provided a highly visible way to demonstrate that something was being done. The first circular advised householders to construct a 'refuge room,' which could be accomplished with the use of inexpensive everyday materials such as tape and newspaper. Government officials believed that using simple means to render ordinary rooms gas-proof would assuage public fear and panic.[41] This advice relied on the assumption that householders had a spare room that could be devoted solely to this purpose, and critics later took issue with this point. Frederick Montague, the Labour MP for West Islington, mocked the 'paste and paper' ARP policy of the government as 'the jest of the moment'.[42]

The publication *The Protection of Your Home Against Air Raids* appeared in 1938 and was intended to address fully the threat of high explosive bombs.[43] As the name implied, in the spirit of Victorian self-help the booklet highlighted government policy that individual householders were responsible for their own air raid protection. Sir Samuel Hoare, Home Secretary from 1937–9, made it clear that the Home Office would only sanction the construction of shallow, splinter-proof shelters. He believed that cellars and basements could be turned into suitable shelters through reasonable adaptations, and a deep trench system in parks surrounded by populated areas would provide emergency shelter for those without home shelters or who were caught on the streets during an air raid.[44] An internal ARP Department memorandum from 1938 stated straightforwardly that 'shelter rooms for householders and shelters in factories are the responsibility of the householder and the factory owner'. Distributed to members of the ARP Parliamentary Committee, it laid out these principles, explicitly stating that 'specially [sic] strong shelters which are bomb-proof or partially bomb-proof have the disadvantage that, apart from excessive cost, they would militate against the policy of dispersal because people, knowing that they provided better cover, would make for them and leave their own homes'.[45] This statement is extraordinary in that it acknowledges that bomb-proof shelters provide the best protection but that they should not be made available for precisely that reason. The construction of permanent shelters for nightly occupation was considered politically inadvisable, and this government memo stated bluntly that public shelters should only provide protection against blasts and shrapnel,

along with reasonable gas-proofing. Geoffrey Lloyd, MP and
Parliamentary Undersecretary of State for the Home Office,
believed that the circular on home protection made the tasks for
householders clear, and that 'it must be assumed that householders,
in light of this advice, will do what they can to increase the
measure of protection afforded by their own homes'.[46]

The most intense stage of pre-war ARP was occasioned by the
Munich Crisis in September 1938 and involved the frantic
distribution of gas masks, the sandbagging of major buildings in
London, and the digging of trenches in central parks. Although
fears of aerial attack often arose in public discourse, maintaining
interest in ARP was another matter. There was a constant tension
between public apathy and fear, particularly in the mid 1930s; as a
political issue it did not really take shape in the public
imagination until Munich acted as a spur to both the public and
government. E.J. Hodsoll later wrote that the crisis was 'a
godsend', which exposed the inadequacy of many provisions and
gave the ARP Department time to admit and rectify
shortcomings,[47] and aided in the recruitment of volunteers as
the probability of war rose. The central government put out calls
for 100,000 volunteers in London alone in early 1938,[48] though it
would only be after September that adequate numbers of volunteers
were listed on government rolls.

The question of employer-provided shelters was particularly
thorny. The ARP Acts required that employers provide shelters, and
the position of the Home Office also pointed to the responsibilities of
employers. However, there was little guidance provided, nor were
measures instituted to ensure uniformity or quality of provisions.
Official ARP handbooks discussing large shelter design, including
Structural Defence and *Bomb Resisting Shelters*, did not appear until
1939, at which point national resources were being secured for
military uses, making it difficult to prepare shelters for factories and
larger workplaces. The Home Office made it clear that such advice
was only intended for such shelters to be provided by private
employers, but the result of supposed 'coordination' with large
employers to build shelters was vague at best.[49]

After 1937, when the need for anti-gas measures was eclipsed by the desire to protect against high explosive bombs, there were increasing calls for deep shelters. The leftist journal *Time and Tide* ran prominent editorials criticizing the government for continuing to concentrate on the gas threat. In October 1938, the publication also detailed the shortcomings of ARP that had been brought to light during the crisis.[50] Following Munich, the demand for deep shelters built at least to a depth of 60 feet with bomb-proof capabilities grew to such an extent that 'ministers felt concern at the opening of 1939 at a growing feeling of restlessness on the part of the public over this question'.[51] Despite the publicized protestations and alternative plans of left-wing critics and councils, the central government remained firm on the policy of dispersal into individual shelters. Sir John Anderson believed that provision of mass bomb-proof shelters was 'mistaken and impossible in practice'.[52]

Yet the government did alight on its own version of an eleventh-hour compromise. The Home Office began experimenting with sectional steel shelters in 1938. These shelters would become the prototype for the backyard 'Anderson' shelter. The Anderson shelter was essentially a curved corrugated steel structure approximately 6 X 5 X 7 feet that was to be buried in the ground and covered by at least one foot of earth, hence providing protection from all but a direct hit.[53] Though visually unimpressive, most technical experts agreed that the Anderson shelter did provide sufficient protection when installed correctly, and the belief was borne out by its wartime performance. The development of this shelter signalled some flexibility and adaptation, but it was also evidence of governmental determination to deal with the problem of protection from high explosive attack in its own way. One Cabinet report on the implications of the Hailey Commission stated that it would satisfy 'reasonable persons', and so official policy remained fixed at the outbreak of war. Officials were immovable in believing that the call for greater provisions for the public was based on the 'mistaken conception that widespread provision of deep shelters was a practical possibility'.[54] The government portrayed its policies as compatible with the British temperament of preferring the private comforts of home and disliking public shelters and being among strangers. The final chapter of this book looks at patriotism and dissent on the subject of deep shelter, revealing the ideological divide between those who held these precepts and the critics who believed that in the circumstances of total war a policy of self-help was immoral.

CHAPTER 3

'THE DEW OF DEATH' – DUELLING PERSPECTIVES ON POISON GAS

Gas may well prove the salvation of civilization in case of another world war. Even with the lethal gases of the last war, the use of which was decried as barbarous by conventional sentiment, statistics show that the proportion of deaths to the numbers temporarily incapacitated was far less than with the accepted weapons, such as bullets and shells! Moreover, chemistry affords us non-lethal gases which can overcome the hostile resistance [...] but without the lasting evils of mass killing or destruction of property.[1]

—Basil Liddell Hart, *Paris: or the Future of War*

This quotation by perhaps the most prominent British military commentator of the interwar years, Liddell Hart, is jarring to the contemporary reader given our views of gas and chemical weapons as barbaric weapons. Since ancient times, those who employ poison have been particularly loathed and viewed as treacherous and cowardly. Chemical weapons have been regarded as illegitimate weapons of war on these grounds, and for reasons that are not entirely rational – but human attitudes towards warfare are rarely rational.[2] As has been presented, the 'doomsday' culture of the interwar years initially appears to present a uniform picture of dread and horror immediately following the First World War regarding the use of gas warfare. Yet the interwar picture was actually far more complex. Attitudes towards gas altered between the 1920s and 1930s. In the former decade it was still possible to think of gas as a mysterious and frightening weapon, but one that was ultimately less deleterious to human life. The publication date of Liddell Hart's book (1925) is therefore quite significant. The more dominant and fearful views of the 1930s have coloured the historical record, and additionally the fact that World War II materialized as 'the gas war that never happened'[3] has also affected contemporary views on the subject. Because the taboo against the use of poison gas has become so entrenched in both military ethics and practice, reopening the debate about the humanity of the use of chemical weapons in warfare is now a non-starter.

This chapter makes a new contribution to the history of chemical weapons by detailing minority 'gas-tolerant' opinion throughout the interwar years. Although these views had limited effect on national and international policy, these contrarians made important contributions to the debate over ARP, particularly through their endorsement of government plans for civilian protection from poison gas. This perspective follows closely on the work of recent historians who have interpreted attitudes to gas warfare from the perspective of its status as a 'taboo'.[4] In A Strange and Formidable Weapon, Marion Girard has also explored the conflicting attitudes towards the use of poison gas as a weapon in the years immediately following the First World War.[5] She argues that the general population was horrified by gas but that military professionals in the 1920s were more gas-tolerant, viewing it as simply another weapon of professional soldiering. They adopted a utilitarian approach to the prevention of gas-related injuries. In fact, armed forces recruits to this day are primarily taught to think of gas as a psychological, rather than a physical, terror during nuclear, biological and chemical training. Convinced that an attack against civilians was inevitable, gas-tolerant commentators believed that the public must accept the threat and prepare effectively. They argued that the physical effects of gas could never be as grave as feared, since climactic and chemical conditions could not render attacks as deadly as had been assumed. These commentators divorced their arguments from the perceived immorality of gas, viewing it dispassionately, and instead focused effect on morale of the possible use of these weapons and on gas as primarily a means of spreading fear and panic. Nevertheless, events of the 1930s guaranteed that the fearful narrative regarding chemical weapons was reinforced and the taboo firmly established.

I seek to bring this narrative to bear on government anti-gas preparations in the 1930s, highlighting two unique aspects demonstrated in the ARP debate. First, this account traces how contrarian arguments demonstrate continuities from the 1920s to the 1930s. Those voicing these opinions, including supporters of government anti-gas measures, targeted their opponents as engaging in needless fear-mongering. Second, I will contrast how their attitudes towards the population – essentially viewed as militarized 'civilian soldiers' – contrasted with the 'innocent civilian' arguments of pacifists and anti-gas campaigners. At the crux of this exploration is the use of public morale as an argumentative tool. The anti-militarist side employed 'dew of death' imagery and argued for the continued sanctity of civilian status. The contrarians countered with charges of fear-mongering and presented a utilitarian perspective that accepted civilians as *de facto* combatants who should psychologically prepare for chemical warfare. Presenting themselves as anti-hysteria, they bolstered government plans for calm and reasonable anti-gas measures. The tenor of this debate would have important implications for the ARP debate as it unfolded.

International attitudes towards gas are simple to relate. As early as 1899, delegates to a Hague Peace Conference voted against chemical warfare, adopting a declaration agreeing 'to abstain from the use of projectiles the sole object of which is the diffusion of asphyxiating or deleterious gases'.[6] Attempts to explain the uncontested 'prohibitory norm' point to fear of the unknown. In general, weapons that imitate primitive violence – bayonets, mortars, even machine guns – are more readily acceptable than mechanized and scientific warfare. The early history of international treaty and prohibition endorses this perspective, and these attitudes remain an entrenched part of the international laws of armed conflict. In the wake of the First World War, a 1920 League of Nations report concluded that gas was 'a fundamentally cruel method of carrying on war, though not more so than certain other methods commonly employed, provided that they are only employed against combatants'. The use of such weapons against civilians, however, was said to be 'barbarous and inexcusable'.[7]

The primary international agreement regarding the use of poison gas was the Geneva Protocol of 1925, banning the use of chemical warfare, although it said nothing of research, development, manufacture and storage. Some commentators have labelled it merely 'a declaration of intent'.[8] The British understood the treaty to ban the first use of poison gas, but not the development or use of gas for defensive purposes, and they continued to investigate new chemical and biological substances and their antidotes.[9] Interwar treaties and proscriptions on gas served simply to make further development in the interwar years, and military plans for its use, all the more secretive.[10] The interwar period was characterized by a shadowy arms race in which rumour of new gases or antidotes occupied many fearful waking hours for military planners.

But as the early beliefs of Basil Liddell Hart illustrate, more neutral and even guardedly positive attitudes towards gas warfare existed. A variety of military and scientific experts, crossing political lines, proposed a radical counter-narrative of the humanity of gas war in the 1920s. Fritz Haber, recipient of the Nobel Prize for Chemistry in 1918 and defender of the German use of gas in World War I, concluded that gas did not cause undue suffering and therefore was not inhumane.[11] Similar commentators included J.B.S. Haldane and military analyst J.F.C. Fuller. Their views focused on gas as it had been employed in the trenches of the First World War — as a weapon against combatants and not civilians, and which had been demonstrated to be less deadly than originally feared. These 'apologists' for gas campaigned, ultimately ineffectually, to educate public opinion on the subject.[12] As enthusiasts, they forwarded their ideas in the mid 1920s, a time of short-lived international optimism and visionary hopes for European collective security and cooperation. Positive diplomatic connections between statesmen such as Gustav Streseman, Aristide Briand, and Austen Chamberlain, and the Dawes Plan agreement to alleviate German financial obligations all seemed to bode well for European cooperation and collective security. International agreements, such as the Locarno Treaties of 1925 and the Kellogg-Briand Pact of 1928, theoretically 'outlawing war', all contributed to feelings of hopefulness. A second world war seemed but a distant and theoretical prospect, and it was in this atmosphere that broader attitudes towards gas warfare were more easily contemplated.

J.B.S. Haldane figures prominently throughout this study of air raid preparations in the interwar years. A professor of genetics and subsequently biometry at University College London, he had experienced chemical warfare as an officer on the Western front during the First World War. Sent to the front lines in 1915, he witnessed the use of chlorine gas in combat and was one of three scientists initially set to work identifying gas and protecting against it. His father, John Scott Haldane, an eminent physiologist specializing in respiration, also arrived in France to carry out anti-gas experiments on himself and his son. Both men subjected themselves to hazardous rounds of self-testing with little thought of the dangers they were undertaking; John Scott Haldane would suffer permanent lung damage. Their findings called for the immediate issue of a higher grade of respirator, but the General Staff did not implement this recommendation.[13] By all accounts, Haldane threw himself into his role as both a soldier and a soldier–scientist. He persuasively argued that capable scientists should be used in the laboratory to contribute to the war efforts, rather than being sent to slaughter in the trenches,[14] and he later characterized his time at the Front as one of great excitement.

In 1925 Haldane published one of his boldest works: *Callinicus: A Defense of Chemical Warfare*. He named it after the legendary Callinicus of Heliopolis, the inventor of 'Greek fire' – one of the first recorded incendiary weapons. Haldane proposed a dramatic counter-narrative of gas warfare. He charged that pacifists who attempted to outlaw chemical warfare were not acting in the national interest and pointed to the 1907 Hague Conference as banning 'the most humane weapon ever intended'. He believed that such laws represented 'one of the most hideous forms of sentimentalism which has ever supported evil upon earth – the attachment of the professional soldier to cruel and obsolete killing machines'.[15] Indeed, fewer casualties were produced from gas than from conventional shells and explosive projectiles, although the lasting ill effects of serious exposure should not be underestimated. Speaking specifically from a tactical military standpoint, there was little indication that the use of poison gas threatened existing military protocols or significantly hindered strategy. *Callinicus*, a slim volume based on a public lecture, represented a significant attack against ignorance, establishment inflexibility, and a lack of scientific knowledge. Though there were flaws inherent in Haldane's arguments – mostly based on his lack of realistic assumptions[16] – he is wholly representative of the gas-tolerant perspective.

The rational and quantitative approach to gas taken by professionals such as Haldane contrasted with the emotional appeals evident in the account of laypeople such as the Earl of Halsbury, whose novel *1944* was often referenced in official circles. These appeals to emotion and humanitarian concerns over the gassing of civilians ultimately superseded the utilitarian arguments of the gas enthusiasts. The receptive audience for *Callinicus*, or the newspapers columns of Liddell Hart or Fuller, was relatively narrow, professional, and ultimately not a highly motivated group. While many of their fellow professionals may well have agreed that gas was not dire, that was an entirely different prospect than actively campaigning for its inclusion in official strategy. Acute motivation to do so simply did not exist. Consequently, acceptance of gas warfare represented a passive ideological stance. On the other hand, the ranks of highly committed anti-gas campaigners grew, and their sense of purpose only increased throughout the 1930s as a new war approached.

Pacifism and the 'Prohibitory Norm'

The 'Dew of Death' was a phrase popularized in the 1930s, referring particularly to the artificial compound known as Lewisite, mixed from acetylene, arsenious oxide and sulphur chloride. Lewisite was easily popularized and demonized as the gas that smelled like geraniums; the contrast between the purity of nature and the concoctions of the scientific laboratory was too dramatic to pass up, as evidenced in graphic posters produced both in Britain and the United States.[17] The danger was stated in the starkest terms by one pamphlet writer – 'one whiff enough for death'.[18] As a fear-laden phrase, the 'dew of death' was associated with the general threat of destruction by poison gas. Obsession with a substance that might kill or incapacitate millions, much like the idea of the 'knock-out blow', became a collective belief that few questioned. Many were terrified by the possibility while others, such as D. H. Lawrence who declared 'three cheers for the inventors of poison gas',[19] saw it as a fitting denouement for the debauchery and sordidness of the modern world. These beliefs, not surprisingly, also fed into the strident and burgeoning pacifist movement.

We have explored the fear of gas warfare as expressed in popular fiction. As the 1930s unfolded, concerns about gas also gathered pace as a political cause and a popular movement. Writers aligned with the centre to far left and the pacifist constituency played up horror scenarios to further political aims. The pacifist left – perhaps better termed anti-militarist – was particularly vociferous in denouncing chemical warfare and governmental preparations for civilian protection. They also resisted the classification of civilians as militarized entities for the purposes of modern total war. They expressed what one observer deemed 'romantic idealism', which played most heavily on visceral anti-gas emotion.[20] These critics emphasized the gas taboo to enforce their anti-war and anti-capitalist messages. It was more difficult, however, to agree on remedies to these ills. Different groups approached the issue with varied positions and priorities. The phrase 'against imperialism and war' demonstrates one element of the left-leaning pacifist critique. The

anti-armament campaign peaked in the early 1930s, most popularly
through the Peace Pledge Union and the League of Nations Union,
which organized the immensely successful 'Peace Ballot' in 1934–5,
garnering the signatures of more than one-third of the British adult
population.

Groups that preoccupied themselves with the prevention of gas
warfare in the interwar years also included the Women's Committee
on Scientific Warfare, the Women's International League for Peace
and Freedom, the Independent Labour Party and the Union of
Democratic Control (UDC). The UDC was a prominent group that
pushed the narrative of fear in the cause of disarmament and
international chemical weapons treaties. A major strain of pacifist
criticism focused on the 'merchants of death' and the broader
political problems they viewed as inherent in the capitalist and
imperialist European order. Pessimistic about the international
situation, disarmament, and the state of collective security, many
pacifists found the armaments industry a convenient target. They
viewed industrialists and private profiteering as the linchpin of the
'war-mongering impulse'. Essentially they forwarded a critique of the
military-industrial complex two decades before President Dwight
Eisenhower coined the term. Although the war in Spain did cause a
shift of rhetoric and a moderation of pacifism as many realized that
Fascism would need to be resisted through military force, this shift
was not evident until just before the outbreak of war.

Organizations such as the UDC produced many books and
pamphlets throughout the interwar years, drawing connections
between government, industry, and war. In its much-cited book *The
Secret International*, published in 1932, it listed the 'war profits' of
British firms such as Vickers and de Havilland. Utilizing a common
anti-armament argument, it depicted government ministers as a 'war
investment class' who held a natural interest in provoking war
scares.[21] The UDC also submitted testimony to the Royal
Commission on the Private Manufacture of and Trading in Arms
in 1935 in an attempt to outlaw the private arms trade. It suggested
that the arms industry, including heavy arms, chemicals, and aircraft
production, should be nationalized.[22] It remarked: 'There is no

remedy for these evils unless the whole industry is taken out of private hands. The abuses are inherent in the system itself.'[23] The Labour Party was also vocal on the subject, producing pamphlets such as *The Sky's the Limit! Plain Words on Plane Profits, Who's Who in Arms*, and *The Hawkers of Death* by pacifist campaigner and Labour MP Philip Noel-Baker.[24]

The UDC published its major critique regarding the issue of chemical weapons in a 1935 work called *Poison Gas*, which criticized the British government's approach as short-sighted and inadequate to deal with possible threats, both chemical and biological. Group members strongly believed that gas was a 'democratic' issue that should be decided by the people rather than politicians, scientists, or war profiteers.[25] They pointed to the dangers of phosgene, mustard gas, or new and 'unknown gases' including the famed 'dew of death'. The alarmist tone used by the UDC was apparent, with section headings such as 'The Perfection of War' and 'The Trio of Destruction'. Writer Kingsley Martin praised the book in a *New Statesman* editorial 'Death From the Air', which enforced his perception that no real air raid protection was available, and that the government simply wished to sanction the build-up of weapons. The *New Statesman* rarely used photographs in the 1930s, and consequently the half-page photo that accompanied the article of a group of individuals dressed in full gas-mask gear would have been particularly dramatic to readers.[26]

By the late 1930s, commentators could draw on actual use of gas in Abyssinia by Mussolini's forces in 1936. The handful of aerial attacks perpetuated by Italian aeroplanes represents a dark chapter in that conflict about which relatively little is known. A contemporary account noted that the Italians were employing a 'peculiarly loathsome form of warfare. Italy denies this, but evidence is corroborated by many witnesses including Red Cross doctors'.[27] Indeed, the Italians consistently denied having used chemical weapons. Although their attempts at concocting mustard-gas bombs were quite ineffectual from a strategic point of view, the bombing of tribal people and Red Cross tents was brutal from a humanitarian one. The account of eyewitness and British Ambulance Service official

John MacFie, *An Ethiopian Diary*, chronicled some of the horrors
visited upon civilians and served as a denunciation of the Italians and
as a warning for Europe.[28] The Socialist Medical Association was an
organization particularly concerned about such events. Founded in
1930, as its name implied its activities were mainly political: 'to
make doctors socialists, to assist in the work of the Labour Party, to
which it is affiliated, and especially to direct propaganda in favour of
a State Medical Service.' Its members also conducted research and
published pamphlets and reports on the medical consequences of the
use of poison gas.[29] Like other campaigners, the Socialist Medical
Association doubted that the Gas Protocol of 1925 would deter
aggression should it prove advantageous to the aggressor.

Some commentators focused on gas and the threat to the civilian
population as a primary reason for pacifism and collectivism – a
widespread passion in the 1930s that reflected a continuation of
the liberal optimism that international law might prevent war.[30]
Norman Angell, the journalist and Labour MP, was prominently
involved with the UDC and the League of Nations Union and was
designated a Nobel Peace Prize Laureate in 1933. His calls for
international policing and collective security were rooted in a belief
that national leaders blindly followed 'hysteria' on the question of the
air danger. His major intervention on the subject of the next war was
his 1934 book, *The Menace to Our National Defence*, in which he voiced
the opinion that it 'will be an affair of widespread gas attacks by
aircraft squadrons and gas carrying tanks'.[31] He believed that frantic
aerial armament bore similarities to a stampeding crowd that
destroys itself rather than taking rational action to escape danger;
mutual deterrence was both useless and destructive. Heinz
Liepmann, a German-Jewish émigré, was particularly affected by
22 April 1915, the date of the first gas attack perpetuated in the First
World War, terming it 'the dress rehearsal for the destruction of
Europe'. Combining fears of scores of chemical bombers wiping out
entire cities along with hints at a conspiracy by an organized group of
'well-paid historians and chemists', he asserted that a mere three
drops of Lewisite would prove fatal. Anticipating charges of creating
public panic, he defended himself against critics who used statistics

to downplay the seriousness of gas-related wartime casualties. He argued that '... I will only repeat that there is no protection against poison gas. Anyone who says that such protection is possible, is a liar.'[32] Aldous Huxley was another individual who believed in the inevitability of chemical attacks against civilians unless war was prevented by international treaty. In *An Encyclopedia of Pacifism*, citing Baldwin's pessimism, he asserted that in the face of modern scientific dangers, gas drill and blackouts were 'futile'.[33] A doctor, writing for a Victor Gollancz (later the publisher of the Left Book Club) volume on the next war, was certain that modern war against civilians would take the form of conventional bombs followed by gas. She felt, in agreement with Red Cross doctors, that no salvation was to be found in shelters, only in instruments like the Kellogg-Briand Pact outlawing war.[34]

One particularly influential book circulated among the pacifist constituency was *Challenge to Death*, edited by the prolific writer Storm Jameson. From 1938–44 she served as the president of PEN (which stood for Poets, Essayists and Novelists) – a group prominently involved in humanitarian activities including the aid of refugees from Germany. She was also a contributor to the war fiction genre, most notably her depiction of Britain as a fascist state in her futuristic novel *In the Second Year*.[35] She was a committed pacifist until resigning as a Peace Pledge Union Sponsor in early 1940, accepting the inevitability and justness of war with Hitler like many of her ideological bedfellows. *Challenge to Death* was well known in political and literary circles, and its essays reflected the dizzying range of approaches and arguments within the pacifist movement. The book included pieces by Jameson, Vera Brittain, Philip Noel-Baker, Julian Huxley, and J.B. Priestley on 'The Public and the Idea of Peace'. The book explored non-violent means of preventing conflict and the threat of modern war, including an essay by Gerald Heard entitled 'And Suppose We Fail? After the Next War?' He portrayed a London destroyed by poison gas and filled with panic as thousands fall dead from 'a whiff of phosgene'. The conclusion of his speculative narrative was 'such, then, is the picture of the Britain which is left, if indeed it can escape complete collapse and dissolution after the next war [...]. At any of these turns order may fail and anarchy win.'[36] The dominant theme of *Challenge to Death* was the advocacy of collective security, including the idea of an international air force, and the idea that poison gas must necessarily be included as a component of comprehensive disarmament. Philip Noel-Baker emphasized the innate immorality of the current arms race and the necessity of an international air force. Pacifists such as Noel-Baker rested their arguments on the basis that no amount of deterrence or retaliatory power would really provide protection against modern warfare, including chemical weapons, being used on civilians.

The 1930s: The Contrarians, Questions of 'Morale' and Anti-hysteria

Despite this darkened mood of the 1930s, some professional commentators continued to take deliberate aim at writers and commentators whom they viewed as exaggerating the threat of poison gas and fear-mongering. They therefore portrayed their ideas as a necessary palliative to fear. A dichotomous discourse was constructed around the subject of gas war, one that pitted the 'alarmists' against these 'rational' commentators, who regarded the threat of gas warfare as more psychological than material. Some of these individuals fit the 'eccentric military commentator' descriptor, but many important contributors were respected professional scientists of the contrarian ilk. Marion Girard has pointed out that the British government prized the expertise of the 'gas tolerant', rewarding some such individuals with important positions.[37] Their legacy in the gas war debate was not a definitive alteration of public attitudes towards gas as a cruel and unusual weapon. This opinion was too thoroughly fixed in the public mind. However, their endorsement of government anti-gas measures as reasonable and sensible was of great value to the Home Office in the interwar period, and therefore of historical significance to the preparation for airborne attack.

It should be pointed out that there was a great deal of concern about gas in both official circles and among prominent scientists, some of whom pressed the Home Office to investigate claims of the production of new bombs and gasses by Nazi Germany. Their 'gas-tolerant' attitudes did not indicate laxity or indifference. Included among these individuals was Frederick Lindemann, the highly influential scientific advisor to Winston Churchill during World War II (and one of his closest personal friends) and advocate of strategic bombing against German targets.[38] In 1935 the British publication of Otto Lehmann-Russbueldt's *Germany's Air Force* appeared, describing apparent German plans for the aerial gassing of Britain.[39] Though some observers doubted that the most sensational rumours of deadly gas production were realistic, no one wished to be caught unaware by any new developments in gas manufacture or usage. The British government had been highly invested in gas defence and deterrence since the First World War. The Chemical Warfare Committee continued to conduct tests and provide guidance against gas. It also undertook experiments to develop new respirators and performed ventilation tests on two Underground stations in 1929.[40] By 1942, the Chemical Warfare Experimental Station at Porton Down had produced many chemical compounds for testing purposes, including about 156 tons of Lewisite deployed in field experiments. It developed a supposedly effective antidote to Lewisite that the Germans were also reputed to have discovered.[41]

Major-General Sir Henry Thuillier, who had been the first Director of Gas Services in 1916, was a primary representative of the gas-tolerant faction who advised the government on ARP in the interwar period. Though he favoured international limitation to the use of gas, he stuck doggedly to the notion that chemical weapons should be permitted on the modern battlefield, entitling one chapter of his 1939 book 'Humanity of Gas Warfare'. Citing the customary historical evidence, he asserted that up to 96 per cent of gassed soldiers during the First World War had been able to return to duty. Proper protection and gas discipline could eliminate the most severe of these injuries, while no protection existed against shrapnel or bombs.[42] By this rationale, no legitimate grounds existed on which to ban poison gas from the battlefield, and furthermore complete prohibition of the use of chemical warfare would never be 'practicable'. Yet the worst effects could 'be averted altogether if the Government and people worked to complete the precautions which are now in hand for saving people from injury and from panic'.[43] Further support for this perspective came from military men and government officials such as H. Montgomery Hyde, aide to Lord Londonderry and later a wartime intelligence officer, MP for North Belfast, and author of *British Air Policy Between the Wars 1918–1939*. Thought to be overly sympathetic towards Londonderry's term as the Minister for Air, he denounced scaremongering about secret gases that could kill millions.[44]

Another military commentator, B.C. Dening, stated that 'the whole British conception as regards the use of gas is a definite fallacy' based on misplaced humanitarian ideals.[45] Writing in *The Spectator*, Brigadier-General E.L. Spears derided the 'lurid pictures drawn of peaceful cities gassed or bombed from the air, and of a decimated civilian population'. While he did not deny that such an eventuality might occur, he concentrated on the positive uses of technology, arguing that

> men in tanks and armoured cars instead of foot-soldiers, and aeroplanes instead of cavalry, will be the protagonists in the next great conflict [. . .]. There will be no need of cannon-fodder such as we knew in 1914–1918. War will be a matter of highly trained experts in elaborate machines of destruction, fighting other experts in equally deadly machines over a wide area of ground.[46]

Some concentrated on alleviating the fear in the public mind of rogue attacks against civilians – some with a greater degree of gentleness and tact than others – primarily believing that the threat of gas attacks was highly overblown and that the greatest danger lay in the likelihood of public panic. In an article in *The Times* in 1934 entitled 'Nonsense About Poison Gas' the author, Dr Freath, asserted that 'more nonsense had been talked about chemical warfare probably than about any other subject in the world'. He doubted that the right climactic conditions for widespread gas use against civilians could ever exist and believed that lurid fantasies had simply seized the public mind with psychological terrors.[47] Some believed that widespread education about gas was the best national defence, arguing that 'the menace to health and life inherent in gas warfare diminishes proportionately as the nature and properties of individual gases become better and more widely known, and as the gas defensive organization based on that knowledge, steadily grows'.[48]

The primary 'anti-hysteria' publication that others drew on and acknowledged in the crafting of their analyses of the poison gas danger was *Don't Be Afraid of Poison Gas* by F.N. Pickett. The author stated quite forthrightly that 'poison gas is not the menace it is popularly supposed to be'.[49] Insisting that the dread of gas was primarily psychological, he cautioned against panic and emphasized the responsibility for calm and countering 'hostile propaganda'. Mustard gas, for example, was highly painful but usually not fatal, and he contended that even a housewife could concoct a rudimentary gasmask in an emergency. In addition, he countered the graphic 'dew of death' rumours, insisting that the laws of chemistry were finite, meaning that no new gases or harmful agents could be produced. Though this assertion was of dubious scientific merit, it was no doubt comforting to think that the possibilities of destructive power remained narrow.

Another author with an especially arresting book title was James Kendall, a professor of Edinburgh University and another government expert who officially advised the ARP Department. In 1938, he published *Breathe Freely! The Truth About Poison Gas* in which he singled out three groups for particular criticism: the left, 'lurid' fiction writers, and military commentators who exaggerated dangers in order to increase the perceived importance of their particular branch of the services.[50] He also categorically mocked the 'dew of death' alarmists as irresponsible fear-mongers, and blasted pacifists such as Bertrand Russell and the hyperbolic predictions he had forwarded regarding gas warfare in *Which Way to Peace?*. Kendall approached the question of morale in much the same way as Pickett, quoting his fellow author at length and emphasizing that if the nation as a whole were to take reasonable precautions against poison gas, there were no grounds for panic. In this vein, Augustin M. Prentiss, a retired army Colonel and the writer of *Chemicals in War*, claimed that the literature on chemical warfare had not kept pace with technical developments. Much in the same vein as Kendall, he argued that '. . . the subject of chemical warfare has been the happy hunting ground for sensational newspaper and magazine writers whose imaginations have furnished lurid pictures of whole populations being wiped out at a single blow with poison gas dropped from airplanes'.[51]

Contrarianism served to enforce official government policy, and this was ultimately the most important contribution these individuals provided to the national debate. Official proposals focused on individual preparations and 'self-help' refuge rooms that would protect occupants against gas fumes. Among the ARP Department's strongest defenders were several chemists and military officials who had previously handled poisonous gases: James Kendall, along with Major-General C.H. Foulkes and J. Davidson Pratt, who had been wounded in the war.[52] Foulkes had been a director of gas services in the First World War, so he had more than a small claim to expertise, even if his account of leading the British Special Brigade against German gas warfare was biased, self-justifying, and ignored important failures.[53] During the 1930s he also acted as a private ARP consultant to factories and businesses, lectured on the subject, and wrote *Commonsense and ARP*, a privately published manual that reiterated many of the official Home Office publication positions in an accessible format.[54] In reaction to the findings of leftist critics detailed later in this book, Foulkes declared in the journal *Nature* that they could do nothing but harm. Such criticisms, he felt, were calculated to destroy confidence in the Home Office's defensive measures.

The contrarians in the poison gas debate fit most naturally with government arguments and imperatives due to their primary emphasis on the dangers of the threat of poison gas to morale rather than its assumed lethality to human life. The official emphasis on the distribution of gas masks and the advice to construct gas-proof rooms demonstrates that the discourse of fear influenced government policy. At the very least, officials had to show that they were doing something to alleviate public fears. At the same time, the Home Office could draw on a professional body of opinion to keep these fears within what it regarded as reasonable strictures. The military men of the 1920s and authors of the 1930s held a common belief that the low morality rates of soldiers who had been subjected to gas during the First World War demonstrated that gas was not an immoral weapon. Most of these men also believed in the impracticality of large-scale gas attacks by air. Though unable to produce any sea change to the prevailing prohibitory norm regarding gas – an unlikely prospect from the outset – the commentators were able to serve as a slight counterweight to some of the more hyperbolic fears of civilian attack. As we now know, the 'dew of death' would fail to materialize during the war, though the advantage of hindsight does nothing to diminish the real fears of interwar Britons. These gas-tolerant contrarians also tended to defend Baldwin's strategic observations about bombing and civil defence by essentially accepting that civilians were now simply combatants without uniforms. They pointed out that, in the world of *realpolitik*, enemy women and children could only be spared at the expense of British women and children. Foreign civilians were no longer immune from attack, so likewise British civilians must accept the threat and necessary discipline of anti-gas measures regardless of personal ideology.

CHAPTER 4

C.G. GREY AND J.B.S. HALDANE – TWO PROFESSIONAL MEN, TWO IDEOLOGIES

Let it be said at once that if one could have eliminated the author's political confusion this could have been by far the most authoritative and complete pronouncement on the subject to date. Dr Haldane is probably, apart from the structural engineering aspect, the most scientific exponent on the problem. He has studied every ramification continuously since he assisted his famous father in the Great War [. . .]. One could wish, however, that he had confined his attention more specifically to pure science, and less obviously to political viewpoints. One cannot help feeling that the scientist in him has had to take second place to the politician seeking his main conclusion [. . .]. It remains to emphasise [sic] that, even though many readers will differ from the author, this is a most important publication on ARP [. . .] and the sooner the various points are taken up by those responsible, the sooner will the man in the street, to whom this book is dedicated, feel that his interests are being adequately studied.[1]

–Journal of the Air Raid Protection Institute, on
J.B.S. Haldane's book *A.R.P.*

... C.G. Grey was the most famous, most pertinacious aeronautical commentator of that time [...]. Much of C.G. Grey's perception of the shape of things to come, whether aircraft or international affairs, has proved remarkably accurate; but it is the pungency of his comments on the contemporary scene which was, and still is, so enlivening.[2]

—Harald Penrose

C.G. Grey and *The Aeroplane* Magazine

The figure of journalist C.G. Grey serves as an appropriate foil to J.B.S. Haldane, the *de facto* leader of leftist air raid precautions (ARP) criticism. He reflects the rightist vision of national salvation through air power and the almost fanatical obsession with flying that characterized the age. He was also a politicking professional who saw no tension between his role as a journalist and agitation at the highest levels of the Air Ministry. Grey spoke to a constituency that prized the notion of the 'new man' of the air. This group was both vocal and influential, believing that Britain needed to boldly advance towards dominance in both civilian and military aviation.

Grey was one of the founding editors of *The Aeroplane*, which was established in 1911, and he remained at the helm of the publication until 1939, when his increasingly right-wing political views forced his resignation. Grey was unapologetically pro-fascist, anti-communist, and undoubtedly anti-Semitic. He wrote in one editorial that Germany and Great Britain were 'the two white nations' of pre-eminent greatness, and as such he believed they should undertake a natural alliance against Fascism. He once claimed to be 'pro-Semitic' but 'anti-Japhetic',[3] whatever such terminological distinction was intended to imply. He was also an open admirer of the regimes, along with the aviation programs, of Hitler and Mussolini. He was particularly impressed with the latter's contributions to flying, and he cultivated personal friendships with prominent individuals in the Italian government and air force. His statements make for uncomfortable reading, although he largely jettisoned them in 1939 at the start of war. Adjectives used to describe him ranged from

the fond to the censorious. To his apologists, the monocled editor
played the role of a curmudgeonly speaker of truth and had the
tempestuous grit to jolt a complacent government into action
regarding air power and rearmament. He was never one to stint in
criticizing the British government in the harshest terms. To
detractors, he was ill-tempered and irredeemably narrow-minded and
xenophobic.

A friendly biographer wrote about Grey's 'common touch', his
lack of pompous attitude, and his many irreverent editorials that
guaranteed that *The Aeroplane* was read far beyond its actual
circulation.[4] His good friend Harald Penrose wrote about Grey
extensively without commenting on his politics. In his book on
British aviation during the 1920s, Penrose quoted Major Oliver
Stewart, also a friend and contemporary of Grey: 'Charles Grey was a
great man. He was witty, incisive, challenging, thought-provoking,
altogether incorrigible, and even people who hated every opinion he
expressed found themselves stimulated by his style and thought.'[5]
Grey's obituary in *The Times* glossed over his admiration for the right-
wing dictatorships. The writer claimed that Grey's views arose not
from a love of Fascism but merely from 'personal friendship with and
great esteem for certain leading Italian airmen, including Marshal
Balbo'. Furthermore, when his editorial position came to an end
'there were many public demonstrations of the affection in which he
was now universally held'.[6] In 1960, the British European Airways
named one of their aircraft the *Charles Grey*. In a history of the BOAC
(British Overseas Airways Corporation), John Pudney labelled Grey
as an 'irrepressible' character with 'a lively mind', whose candour was
vital to aeronautical writing in his day – again, without even hinting
at his politics.[7] The air of irascibility no doubt helped to secure his
reputation as 'far and away the most remarkable, controversial, and
oft-quoted aviation writer of his day'.[8] He wrote in a purposefully
provocative style, describing the Great War as a minor conflict that
lasted only four years and did 'comparatively little damage'.[9]

While Grey's more extreme views naturally cannot be held as
representative of the larger group of aviators, he did enjoy an
extended tenure of pre-eminence and influence through his editorial

post and unofficial connections with both military and civilian aviation. His sub-editor, Geoffrey Dorman, had been a friend of Oswald Mosley at the Royal Flying Corps Flying School in 1915 and later became a supporter of the British Union of Fascists.[10] As a prominent figure, Grey allows us to access complex and sometimes contradictory expressions of British nationalism, not all of which were fixed or absolute. It is clear that Grey's readers, as well as admiring historians and commentators, viewed him as an excitable though fundamentally harmless commentator, and he was warmly appreciated as a friend and colleague. Yet at the same time his views on political and racial questions, even for his time, were undoubtedly risible. The fact that these views were hardly touched on by biographers perhaps signals that there was something about aviation in particular that promoted an acceptance of them. It begs the question of how normalized these more extreme political positions were within aviation circles. For Grey they seem to have been a personal conviction tied to his views on military aviation and rearmament. As the *Sunday Express* noted when he stepped down from the editorship of *The Aeroplane*: 'He believes and has never hesitated to say so – that we should be governed by a strong party of the extreme Right.'[11] Grey certainly did not belong by any means to a 'Cliveden Set' pro-German aristocratic milieu, and there is no particular hint that he actually sought links with any fascist groups active in Britain.

One dominant theme in interwar British aviation was the notion of aviators as a breed apart, a multinational cadre of individuals who were more loyal to each other than their own nation-states. These ideas had deep roots in the mythology of the flying Aces of the Great War, serving as a foil for the deadly and unheroic ground war. Tales of man-to-man battles proved irresistible fodder for newspapers and contemporary writers. The recounting of near escapes, off-duty antics, and the chivalric treatment of a vanquished foe were dedicated to the gallant flyers. These flyers were gentlemen not only by social class but also in the perceived nature of their undertakings. The air was not a working-class realm. The official historian of aviation in the First World War noted that 'an immense service was rendered in those early years by gentlemen adventurers, engineers and pilots, who all for love and nothing for reward, built machines and flew them'.[12] Flying was conceived of as an aristocratic activity associated with pursuits such as horsemanship. Flying was also aristocratic because the costs of training as a pilot were exorbitant and were borne by the individual candidate until quite late into the First World War. This excluded those lacking private means.

Grey had long demonstrated susceptibility towards the narrative of chivalry in the air. He equated piloting with the 'glorious cavalry' in his book, British Fighter Planes, written in 1941 after the triumph of the Battle of Britain.[13] Penning the preface to the English translation of Manfred von Richthofen's autobiography The Red Air Fighter, he painted aerial combat with unabashed romanticism. Grey portrayed Von Richthofen as a sort of slightly 'unevolved British schoolboy' who might have been a country gentleman had he had the good fortune to have been born British.[14] Grey wrote: 'It is one of the accepted facts of the war that the German aviators have displayed greater chivalry than any other branch of the German services.'[15] Grey corresponded with German officials throughout the mid-1930s after Hitler's revival of German military aviation, offering expressions of friendship. The German Air Attaché, writing to Grey in 1936, hoped that the good relationships and friendly feeling that existed in both nations in the field of aviation would 'become real guarantors of friendship and peace'.[16]

Similarly, Grey extended this feeling of the 'brotherhood of aviators', towards the efforts of German flyers participating in the Spanish Civil War. Spanish Nationalist pilots who supported General Franco also viewed the conflict in terms of the heroism of the flyer. One of them, Captain Jose Larios, dedicated his memoirs 'to keep alive the memory of gallant airmen'.[17] Fascist sympathizers, along with Catholic publications who supported Franco as a protector of the Church against anarchistic and anti-clerical violence, undertook a concerted propaganda effort to portray the Nationalist cause and the aerial bombing of cities in a more favourable light. Among the outright lies spread was the allegation that fires and other destruction had been wrought by the Republican side itself, anarchists, communists, Jews, or homosexuals.[18] Grey was among those who wholly propagated this view. From his point of view, Republican forces were anarchistic and antisocial rebels and the pilots who patrolled the skies were acting for the good of civilization.

No aspect of Grey's work was more important to him or valued by his supporters than his advocacy of British aviation and a strong Royal Air Force (RAF). Grey was an industry man, and his opinion reflects at least a portion of what members of the Royal Aeronautical Society, those with financial interests in aeronautics, or those simply enthralled with the mechanics of the aeroplane, felt about their endeavours. He campaigned for increases in both the RAF and government-sponsored research and development in the field of aircraft manufacture. His editorials routinely denounced disarmament, and he firmly believed that a world without weapons was but a fantasy and entirely impossible in practice. He also lamented attacks on the Air Ministry, the short-sightedness of British policy, and affirmed the necessity of the RAF retaining its independence from the army.[19] He once wrote 'the fact that I know my articles infuriate so many people has been one of my chief incentives [. . .]. I always have a hope that the unpleasantly abrasive qualities of these articles in *The Aeroplane* many have helped a number of people concerned with British aviation to think a little more sharply than they might have done otherwise.'[20]

Grey was part of a coterie of aviation enthusiasts who viewed themselves as saviours of the nation. As Martin Pugh describes, 'airmindedness relied on a collection of peers, entrepreneurs, and propagandists, many of them characterised by extremism and eccentricity'.[21] These included aristocrats such as Lord Rothschild, the Duke of Richmond, and Lord Montagu of Beaulieu. Tommy Sopwith, an early flyer and founder of the Sopwith Aviation Company that produced the famed 'Sopwith Camel' single-seat fighter during World War I, was another important contributor. Outspoken socialite Lady Houston became a patroness of British aircraft design when the national government refused funding. Some of her largesse contributed towards the prototypes that led to the building of the Spitfire aircraft. She later became known among admirers as 'the woman who won the air'.[22] While this moniker is no doubt hyperbole, it does reflect the influential role that dedicated individuals played in interwar aviation. The fact that most were iron-willed, stubborn and indefatigable undoubtedly helped their cause. While at times many made themselves a sheer nuisance to officialdom, they contributed a great deal towards promoting aviation.

Sir Samuel Hoare, at the time Secretary of State for Air, called Grey a 'helpful critic'. Writing to his friend Grey, Hoare said, 'You know better than anyone the difficulties with which we have been faced, the internecine battle, for instance, with the Admiralty and to a less degree with the War Office, the atmosphere of personal bitterness that in the years immediately after the war had entered into many corners of the Air Force and the British world, the constant pressure to reduce expenditure...'.[23] At Grey's memorial service, Lord Tedder, long-time Marshal of the RAF, stated that his 'driving force was the belief that Britain must be at the top and that what Britain did and produced, should, could and must be the best in the world'.[24] This reflects the fact that Grey primarily saw himself as a patriot and saw his attachments to European dictatorships as secondary. After his dismissal at the beginning of World War II, Grey reportedly expressed to a friend his relief that he did not have to edit *The Aeroplane* during the Phoney War. He wrote that it would have tested his patience 'to bust up that absurd official truce when our bombers were forbidden to drop bombs on German land but were shot down by the dozen by reconnaissance'.[25] Grey proved himself to be a bulldog of a nationalist.

Grey also spoke to the question of ARP, stating that 'an efficient system of passive defence is of the utmost importance to those who take part in the active defence of the country [... it serves to] help to prevent panic, alleviate suffering and to reduce the number of casualties and the amount of damage'.[26] He did, however, fly his true colours in an editorial some six months later regarding the psychology of bombing and the inevitability of civilian populations being attacked. Regarding the former point, he did not think there was much more to be discovered about the mass psychology of populations in wartime that had not been discussed in the nineteenth century by Clausewitz. Echoing Baldwin, he delivered his firmest pronouncement on the subject:

There is only one sure protection against being bombed and that is to have such a bombing fleet that the other fellow will never dare bomb you. You can have all the Archie guns, balloon barrages and interceptors you like, but you will never stop the bombers from getting through.[27]

Friendly commentators have seemed to suggest that Grey's abrasiveness was in keeping with the emergence of the brash and bold new world of flying. Some truly believed that such a figure was intrinsically required in order to ruffle traditions and to oppose an establishment that was resistant to change and blind to the reality of international aerial competition. Indeed, Grey's views on rearmament and the role of the RAF were predominant in the field of aviation. W.E. Johns, author of the *Biggles* stories and editor of *Popular Flying*, provides an interesting counterpoint to C.G. Grey. Although of decidedly different political beliefs than Grey, he voiced many of the same themes regarding rearmament as did his fellow aviation editor. Despite the fact that he was a pacifist and arch critic of the British government's policy of non-intervention in Spain, Johns believed that war was inevitable and that the nation must be prepared. He also sustained a call for rearmament in *Popular Flying*, with statements such as: 'Rightly or wrongly I hold the view that the more aeroplanes we have the more likely we are to avoid war.'[28]

When Grey stepped down from *The Aeroplane* on the eve of war in August 1939, tributes to his editorship read like obituaries of sorts, such as the following published in the rival journal *Flight*, reflecting on Grey's role in promoting British aviation:

The names of C.G. Grey and *The Aeroplane* have been synonymous for so long a period that one had come to regard them as inseparable. Many will regret the retirement of C.G. Grey. He has served a long term of activity in the great cause. If his outspoken and fearless criticism has aroused the ire of many sections of the community, both at home and abroad, his views have often been respected and have acted as a goad to further effort.[29]

It the end it might be tempting to leave off with the opinion that individuals such as Grey were 'good chaps' at the end of the day, whose extremist claims were just a bit of innocent dilettantism. Yet their incendiary and offensive rhetoric had real effects, if not influence, and they might have had rather more impact if the fledgling British fascist movement had been more successful. His grievances against the establishment predisposed him to the extreme right and to wild conspiracy theories combining his anti-Semitism and antipathy towards big business.[30] At the same time, Grey does embody many of the contradictions inherent in such political beliefs in 1930s Britain. When it really did matter for his country, he did realise the over-exuberance of his embrace of the fascist 'new man.' As such, C.G. Grey just barely landed himself on the 'right side' of history, assured of positive remembrances from colleagues in government and industry.

J.B.S. Haldane and the Leftist Critique of Science

J.B.S. Haldane belongs to a bygone generation of scientific and intellectual polymaths, of which Bertrand Russell was another important example. These individuals published respected books and publicly commented on an astounding range of subjects. Both Russell and Haldane were intensely political, combining their public intellectual work with advocacy for leftist and even radical issues. Especially during the First World War, Russell had become prominent as a pacifist, secularist, and antiwar campaigner, and in the interwar period he forwarded controversial ideas about modern love and marriage in tandem with his reformist second wife, Dora. As a high scientist, Haldane's bold forays into politics and popular publishing did not go entirely unremarked. Convention dictated that nationally-prominent scientists at prestigious research institutions such as Cambridge should neither popularize their work for mass audiences nor sully their hands with partisan squabbles. Haldane challenged this ethos, undaunted in presenting himself as a political agitator and a public intellectual.

Haldane reflected a move towards 'leftist science' in the 1930s – the movement that forms a partial background for this narrative of ARP criticism. Gary Werskey chronicled some of this movement in his book *The Visible College*, focusing on J.D. Bernal, J.B.S. Haldane, Lancelot Hogben, Hyman Levy and Joseph Needham. These individuals sought to ameliorate the worst products of scientific genius, which Bernal was to characterize as 'a super-efficient machine for natural destruction with men living underground and only coming up in gas masks'.[31] As prominent members of the Cambridge Scientists' Anti-War Group, whose activities are explored later in this book, Bernal and Joseph Needham promoted a model for the cooperative and peaceful uses of science. Indeed, pacifist causes were the initial focus of attention for most 'leftist scientists', also incorporating critiques of capitalism, imperialism, and war profiteering that were products of that time. All these elements were evident in the campaign against the 'Merchants of Death' referenced in the gas warfare debate. From 1936, however, this group shifted its activities to encompass an entire movement 'Against Fascism and War' as part of the vaguely defined Popular Front that was prompted by the Spanish Civil War. Despite the drift away from pacifism, the belief that scientific progress could only occur with socialism remained a defining feature of the movement. Bernal himself stated as much in his landmark 1939 book *The Social Function of Science*, and he firmly believed that capitalist societies wasted human potential through competition and non-rational production.[32]

Following a conversion to this vision of the radical scientific left in 1931, Haldane pursued politics with the eagerness he had previously devoted to arguments such as those epitomized by his book *Callinicus*. The arena for this conversion was the second International Congress of the History of Science and Technology, held in Kensington in 1931. The Congress included a lecture by the Soviet scientist Nicholai Bukharin on the role of scientists creating socialist culture in the Union of Soviet Socialist Republics. Haldane had finally identified the cause for which he had been waiting. Zealously taking up his new identity as a credible revolutionary, he attempted to expunge the signs of his upper-middle class background. For example, he insisted on travelling in a third-class railway carriage to demonstrate newfound distance from his true class origins.[33] It was somewhat reminiscent of the character of Philip Ravelston, the well-off Marxist publisher of '*Antichrist*', featured in George Orwell's 1936 novel *Keep the Aspidistra Flying*. He seeks to demonstrate reverse snobbery and working-class solidarity by slumming in a comfortable flat in 'the wilds' near Regent's Park.

Befitting the range of his scientific knowledge and interests, Haldane's views were decidedly complex, even if his political rhetoric often was not. While he continued to downplay the threat of poison gas, he was also critical of government and military policy. He openly questioned the offensive first-strike policy of targeting enemy civilians, deeming it to be 'murder'.[34] His first-hand experiences in Spain and his study of air raid preparations in both Spain and Britain further deepened his thinking on military issues and his commitment to leftist politics. He approached both issues primarily as a chemist and as a former military officer. These combined sets of expertise made him, in the words of his biographer, 'tailor-made for the campaign which the Communists now led'.[35] Haldane travelled to Spain as an expert and advisor to the Republican government on the issue of poison gas protection, visiting Madrid in December 1936 and again in March 1937. His time in Spain convinced him that the Spanish had more to teach him on the subject of ARP than *vice versa*. The grand cause of Republican Spain allowed Haldane to display his sweeping political rhetoric – he claimed solidarity with the Spaniards simply by having experienced an air raid. As he claimed in a BBC broadcast, 'If I lived for a thousand years, it might still be my proudest boast that on Christmas day, 1936, I was a citizen of Madrid'.[36] The subject held deep emotional resonance for him; on one occasion during a meeting on Spain, he railed against the local Conservative MP for Hampstead, George Balfour, as 'one of those responsible for the massacre of the women and children in Madrid'.[37] He was no more courteous towards the Labour Party, accusing it of being complicit in the suppression of information regarding Spanish air raids. In his opinion, mainstream Labour refused to tackle the issue as the Communist Party did and was particularly spineless in supporting the British government's official policy of non-intervention.

In rallies held throughout England to publicize his book *A.R.P.*, Haldane spoke about the role of leftist scientists in promoting the truth about ARP, a truth that he felt was being 'kept from the British people'.[38] Based on his experience in Spain and his enthusiasm for deep shelters, Haldane was the key leftist critic who instigated this debate. His approach was based on a fundamental belief that mass deep shelters were the only morally acceptable way to proceed, as not even the moderately well off could provide their own shelters. This moral basis reflected leftist and socialist definitions of mutual obligation, in contrast to the individualism promoted by government plans. As such, he led a campaign that emphasized both left-wing social issues and his alternative scientific basis for ARP based on personal observation.

Though he defended the technical merits of government gas-proof rooms, he nevertheless believed that their widespread use did not constitute a useful and sound ARP policy. Following what he had witnessed in Spain, he stated, 'I doubt if gas protection in ordinary houses is worth worrying about in comparison with protection from high explosive'.[39] Furthermore, he came to believe that the refuge room advice was counterproductive, since it would encourage civilians to remain inside these rooms within their homes and therefore render them vulnerable to high explosive bombs. He wrote in the forward to a Communist Party publication:

Six months ago we were to shelter in gas-proof rooms. The Communists were attacked as panic-mongers for saying that these were useless against explosives. To-day we are offered steel shelters, which are a little better than nothing, and propped basements, which are probably rather worse. Six months hence the Government will doubtless admit that propped basements are eyewash, like refuge rooms.[40]

Haldane wrote two volumes for the Left Book Club (LBC), his book *A.R.P.* and a small pamphlet *How to be Safe from Air Raids*, which was offered to members but not published under the LBC label. *A.R.P.* was published in August of 1938, just one month before the Munich Crisis, and it became one of the most important contributions to the critique of dispersed shelter policy. A LBC agent proclaimed that Haldane was 'the greatest living authority in England on this subject'.[41] It is unlikely that many would have seriously disputed this notion. Victor Gollancz declared in advance that the immediate political significance of *A.R.P.* would probably surpass anything yet published by the club,[42] emphasizing that the critique of ARP was to serve the larger goals of the interwar left.

Haldane began his critique by focusing on official Home Office publications, particularly the circular entitled *The Protection of Your Home Against Air Raids*.[43] Aside from disputing the notion that the home was the ideal place to offer protection from air raids, he also declared that these pamphlets contained misleading and incomplete technical advice: 'There is a good deal of "padding" in some of these documents, which is natural enough, for there is very little substance.'[44] He consequently set up his 'scientific' ideas in opposition to the vague and flexible plans for ARP, which the Home Office believed was the best way to prepare individuals and local authorities for an uncertain situation that was subject to abrupt change in wartime. Haldane sought to portray government policies as both inaccurate and slightly ridiculous.[45] In the circular on home protection, two pages were devoted to the question of preparation against the effect of explosive bombs, advising householders to reinforce walls and windows against splinter damage. Haldane remarked that 'in practice people in houses are rarely killed by splinters which penetrate the walls. They are killed because the house is knocked down'. He also criticized the Home Office's list of refuge room essentials for including items such as books, cards, and a gramophone – all, in Haldane's opinion, reflecting a middle class bias. Crucially, however, the guides had neglected to mention the provision of a pickaxe. In Spain, the provision of strong tools had proved essential for victims to escape from houses that had been demolished by high explosive bombs. He concluded that 'the official handbook does not distinguish very sharply between an air raid and a picnic. In Spain the distinction is quite obvious.' The only advice the government guides provided was that emergency trenches should be at least an adequate distance 'to avoid falling debris,' which Haldane derided as 'presumably [the] debris of the refuge-room and those who have taken refuge there'.[46]

Haldane also challenged the government's theory of dispersal, the principle that was fully accepted by supporters of government ARP. He, along with other scientists on the left, insisted that the effect of dispersal would merely be to increase the possibility that each enemy bomb would find a human target, especially if the majority of the population had no access to deep shelter. Joseph Needham, a fellow leftist scientist and prominent member of the Cambridge Scientists' Anti-War Group, noted that careful statistical analysis had demonstrated that:

The principle of dispersion per se is valueless. For although more people are killed if a shelter is hit, the chance of its being hit is at least proportionately smaller. It has been calculated that if a one tonne bomb fell in certain parts of Cambridge, 750 people would be killed or wounded in their homes, if they stayed in them. With proper shelters not more than, say, 300 would be killed in one shelter if it were hit.[47]

Haldane supported this logic, believing that 'dispersal within a dangerous area does not reduce the probable number of casualties. Whilst ensuring that no single bomb will wipe out a hundred people in a fraction of a second, it also ensures that almost every bomb will find a human target of some kind.'[48]

In A.R.P. Haldane analysed ten different types of shelter including refuge-rooms, steel frame and other strong buildings, splinter-proof rooms, trenches, brick shelters, underground railways, tunnels, and other bomb-proof underground shelters. Throughout much of this material it seems clear that he was simply setting up 'straw men' – clearly inferior shelter schemes such as splinter-proof rooms and trenches, which he could then discredit in favour of his desired deep shelter plans. He dismissed the conversion of large buildings to ARP shelters as an ineffective proposition, and he also believed that private rooms would provide only the most limited of protection. Nor did he hold much store in vague assurances that new buildings would be reinforced and be fitted with underground shelters, since these measures would do nothing to provide immediate protection. In fact, Haldane expressed general scepticism over many plans for shelters being advertised in the architectural press. He believed that 'on the principle that most theologies are untrue, we can conclude that most of it is worthless, because the different statements disagree with each other'.[49]

Haldane's own comprehensive plan for London was grand in scope if not in detail. He advocated the use of underground tunnels, tracks and other existing structures as deep shelters. In addition, he believed that new tunnels could be dug in areas such as Paddington and that properly designed trenches in London parks could provide additional shelter. He projected that 'in London the shelters would consist of 1,400 miles of brick-lined tunnels at a depth of about 60 feet, with multiple entrance tunnels sloping down to them, and a system of ventilation which would ultimately render them gas-proof'.[50] Soils in various areas would need to be surveyed to decide on the best construction methods, and he insisted that shelters be deep enough to be bomb-proof, fully ventilated, and have at least three or four separate entrances.[51] Acknowledging that in practice some civilians would be forced to use backyard shelters, trenches, or even their own homes, he nevertheless insisted that they must be given the best advice and scientifically sound information regarding these options.

Haldane's *A.R.P.* was admittedly short on technical details, leading to some professional criticism on this score. *Keystone*, an architectural journal, editorialized that 'Professor Haldane is disappointingly weak in his technical detailments,' since he did not cite professional sources and it is unclear the extent to which he consulted with engineers or architectural experts. The journal's editors believed that some of his statements would cause architects to 'squirm'.[52] Yet Haldane did receive select endorsement from some unexpected sources. C.G. Grey actually cited Haldane's work as an elegant appraisal and critique of the hysteria regarding gas warfare.[53] James Kendall, who later lambasted other leftist critics in his 'anti-hysteria' book, cited *A.R.P.* as a reasonable and reputable source about the probable dangers of gas.[54] The Air Raid Protection Institute, a mainstream, non-political 'professional body versed in ARP',[55] leant qualified support for Haldane's scientific findings. A review of Haldane's book by the Institute emphasized that the LBC ARP books were being read in professional circles and that the expertise of individuals such as Haldane was held in high regard.

His plan was picked up by the Communist Party and detailed in the pamphlet *A.R.P. for Londoners.*[56] The Communist publication *Labour Monthly*, edited by the leading Marxist intellectual Rajani Palme Dutt, stated that *A.R.P.* 'could not have been published at a more opportune time'.[57] Communist pamphlet writers and ARP campaigners used many of his statements verbatim, and Haldane was asked to write the forward to many of these publications, a measure of his premier status among this constituency.[58] Various versions of tunnel plans became popular with local leftist and Labour officials, although experts acknowledged that a great deal of conversion work would need to be done to make existing structures serviceable for the public, not least of which was the need to provide safe entrances to prevent the possibility of stampedes at narrow points. Aware that his plan would constitute an enormous undertaking, Haldane suggested that it should be carried out in two stages, one to be instituted immediately with the remainder requiring two or three years to complete. His administrative plans included the appointment of a Minister of Civilian Defence, and the reorganization of ARP on 'technical' rather than political grounds, although he did not detail many specifics. Haldane also favoured new guidelines for air raid wardens and provisions for evacuation including road-widening schemes.[59]

Haldane, however, did not seem to really understand the difficulty of making such enormous administrative changes, even if they had been instated over a period of many years – a point noted by his detractors. *The Times* published a mixed review of *A.R.P.*, criticizing the 'left bias' and obvious ideological slant of the book. The reviewer additionally believed that Haldane demonstrated 'next to no appreciation of the training and organization problems which even small schemes of protection raise' – a point that the government echoed continuously throughout the debate. Yet the reviewer still felt that Haldane's personal experience was valuable and that the emphasis on deep shelters was the correct one. The conclusion was that the book was 'most valuable material for critics and supporters of ARP,'[60] a vague statement perhaps suggesting that all parties could find elements in the book to bolster their own position. The supporters of government ARP could use it as example of irresponsible politicking, and critics could point to a scientific basis for deep shelters.

Haldane's contribution to the ARP debate in the 1930s was therefore a wide-ranging focus on technical points of policy tinged with charges of irresponsible political motivation, though he was more nuanced than his harshest critics would have given him credit for. With his fellow leftists he waged a long and often vitriolic campaign on the issue of deep shelters and civilian protection against air raids, but it was one reflecting their vision of the socialist balance between the rights of citizens and the responsibilities of the state.

***

There are some similarities between C.G. Grey and J.B.S. Haldane – both men flirted with extremism but remained mainstream within their professions. However, it is worth pointing out that C.G. Grey, both during and after his editorship of *The Aeroplane*, was largely forgiven for his politically extreme views, and they weighed little on the reception of his critiques of aerial policy. For Haldane, on the other hand, charges of politicking went hand-in-hand with discussions of his work on ARP, even if ultimately this did not harm his government standing during World War II.

Both men contributed in opposing ways to the particular cast of the intersection of politics and professionalism in the 1930s. They demonstrate the influence that a dedicated professional man could exert on policy and politics during this decade through sheer dynamism and personality. The debates in which they participated were often cast in extreme terms: disaster or salvation, freedom or tyranny, aerial triumph or aerial disaster. Both figures were representative of their constituencies. Grey reflected pro-militarist policies, infused with a dash of RAF-building 'Trenchardism'. The only defence was offense and strength. Such opinions were particularly influential in the negative sense, reflecting deep-seated pessimism within the circles of British aviation. Even the leftist critics to some extent reflected these gloomy prognostications and based their prescriptions for public defence on them. Haldane envisioned redemption in the next war through democratic action and the protection of the civilian population. The remainder of this narrative largely follows Haldane and others who subscribed to a similar emphasis on civilian protection. The next chapter deals with an event that galvanized both constituencies and prepared the ideological ground for the People's War: the conflict in Spain.

CHAPTER 5

THE PSYCHOLOGY OF THE
TERROR VICTIM IN SPAIN –
MORALE AND DEFIANCE

It's Guernica today, it'll be Paris and London tomorrow...
> —Isabel Brown, Spokesperson and
> fundraiser for Spanish relief[1]

... From what I and others have seen in Barcelona, it was
obvious that something drastic was necessary if [shelter]
security were to be guaranteed to the civilian population.[2]
> —MP for Finsbury, George Woods

We know that terror is intended to inflict a disproportionate impact
on morale and public confidence in proportion to the actual
destruction and loss of life that may be inflicted. The cliché that we
must not 'let the terrorists win', echoes the concerns about morale
that characterized preparations for World War II and the terror of
aerial bombardment. The voice of expertise maintained that the
physical machinery of the state could withstand bombardment but
that the reaction of citizens was the weak link in the chain. Individual
and collective psyches were viewed as dangerously unstable, yet
simultaneously of supreme import to the war effort. Yet the bulk of
the evidence from twentieth-century conflicts demonstrates that

morale is not nearly as fragile as imagined. Even when civilians suffer terribly during conflict, such suffering does not unduly affect the ability of states to compel these citizens to support war efforts, whether voluntarily or through coercion. In fact, adverse physical conditions and collective suffering can strengthen national resolve. Anger and a desire for revenge can easily supersede feelings of helplessness or disappointment with one's own government. Observers of the First World War believed that a stiffening of resolve and an increased willingness to fight quickly followed major raids.[3]

Nor do fear, dread and small-scale bouts of panic necessarily correspond to a lack of courage or the fatal collapse of morale. Fear is an entirely normal part of such a complex and intense experience, and the random nature of attack could traumatize even the most stoic. During the First World War the writer H.G. Wells, an early prophet of aerial destruction, admitted to his friend Arnold Bennett that 'in air raids he was afraid of going to pieces altogether'.[4] During the First World War the British public 'had reacted to air bombardment in a mood of indignation; at other times and places it had shown some tendency to panic'.[5] Memory is selective, and dramatic events invariably tend to overshadow more banal experiences. While officials were worried about civilian morale and the rebellious potential of crowds, contemporary accounts suggested that worry and frustration, along with anger over the inadequacy of British defences, were erroneously conflated with panic by the press during the First World War.[6] The official historian Richard Titmuss suggested that military planners were 'too remote' from the ordinary people and that this may have influenced their accounts. He argued that flocking to Underground stations was not necessarily a sign of panic at all. Rather than waiting for official shelter measures to be implemented, the population was merely adapting to the dangers and acting in a logical and rational way.[7]

The British narrative of the Spanish Civil War and World War II in Europe incorporates two important and powerful mythologies: memories of humanitarian atrocities coupled with civilian defiance during the Spanish Civil War, and the 'Spirit of the Blitz' and British stoicism. By the 1930s, the dialogue surrounding mental health and wartime behaviour had definitively shifted from the earlier terminology of 'primal instinct' to the somewhat kinder and gentler language of 'psychology'.[8] The notion of psychology and its related sciences as a cure-all for neuroses and other ailments of modernity became prevalent. Consequently, there was less talk of the animalistic mob, but more emphasis on how the mind could and should be manipulated to curb unhelpful behaviours. The accepted emotional regime of wartime was that of bravery and stoicism; fears were to be kept private. Civilians, particularly in London, were furthermore wholly conscious of their important role in waging the war and expressions of fear may well have been a source of social embarrassment.[9] As Joanna Bourke reflects, the image of 'terrified Londoners' fleeing Zeppelin attacks during the First World War was transformed into praise of the 'stoic Londoners' of World War II.[10] The cheerful cockney, the bold declaration that 'London can take it', and the defiant symbol of St Paul's rising unscathed through the destruction of the bombs all form the basis of public memory of the war.

Beyond the horror that many Britons felt towards atrocities such as Guernica, the Spanish Civil War served as a reminder of the air peril and as a rehearsal for aerial bombardment in a general European war. Accounts of the Spanish Civil War and aerial attacks on Britain finely balanced the humanitarian sympathies directed towards the suffering of innocent civilians with a more triumphal account of fortitude and inner strength. It must be acknowledged that these were all essentially propaganda images crafted by participants, governments, writers, and newspapers. 'Propaganda' need not necessarily be taken as a pejorative term, though it usually is. The British understanding of the Spanish Civil War was almost entirely shaped by one side of the conflict – the cause of Republican 'democracy and freedom' against General Francisco Franco's Nationalists. It is not necessarily a right or wrong account of the conflict, but it certainly is a statement of the dominant values of those who wrote the narrative. Conceptions of British national identity and Spanish 'otherness', had a profound influence on how participants and

THE PSYCHOLOGY OF THE TERROR VICTIM IN SPAIN

historians alike viewed the conflict. In fact, Spain 'was still a country about whose politics, history, religion, culture and customs [the volunteers] knew very little. Theirs was an outside view, inevitably a simplification, that filtered out the Spanishness from the struggle and made it more manageable.'[11] The reaction to the civil war in a country such as Britain must be understood in the contemporary context, rather than through ideas imposed by later commentators. The assumptions that observers brought to Spain were 'informed by notions of "Englishness" as much as by any understanding of "Spanishness."'[12]

The literature of British involvement in Spain has an extensive range and is reflective of the support of Republican Spain. Many accounts are a direct product of a generation of scholars in the 1960s rediscovering Spain and using it as an analogue for their own political struggles. Other studies focus on politics, ideology and the culture produced by the Spanish Civil War – poetry and verse in particular.[13] This chapter has a different focus, instead expanding on how observations regarding ARP in Spain were translated into the British context. I emphasize that British views of Spain were, at their core, directed towards internal British politics and aspirations for social change – a theme that will be further explored in Chapter 8. For all the rhetoric about international solidarity, Spain functioned primarily as a venue to reassert British democracy. Spain facilitated the application of the lessons of air warfare to Britain, through advocacy for improved ARP and the hailing of Spanish civilians as models of fortitude and stoicism in modern warfare. The conflict served as a model for how British citizens should approach their roles on the Home Front during wartime. Most importantly this was a highly active conception of citizenship, in which civilians took the lead in providing for themselves. These themes run throughout the ARP critique as it will unfold in the remainder of this book. The experience of Spanish civilians under bombardment coincided with how British critics wished to perceive themselves and their society, and they exploited these examples at every available opportunity.

Air Raid Victims in Spain: Terror and Fortitude

The Republican opposition to the Nationalist coup instigated by General Franco in the Spanish Civil War (1936–9) was a cause that galvanized British leftist activism, allowing this divided constituency to unite around a 'Popular Front' directed against Fascism. It was immediately painted as a simple conflict between 'Fascism' and 'democracy' and the fact that the situation was infinitely more complex and rooted in arcane political feuds was of almost no consequence at the time (or now, for the memory of the war). The Republican cause gained the favour of most canonical writers[14] from Ernest Hemingway to George Orwell, though the latter's classic *Homage to Catalonia* is anything but a simplistic endorsement of the left-wing side he fought for in Spain. On the other hand, Nationalists had to make do with sympathetic newspaper columnists and clerical tracts endorsed by the Roman Catholic Church – the support of Evelyn Waugh notwithstanding. As such, these accounts simply did not have the historical staying power of the compelling declarations of Republican supporters – W.H. Auden, Stephen Spender and Louis MacNeice among them.

This powerful rhetoric was combined with the fact that over 3,000 left-wing Britons travelled to Spain to volunteer to fight for the cause, though many went with quite naive notions of what they were actually going to do once there. The very act of travelling to Spain was one of defiance for British citizens; their government's official policy of non-intervention rendered their involvement illegal. Some fought with the International Brigades that included British and American Battalions, and others fought with independent militias, such as the Marxist POUM that Orwell joined. Around 80 per cent of the volunteers were ordinary working-class Britons, but the remainder were poets, writers and journalists, such as Miles Tomalin and the Marxist military commentator Tom Wintringham. The writers and poets John Cornford, Julian Bell (a nephew of Virginia Woolf), Charles Donnelly, Christopher Caudwell, and Ralph Fox all died on the Front. Many were very young, such as Cambridge-educated Cornford, who perished at the age of 21. No doubt some imagined themselves as a type of romantic latter-day Lord Byron, writing literature and fighting in distant lands for that great eternal cause: liberty.[15] Spain was viewed by most of the British as a fantastical, exotic, otherworldly country and was commonly described by words such as 'sultry'. It was also perceived of as an 'old country' dominated by tradition and untouched by the ills of modernity.

The strategic and military contribution of the international volunteers to their purported cause is doubtful. In addition, even though their version of events dominated the narrative both then and since, it failed to translate into any material support for the Spanish government from Western democracies, even as Nazi Germany and Mussolini armed the Nationalists. Worldwide sympathies were perhaps cold comfort for the losing side, but there is little doubt that English and American writers helped to cement foreign disapproval for the Franco regime that endured until the dictator's death in 1975. What these British volunteers accomplished for their *own* ideas of citizenship and war was, however, more immediate in fruition. Spain rehabilitated the notion of the 'just war' and the independent militias were seen as truly heroic – in contrast to the regimented slaughter of the First World War.[16] This helped, in part, to unite somewhat an otherwise fractured leftist constituency in Britain. But the most important aspect of war in Spain for the British was the spectre of what future aerial warfare might entail, particularly its impact on individual citizens.

Air attack in Spain began in fits and starts, soon after the civil war commenced, with 35 air raids of various intensities on Madrid occurring between October 1936 and January 1937. The conflict has entered popular memory through the image of helpless civilian victims of aerial bombardment, most prominent with the bombing of Guernica on 26 April 1937. It was an attack that claimed an estimated 1,650 lives, though it is now thought that the actual number may have been around 800. The brazen nature of the daytime raid rocked worldwide opinion. Lieutenant-Colonel Wolfram von Richthofen, cousin of the famous First World War 'Red Baron,' and chief-of-staff of the Condor Legion casually noted that the 'usual mix' (one-third incendiary bombs, and two-thirds 250-kg high explosive bombs) proved to be a 'technical success'.[17] Pablo Picasso's famous mural depicting the horrors of the attack symbolized the shock of the event; the very abstract nature of the work reflecting the bafflement at the co-mingling of technology and barbarism that many felt was being realized in Spain. Predictions of brutal aerial attack in novels or films had foreshadowed this outcome – and even worse – but the actual cold-blooded practice of murder from the air stunned observers.

The first British journalist to witness the carnage was G.L. Steer, correspondent for *The Times*, who wrote a starkly grim account of the attack. He declared the air raids to be 'unparalleled in military history'. It was popular among the British to romanticize the Basques as both exotic and a truly 'democratic people',[18] and Steer proved to be no exception. He also did not stint in attributing the attack to German involvement, and was one of several eyewitnesses and foreign reporters whose records forestalled attempts by the Nationalist government, the Germans, and right-wing apologists to spread the rumour that fires in Guernica had been started by supposed 'subversives'.[19] His account stirred powerful emotions and likely impacted reports about Guernica around the world, as did his later book *The Tree of Gernika*. W.E. Johns used his position to pen furious editorials denouncing the policy of non-intervention and Nationalist aerial bombing atrocities. Though hardly a radical, he eulogized foreign volunteers who risked everything 'fighting for that most hopeless of causes – Freedom'.[20]

Attacks in Spain famously served as a test case for the Luftwaffe in pioneering new tactics and observing the effects of bombing on cities. In fact, during the Nuremberg Trials, Hermann Göring confirmed that Hitler's advisers had urged support for General Franco for this purpose. The result was the Condor Legion, the German aerial expeditionary force to Spain that consisted of 5,000 men and 100 first-line aircraft. The force, as well as the German Luftwaffe in general, had developed new and innovative ways of thinking as a secretive body divorced from the old imperial army system.[21] For this motivated force, Spain provided the perfect opportunity – both strategically and ideologically – to hone aerial attack skills. The Messerschmitt Bf-109B fighters and Heinkel He-111 bombers of the Condor Legion quickly established air superiority over the aerial defences that the Republican side were able to muster.

Despite Guernica, aerial attack did not become systematic until September 1937, when the collapse of the Asturian Front and a shift in strategy caused the Nationalists to attack Barcelona. Though on a much smaller scale, these raids more closely resembled those that would be perpetrated on Britain and demonstrated how German pilots had become routinely expert in mounting urban attacks. A variety of ordnance was tested, although incendiary bombs initially proved ineffective at setting fire to cities – a technical difficulty that would be resolved with the outbreak of World War II. These bombs, however, were relatively effective at setting wheat fields alight as part of a strategy of economic warfare that was crucial in a largely rural country with inadequate external supply routes. Of far greater consequence was experimentation with high explosives, machine-gun strafing of civilians, and the tactic of purposefully targeting populated city centres – not merely 'military' installations that may or may not have overlapped with civilian residential areas.

J.B.S. Haldane believed that defenceless Spanish cities served as 'test cases' for fascist pilots, and that 'this may be regarded as a dress rehearsal for a similar attempt on Britain'.[22] In a future war, he warned, attacks would be much more devastating. A fellow leftist John Langdon-Davies, who was a long-term expatriate living in Catalonia, forwarded somewhat similar notions in the second of two books he wrote about Spain, *Air Raid: The Technique of Silent Approach, High Explosive, Panic.*[23] Haldane and other aviation experts disputed the plausibility of Langdon-Davies' 'silent approach' theory of aeroplanes turning off their engines for stealth attacks. Nevertheless his book was highly indicative of the type of commentary that emerged after Spain. Observers immediately drew parallels between Spain and future perils for Britain, employing analogies to emphasize the gravity of aerial destruction. For example, G.L. Steer noted that attacks on small Basque towns could easily presage the total destruction of smaller British industrial towns, giving the example of Hull in the Northeast.[24] Indeed, many of these towns were subject to randomized attack after the main Blitz on London was thought to be over. These commentators believed that military events in Spain were of direct import for Britain, emphasizing strategic as well as moral reasons why fascist involvement threatened British democracy.[25]

There were three primary conclusions drawn by British observers from the aerial bombing of Spanish towns. First, there were no instances of mass panic to the extent that civil order was in jeopardy. And this, it should be noted, was among 'emotional, dramatic, excitable' Spaniards, as many Britons would have stereotyped them. This fact demonstrated that civilians might be more resilient than anticipated, particularly those who truly believed in the rightness of their cause and in their democratic freedoms. Second, technical observers highlighted the absolute necessity of deep underground shelters and the inadvisability of using cellars and converted basements for civilian protection, a subject explored in the following chapter. Finally, the ability of local communities to provide for their own shelter under extremely trying conditions was praised, providing a model for spontaneous action that leftist boroughs attempted to follow in the short time remaining before the start of war in 1939. This account will later discuss how British politicians and activists attempted to shame the wealthier British government by pointing to the shelters built by Spanish municipalities.

British observers agreed that, contrary to general expectations that civilian bombing would quickly destroy morale, the Nationalist bombing of Madrid actually increased the determination and defiance of the population. Air raids provoked fear and outrage, but on the whole they failed to dent morale. Although the example of attack in cities such as Guernica again raised the spectre of the 'knock-out blow' among many commentators in Britain, actual experience in Spain demonstrates that this type of strategic blow to morale was not in the offing. Aerial historian Stephen Budiansky argues that the 'failure of strategic bombing' was one of the lessons that close observers could have derived from Spain if a careful study of available data had been made. The Luftwaffe's own studies demonstrated that systematic ARP went a long way towards blunting any sort of terror perpetuated by bombers.[26] Completely contrary to official expectations, it was actually the human element of the equation that proved most defiant and resourceful. Air raids against military installations, supply routes and frontline troops naturally attained the desired military effect. Raids against civilians in cities, however, proved far less important and could crucially unite populations that might otherwise be prone to division.

The leftist writer Esmond Romilly travelled extensively through Spain and experienced air raids in Barcelona. Taking shelter in a Metro station with local residents, he observed that 'the fear of suffocation was stronger than that of the bombs,' and that people calmly left shelters following air raids.[27] The city had undertaken extensive shelter-building measures, and its mayor was particularly prominent in extolling the necessity of purpose-built shelters for as much of the population as possible. He was often cited by British critics, but he also undertook his own campaign to make the British press aware of the plight of the Spanish people and their accomplishments in ARP. In a letter that was published in *The Times* in February 1938, he claimed that his city had constructed around 400 shelters of varying sizes, which were capable of housing nearly 350,000 people – though these figures were not independently verified.[28] Philip Noel-Baker at one time bandied about figures in the Commons that Barcelona was constructing shelters that would house 1 million people.[29]

Dr E.B. Strauss, a British physician and psychologist who was in Spain during the conflict, concurred that contrary to expectations, morale remained very high. His professional explanation was that:

The bombed become automatically united in a common hatred and terror of the invisible and intangible enemy from the skies. Observers state that one of the most remarkable effects of the bombing of open towns in Government Spain had been the welding together into a formidable fighting force of groups of political factions who were previously at each other's throats.[30]

J.B.S. Haldane also remarked that he expected to find panic in Madrid due to the air raids, but although a few people stayed overnight in the Metro stations, 'I never heard of anyone sleeping in a cellar. It simply 'wasn't done' to be frightened [...]. On the whole everyone carried on.'[31] He was most vocal in his praise of Spanish stoicism, arguing that the only instance in which an air raid produced significant panic was when a large population of refugees, driven from towns with little planning and protection, overwhelmed certain areas of Barcelona. When this occurred, it became impossible to provide bomb-proof shelters for even a fraction of the refugees. Yet a huge effort was exerted to create shelters even in the midst of attack. As he related: 'The Government kept its head, and there was no threat of a revolution to end the war.'[32]

It was thought that the government 'keeping its head' led to individual citizens following suit. Complex psychological reactions to raids were to be commonplace in accounts of the Blitz and manifested dramatically in accounts of bombing in Barcelona and Madrid. The assistant ARP medical officer for the Borough of Battersea, G.B. Shirlaw, noted that Spanish aerial bombing led to a range of civilian reactions. Some individuals felt most reassured taking refuge under any sort of cover, while others preferred to be out in the open where they could see the sky.[33] Curious rather than terrified, many boldly ventured outside to observe raids and had to be dissuaded by authorities from air raid spectatorship. The poet Louis MacNeice reported that, to his surprise, air raids caused feelings of 'excitement' rather than fear.[34] This foreshadowed a common experience during the Blitz; many Londoners found that their undoubted fear was also mixed with a palpable excitement and desire for 'spectatorship'. The Canadian diplomat Charles Ritchie recalled watching raids from the roof of a central London hotel with a sense of exhilaration. On occasions when he took cover, however, he felt 'annoyed with myself for taking shelter not because I was afraid but because the others had run for shelter and I had instinctively imitated them'.[35] Of course, among the most famous of the spectators was Prime Minister Winston Churchill, who alarmed his ministers by braving danger on the rooftops of Whitehall to watch the spectacle of bombs raining down on London.

There was also an element of public performance inherent in many accounts – a psychological influence that dictates behaviour, acting almost independently of individual preferences. This was particularly relevant to the British experience during World War II. George Orwell suggested that although air raid shelters had been dug all over Barcelona, it was only 'timid' individuals who dived into shelters and cellars.[36] No doubt many individuals felt rather more timid and uncertain than they acted, but the public expectations of neighbours and fellow citizens restrained them from showing fear. It is much the same with soldiers, who in the first contact of battle will stand their ground due not to great wellsprings of courage, for few are truly courageous in such circumstances, but because they know it is expected of them by their fellow comrades. They wish neither to let down those who depend on them, nor to prove unworthy of their designated tasks.

Aware of the unique value of air raids in Spain as a test case for current bombing practices, the British government sent observers to cities such as Madrid and Barcelona. The MP Geoffrey Lloyd, who represented the Home Office, assured his colleagues that 'reliable reports' were being made on the events in Spain.[37] Duncan Sandys, a Conservative MP and the Chairman of the Parliamentary ARP Committee, declared, 'those who are responsible for the organization of air raid precautions in Great Britain would do well to study in the minutest detail the technique of air raids in Spain and the measures which the Spanish people [have used] to protect themselves against the menace of the modern bomber'.[38] The Committee invited the mayor of Barcelona to relate ARP provisions in his city in early 1938, and British politicians and reporters greeted his accounts with interest.[39] However, expressions of interest did not mean that British officials were prepared to institute the same protective measures for British cities. As Wing Commander J.N. Fletcher, ARP officer for Guildford, explained, 'Shelters give no better protection than houses, but make it certain that large casualties would occur if a shelter were hit. This happens in Spain. Those who try to reach shelters, and leave their homes for the purpose, are exposed to several additional and unnecessary perils.[40] In addition, the members of the 1939 Hailey Commission, discussed in the final chapter of this book, believed that:

> It seems clear that protection designed to be bomb-proof was available for only a relatively small proportion of the population, and that its bomb-resisting qualities were not effectively tested. In the second place, the conditions of the problem, here in Barcelona, are so different that comparisons are of no great value. Barcelona enjoys a climate very different from ours, and exposure to it by night involved little hardship.[41]

These practical considerations represent an equally valid perspective on the lessons of the war in Spain. The bomb-resisting qualities of Barcelona shelters were indeed untested from a quantitative scientific point of view. In addition, there remained no means of fully ascertaining how many people were actually sheltered in Spanish cities, since much information was based on anecdote or hearsay. Nor was it possible to assess how these shelters affected casualty rates.

Some interpreted the lessons of Spain as pointing towards the necessity of increasing armaments and the fighter force of the RAF rather than investing in shelters.[42] It was a sentiment that commentators such as C.G. Grey endorsed. At the same time, air raids carried out by Japanese forces on cities such as Nanchang and Chungking were also reported on in the British press and investigated by the government. They remained, however, little-discussed in the public sphere for several reasons. This is partially attributable to distance, as opposed to the shocking nearness of European conflict. At the same time it is impossible to ignore the fact that racialist ideas no doubt played a role in perception. As in the case of Arabia and Iraq, views of racial difference often meant that far-flung bombing victims were viewed in a different light than European victims. Like Spain, information from Chinese raids might have tended to discount the value of strategic bombing, reinforcing the idea that people react with a hardening of resolve under bombardment. Yet military authorities may have been hasty to dismiss China as an 'Other'; a country and people so dissimilar to Britain as to be unsuitable for comparison.[43]

Nevertheless, British analysts of all political persuasions were quickly convinced of the value of deep shelters. The *Evening Standard* endorsed the provisions of Spanish cities, believing that surface steel shelters of the type proposed by Sir John Anderson had 'already been condemned in Barcelona'.[44] The value of trenches to the civilian population was also highly discounted. Cyril Helsby, a structural engineer, informed colleagues in a professional lecture that the Spanish 'have no use to-day for trenches in the manner recommended in England'.[45] Though he was careful as a representative of the Institution of Structural Engineers not to bring government plans too thoroughly into question, he did tentatively endorse the notion that shelter provisions must 'go deeper' than presently advocated.[46] J.B.S. Haldane made a case study of the Catalan town of Reus that was relatively well-prepared for aerial attack, with underground concrete shelters for 9,000 people, shelters under homes for 11,000 people, and with shelters that would house a further 1,200 under construction. This would accommodate most, though not all, of the 27,000 inhabitants.[47] Such a study applied especially to smaller towns, like those in coastal areas or in the Midlands, which might have felt that a disproportionate ARP emphasis was paid to London. The Welsh Liberal MP Megan Lloyd George used Haldane's findings to emphasize that although these provisions were incomplete, they were nevertheless impressive. She believed that the construction of these shelters meant that only three deaths occurred during an air raid that destroyed 35 buildings.[48] If residents had taken refuge in cellars or basements they most likely would have perished.

At the same time as the British government was reiterating that mass underground shelters would not be provided for residents of London, observers in Spain felt that easily available shelters helped rather than hindered the public in the performance of vital war duties. They proved vitally beneficial to the psychological wellbeing of the populace. Although people availed themselves of the shelters if they were caught on the streets during a raid, in general a 'business as usual' attitude prevailed in the city.[49] It was thought to be psychologically reassuring that people understood that there *was* an option of shelters close at hand, even if they did not choose to utilize them. G.B. Shirlaw noted that the mere presence of bomb-proof shelters with large signs on the exterior had 'a strong psychological value in allaying the fears of the nervous civilians'.[50] Major Noel de Purton MacRoberts, the ARP officer for St Pancras, penned a technical account called *ARP Lessons from Barcelona*. In it he forwarded the theory that a well-prepared citizenry would actually dissuade enemy bombing, and consequently that preparing shelters for citizens was an essential part of military preparedness and not an area in which civilians should be left to fend for themselves.[51] The building of public shelters was also a confirmation that citizens' needs were being taken into consideration, and that they were not regarded as unimportant or disposable civilians by their local governments.

Although the basis of alternative ARP plans involved the construction of very large shelters that could accommodate thousands of people, the example of Spain proved that even smaller underground shelters had a place in a comprehensive ARP plan, particularly in mid-size towns. This theme was picked up by architectural professionals, including Serge Chermayeff, one of the Finsbury shelter planners discussed later in this book. He believed that a study should be made of shelter plans in the town of Cartagena. They were designed to accommodate 75 people and were built to high professional standards, protecting occupants from all dangers except that of a direct hit by high explosive.[52] A special ARP supplement of the professional publication *Architectural Design and Construction* highlighted the calm demeanour of the residents of Barcelona and the effectiveness of shelters:

> The deaths occurring in raids less than a year ago were never less than several hundreds in each raid [...] the casualties to-day are relatively [minor]. It is worth considering for a moment the psychological value of air-raid shelters. Some people are disposed to condemn what they call funk-holes on the grounds

that pampering the populace in this way will undermine its morale. This was not the case in Barcelona, where the population remained calm.[53]

The Barcelona correspondent for *The Times* agreed, reporting in March 1938 that enemy air raids did not succeed in bringing the intended 'horror and panic' to the civilian population. He claimed to have seen a dying man on a stretcher raise his fist in a defiant anti-fascist salute.[54] This imagery was common in left-wing propaganda posters. It echoed the battle cry '¡No pasarán!' ('They shall not pass') which was employed frequently by the Republican side, most particularly by the Communist leader Dolores Ibárruri Gómez in her famous speech at the Siege of Madrid early in the hostilities. Other images featured the defiant militia or even solitary figures raising their fists in defiance at German bombers. The use of artistic perspective could accomplish what was impossible in reality – to dwarf the might of the aeroplane and elevate the power of the individual.

For British observers, these images combined all the elements they found most heroic in Spain; they universalized the experience to prepare their own population for air warfare. One military commentator believed that civilians in the future would react with even greater calm than had the Spanish, who had been vulnerable to the novelty and surprise of aerial attack. Once ordinary people accepted air attack as inevitable and prepared adequately for it, fear would mostly subside.[55] These accounts of the resilience of civilian morale confirmed that people would become more accustomed to the psychological strain of unpredictable bombing, to the extent that some 'normalcy' would persist.[56] Furthermore, the combination of reasonable shelter provisions with the innate resilience of populations in the face of attack could in fact turn the tables on the 'morale destroying' aims of the bombers. The narrative of Spain was ultimately influenced by the approaching inevitability of war with fascist powers. In contrast to the despairing accounts of the fiction writers and peddlers of fear that characterized most discussions of the next war, the image of heroic Spaniards was *necessary* to provide a model of wartime Home Front heroism. The continental idea of a *levée en masse* served as a prototype of 'democratic defence' – an idea woven throughout the remainder of this book. Many of the notions advanced by the Republican cause in Spain, such as civilian self-sufficiency, ARP-building local authorities, and poets- and artists-in-arms, broadened the range of what was considered true wartime heroism. Even non-combatants, through their efficient organization of the Home Front or participation in civilian defence, could lay claim to this status.

PART II

CHAPTER 6

CRITICISM FROM THE LEFT – GAS MASKS, REFUGE ROOMS AND DEEP SHELTERS

We have to lead mass pressure to ensure provision of adequate protection for the people against air attack, at the expense of the Chamberlain Government and to lead mass participation in the work of the ARP wardens and organization so as to prevent it falling into the hands of reactionary military and police officials.[1]

–Communist Party of Great Britain, *London District Congress 1938 Discussion Statement*

Since the images of destruction and fear associated with bombing, especially from Spain, were so immediately compelling, many realized the potential of the issue to be popular and emotive with the British people. The recommendations of leftist writers such as J.B.S. Haldane were quickly picked up on by the communists, among others, to critique government provisions for protecting the civilian population. These individuals and groups began agitating on the issue of home defence, and the Communist London District Congress declared its intent to make civilian defence a primary domestic concern. The representatives at the congress believed that civil defence might provide a way to mobilize the working class and challenge the government in a way that other issues had not done during the 'failed revolutions' of the interwar years. The General Strike of 1926 provides the best example of how British progressivism did not go according to plan for the reform-minded in the interwar years.

The leftist air raid precautions (ARP) critique evolved to combine technical observations from Spain and theories of deep shelter with collectivist and communitarian ideals. The discussion about ARP could be tailored to specific issues dear to leftist constituencies, such as class bias, the role of local authorities, and the status of civil liberties. Throughout this period the Communist Party's newspaper, the *Daily Worker*, expressed displeasure with government ARP provisions in stark terms, highlighting the inadequacy of civilian defences and pairing their critique with strong pacifist undertones. Its writers declared that £22 million was being made available for 'air attack', by means of Royal Air Force (RAF) rearmament, while the population demanded that funds be instead allocated towards civilian defence.[2] The justification for increased ARP funding played out in different ways, with the Communist Party, scientists such as Haldane, the Labour Party, and local authorities forwarding various arguments for alternative civil defence. There were two major facets to the discussion of technical ARP: the critique of government recommendations for gas-proof refuge rooms and the debate over deep shelters. In the case of gas-proof rooms, the 'Cambridge Scientists' Anti-War Group' (CSAWG), nominally headed by J.D. Bernal took the lead, challenging the technical value of government-issue gas masks and the protective merits of Home Office guidelines. Yet the gas debate was quickly becoming a secondary consideration by the time their work was published by the Left Book Club (LBC) in 1937.[3] In addition, charges of harmful and irresponsible politicking dogged the critics to the extent that they were often seen as agitators first and professionals second. The critique of dispersal and advocacy for mass deep shelters was relatively more successful, garnering a measure of public prominence that continued into the war.

Gas Hysteria: Government Plans and the 'Gas-Proof Room'

The images of destruction and catastrophic loss of life that we have seen displayed in interwar literature and culture captured the public imagination. Visions of the 'troglodyte' masses wandering about with gas masks were both repellent and fascinating. Anti-gas measures were the focus of the first ARP circular, in keeping with the disproportionate fear of poison gas. And as Wing Commander E.J. Hodsoll of the ARP Department publicly declared, gas was 'easier to defeat than bombs'.[4] This sentiment reflects the 'contrarian' opinion discussed in Chapter 3, as it endured in the 1930s and bolstered government ARP planning. The CSAWG instituted the primary critique of the government's anti-gas protection measures. The founding organization included 80 left-leaning scientists and charged itself with the purpose of protesting 'the prostitution of science for war purposes'.[5] Their first public action was a letter of protest to the *Cambridge Review* in June 1934 against the militarization of scientific research. It was signed by 79 individuals, including faculty, research workers and graduate students, but this number represented a tiny minority of Cambridge scientists and only 12 per cent of 'pure scientists'.[6] It did, however, count some prominent scientists as members, such as Joseph Needham and J.D. Bernal, who served as its public figurehead.

The Cambridge Scientists formulated a project to evaluate preparations for gas attack by testing gas masks and the merits of 'gas-proof' refuge rooms. There is little indication of exactly how this critique came about, given that extant records of the CSAWG are scant. It seems to have been conceived by members J.H. Fremlin and R.L.M Synge following the government's recommendations that individuals construct 'gas-proof' refuge rooms as their primary defence against aerial attack.[7] The focus on gas also reflected the arguments simultaneously forwarded by fellow leftist groups, such as the Socialist Medical Association and the Union of Democratic Control.[8] The CSAWG contracted Victor Gollancz to publish its findings, beginning the ARP crusade spearheaded by the LBC. The results were first published in the volume *The Protection of the Public From Aerial Attack* and secondarily in a less technical publication that answered some of the criticism directed against their study. The preparation and writing of the group's LBC book began in 1935, although it was only published in February 1937. National discussions regarding ARP soon drifted from gas to shelter protection, casting the CSAWG's gas test results in an anticlimactic light. In addition, the identification of the Cambridge Scientists solely with the issue of gas and their depiction as antiwar extremists had lasting implications for the success of their ARP criticism. The Home Office was able to portray the CSAWGs Scientists as rabble-rousing communists whose sole motivation was to undermine confidence in government plans. Though the gas critique was a non-starter, it importantly constituted the first attempt at independent verification of the government's ARP claims. The gas-proof room critique gave leftists their first entrée into the issue and was useful in initiating criticism of other measures.

The researchers conducted at least 14 separate tests, using the accommodations of Cambridge postgraduate students to demonstrate the inadequacy of gas-proof rooms. They concluded that these rooms, constructed according to Home Office instructions, did allow for the passage of gas, perhaps fatally so. Their test methodology involved sealing door and window seams in the room according to the Home Office advice in the first circular, and subsequently measuring concentrations of gas in the room over time as it seeped *out* of tiny cracks in the structure. The CSAWG was forced to use this methodology since it was all but impossible to simulate the conditions of a possible gas attack and measure gas seepage into a building or room. This technique also failed to account for climactic conditions such as temperature and wind, and these facts later provided ammunition for government officials to rebut the scientists. The CSAWG concluded that under the conditions of a sustained mustard gas attack 'it would be possible on an average to remain alive for about three hours in the gas-proof room; in other words the "gas-proof room" is not gas-tight'.[9]

The CSAWG also tested the quality of government-issue civilian gas masks; as the official historian later noted, they only had access to the open-market 'civilian type' mask.[10] They had chided the British government for refusing to release test figures on their gas masks and not allowing them to be subjected to independent tests. The CSAWG determined that the civilian masks would only work effectively for several hours with moderate to strenuous breathing, and they pointed out that there was no provision for children under the age of five.[11] They believed that the Germans, French, Swiss and even Russians had stockpiled a higher standard of gas mask that was more comfortable and closer fitting. The French masks even enabled the user to exercise for one half hour, and had strict requirements for the percentage of gas that was permitted to pass through the filter.[12] This criticism was despite the fact that an extra £850,000 had been allocated in the 1936 Civil Service estimate 'to produce, as near as possible, the perfect gas mask'.[13]

The test results were used prominently in Communist Party publications, which cited their statistics on the effectiveness of gas masks,[14] and the findings were also endorsed by the predominantly leftist Association of Scientific Workers, many of whose members were also affiliated with the Cambridge Scientists. The scientific union published an article in *Scientific Worker* calling for further investigations into anti-gas measures.[15] However, it is important to note that leftist scientists did not uniformly endorse the work of the CSAWG. J.B.S. Haldane believed that the CSAWG's conclusions were far too absolute. He was also troubled by its complete dismissal of the gas-proof rooms, although he continued to believe that deep shelter should be made a higher priority. Often erroneously assumed to be a member of the CSAWG, he sought to distance himself from it.[16]

Other scientific and gas experts were overtly hostile to the implications of the CSAWG's work and emphasized their belief that its members had subversive political motives. The most unflattering review of the Cambridge Scientists' work was penned by Major-General C.H. Foulkes of the gas-tolerant 'contrarian' faction. In the journal *Nature* he declared that proclamations such as those undertaken by the CSAWG could do nothing but harm, because they were calculated to destroy confidence in Home Office measures. The *Daily Mail* picked up the branding of the CSAWG as possessing a radical political agenda and published refutations of the CSAWG's findings, including a piece in which an expert, Mr R.K. Law, stated that:

> I don't know what constitutes a Cambridge Scientist, but I know that a scientist is supposed to be somebody interested in one thing only – and that is knowledge and truth [. . .] the Cambridge Scientists avow openly that theirs is not a scientific aim but a political one. They are representatives of an extreme Communist body of opinion [. . .]. These experiments they have done, I am told by the Home Office, are really completely farcical. They made all kinds of most elementary mistakes and ludicrous blunders. The results which they got are, for all practical purpose, worthless. . . .[17]

The Home Office likewise emphasized the recurrent menace of extremist 'Red' politics. Geoffrey Lloyd, speaking on behalf of the Home Office, commented on the CSAWG's charges several times in the Commons. The opening salvo was simultaneously dismissive and censorious: 'I am aware that some persons calling themselves the Cambridge Scientists' Anti-War Group have made some observations on this subject, but it is not clear whether their interests are primarily scientific or political.'[18] He also stated that the Cambridge Scientists did not have hands-on experience in anti-gas measures, in contrast to over a hundred scientists employed by the government.[19] The ARP Department mobilized its own set of experts, including C.H. Foulkes, J. Davidson Pratt, and James Kendall, author of the memorably entitled *Breathe Freely!*. Kendall accused the CSAWG of irresponsible fear-mongering which adversely affected public safety. He feared that some individuals might abandon attempts to construct protective refuge rooms, thus placing themselves at increased risk.[20]

The charge of fear-mongering and undermining public confidence was a particularly difficult one to refute, but members mustered their finest arguments with this aim. J.H. Fremlin, a Cambridge research student and an initial instigator of the gas tests, was called to address the Gas Sub-Committee of the ARP Department in July 1938. Fremlin denied that the tests were intended to impugn all Home Office advice, but felt that it was only fair to note that governmental conclusions contained omissions and were too difficult for ordinary citizens to implement. He expressed regret that political arguments had entered into the discussion, claiming that their experiments were purely of a technical and scientific nature. The conclusion of the sub-committee, as expressed in the Home Office report, was that 'although [Fremlin] answered very cleverly, the Sub-Committee were not prepared to accept the tests as very significant'. It was also dryly observed that the Cambridge Scientists' assertions that their group was scientific and that their work was apolitical and purely in the interest of scientific discovery 'did not cut very much ice'.[21] In addition, the report reiterated the major complaint against the CSAWG – that their tests measured gas seepage *out* of a sealed room, an entirely different prospect than predicting gas leakage from the outside in. Yet this type of test was the only one that could feasibly be carried out, given the amount of gas that would be needed to attempt to measure the reverse occurrence. Of course, this very reason also could be used to minimize the danger of gas in the first instance. The CSAWG had no choice but to defend its methodology and insist that the two conditions were scientifically equal. As Joseph Needham had written in his notes, gas flowing out of a room did indicate that gas could flow in: 'Since Nature abhors a vacuum, gas would flow in through the pores to fill the vacuum.'[22]

Needham noted that CSAWG members were particularly affected by the charge of being a 'politically motivated' minority of scientists.[23] An attack on the group by Geoffrey Lloyd in the Commons reflects this type of rhetoric: 'The Anti-War movement is, of course, well known to honour-able [sic] members. It was condemned as a Communist-inspired movement by the National Executive of the Labour Party, and I do not know that it is necessary to go further than that….'[24] The scientists sought to distance themselves from other leftist critics, in particular the communists, even though most of its members had close, if unofficial, ties to the Communist Party of Great Britain. In their second book they attempted to make clear that their work stood apart from 'sensationalist brochures'.[25] This broad depiction of all critics of government ARP as extremists greatly troubled the CSAWG, as it had grave implications for the reception of its work. The official postwar historian reflected the general opinion that '[*The Protection of the Public from Aerial Attack*'s] declared aim of offering a critical examination of ARP measures was faithfully followed, to the exclusion of any positive counter-suggestions'.[26] The CSAWG's claims of non-political intent were therefore not to pass scrutiny easily, and the members found it difficult to refute charges of being unpatriotic.

The Cambridge Scientists launched their defence in the forums available to them and sent out further calls for research into other areas of ARP. They justified their scientific findings in the magazine *Nature*, in response to Foulkes, proclaiming that their aim was 'to provide some scientific data concerning the published precautions – because no such data had been published and we felt that the unsupported statements of the government spokesmen concerning their efficiency were no substitute for scientific fact'.[27] They also sent letters of defence to other publications such as the *New Statesman and Nation*, highlighting the importance of their scientific findings and appealing for £600 to finance a film calling for 'balanced and reasonable action' by the government. The scientists also took umbrage that they had published their findings under their own names, risking their professional reputations, but had 'been refuted by anonymous Government experts in an unpublished report'.[28]

The Cambridge Scientists first published *The Protection of the Public From Aerial Attack* with a great degree of confidence. J.D. Bernal was sufficiently impressed with the CSAWG's work to send advance copies to important military and policy commentators such as Basil Liddell Hart. He prefaced the findings with a letter proclaiming that 'the results of the investigations seem to dispose fairly conclusively of certain of the Government's proposals of Air Raid Defence'.[29] Before long, however, the CSAWG and its members were forced to defend their tests and their professional reputations against charges of political motivation, ineptitude and even fraud. They did, however, find some prominent defenders among the 'usual suspects' – Labour MPs, for example. The CSAWG was defended in the House of Commons by the emotive rhetoric of Philip Noel-Baker, who denied that the scientists were a subsidiary of the Communist Party and emphasized the importance of current research rather than relying on First World War data.[30] This line of argumentation emphasized the scientists' professional identity and the importance of opening independent discussion of these issues.

Nevertheless, the gas critique proved to have limited purchase. As much as the CSAWG insisted that its test criteria were sound, it was soon clear that the gas critique could not serve as a basis for a larger campaign, and the debate moved on to the problem of deep shelter and high explosive bombs. The government and its supporters found that the charge of political extremism was easy to employ and that accusing opponents of attempting to undermine national confidence in ARP was an effective criticism. The contrarians again showed their limited influence in arguing that the danger of gas warfare could be calmly countered. Following 1937 there were no significant leftist commentaries on gas warfare because the discussion of ARP had shifted to the question of deep shelters. Naturally, a range of pacifists continued to decry the potential use of gas, but gas-proof rooms ceased to be a major concern. Technical criticisms developed into sustained political attacks against the government based on financial demands and the need for citizen-instituted air raid shelters as had been constructed in Spain.

Deep Shelters – Modern Warfare and the Urge to Go Underground

The call for deep shelters in British cities began immediately following the first air raids in Spain and reflected an acute awareness that, sooner or later, war would reach British shores. The Cambridge Scientists, realizing this shift, emphasized deep shelters in their second publication, arguing that 'the almost complete lack of reasonable protection against high explosive is the main shortcoming of the ARP scheme'.[31] Similarly, in a February 1938 letter to *The*

Times the CSAWG insisted that the issue of high explosive protection was the most crucial component of civilian defence.[32] This was the issue that would enable it to forward the model of active citizenship observed in Spain. The leftist critics were keenly aware of the criticism that they merely derided the government without offering feasible policies of their own, and their shelter plans aimed to provide a programme for action. The deep shelter programme proposed by J.B.S. Haldane demonstrates the fruition of the technical lessons from Spain as applied to Britain. Local councillors and officials picked up his plans and worked within the institutional mechanisms to press the government on the issue. For example, the Air Raid Protection Institute included Labour politicians such as Dr Richard Tee from Hackney. He lectured at the Institute on ARP for the borough, studied the issue of gas decontamination, and also worked on the Air Raid Precautions (Policy) Sub-Committee of the Committee of Imperial Defence.[33] These local officials would become important players in the nationwide debate.

The LBC also conducted an extensive campaign on the issue of ARP following the publication of the books by the Cambridge Scientists and J.B.S. Haldane, using these works as primary texts of their movement. The technical critiques were intended to form the basis of an integrated campaign to raise awareness of the issue as one of grave national importance – for example through 'Peace Councils' under the aegis of the Left Book Club.[34] Haldane and John Langdon-Davies, his colleague who had observed air raids in Spain, also cooperated on the issue of deep shelters, calling for bomb-proof shelters in London, increased protection for the vulnerable, and a clearer evacuation policy.[35] In 1938, John Strachey, a founder of the LBC, along with Victor Gollancz and Harold Laski, urged LBC members to lobby the government to adopt Haldane's recommendations for deep shelters.[36]

Issues of class and the financial obligations of the government towards its citizens were at the core of the leftist ARP critique from its inception. As we have seen, the 'self-help' basis of government plans was evident in the titles of Home Office circulars such as *Make Your Home Safe Now*. The unwavering message of ARP was that the householder should be responsible for the defence of his or her family in his own home. The Cambridge Scientists pointed out that a large percentage of the population simply did not have a spare room at their disposal that could be set aside for gas-proofing. Later on, critics pointed out that many urban Britons lacked outdoor spaces to install government-provided Anderson shelters. Consequently, they felt that government plans were biased against the urban poor, those very civilians who were at the greatest risk from aerial warfare. They believed that current ARP policy only exacerbated the economic disparity between the rich and poor and between wealthy and impoverished boroughs, especially since the burden of communal costs would disproportionately affect poorer areas. British leftists were particularly riled by the appearance of preferential treatment for the well-connected, while self-help seemed to be the prescription for ordinary citizens. For example, it came to light that the armed forces would receive the highest quality gas masks. In addition, deep shelters were being constructed under Whitehall for government officials and for the protection of the Royal Family near Windsor.[37] The British Movement Against War and Fascism and the Union of Democratic Control both argued that government officials, military personnel, and essential workers would be provided with prime shelter provisions, gas masks, and protective clothing, while the general public would only have the best protection they could afford.[38]

These critics first targeted their appeals to the urban householder who would likely find the Home Office advice difficult, if not impossible, to undertake. Haldane cited a statement by Conservative MP Duncan Sandys to drive home the point that the present government had no intention of helping the urban working class: 'The Home Office should abandon its hesitant attitude and tell the public plainly that, wherever it was reasonably possible, and within the limits of their means, it was the duty of every individual to provide protection for himself and his family.'[39] In the words of the Cambridge Scientists, the poor would 'get the least protection and pay relatively the most for it. To permit and advise people in the building of protective shelters instead of providing state shelters on an equal basis for all is to deprive the poor of shelter to the advantage of the rich.'[40] The CSAWG also found the government advice on constructing one-foot thick walls to protect from splinters to be alarming, since virtually no homes, and certainly not those of the poor, conformed to this standard. They concluded, 'This means in practice that the inhabitants, unless they are well off, will have no effective protection even against splinters'.[41] The critics believed that the structure of government ARP reflected all the worst class inequalities of British society that they were sworn to oppose.

The *Daily Worker* also focused on the economic aspects of government ARP policy, appealing directly to the bread and butter issues of the urban working class. An article entitled 'Skin Flint Attitude of the Air Raid Chief' charged that civilian protection, including the need for the preparation of vulnerable schools, was being subordinated to military needs. Despite the assurances of E.J. Hodsoll that school protection was a government priority, the *Daily Worker* writers believed that he was 'anything but anxious to spend money in affording the necessary protection'.[42] Bernal expressed an even more extreme view of the situation, possibly borne out of frustration at the government's intransigence, when he stated, 'the public cannot be protected without enormous cost and the abolition of all rights of private property. This is something no capitalist government has any intention of doing.'[43] More moderately, Haldane pointed out that one of the primary functions of the capitalist state was to 'preserve the existing class structure,'[44] but that this tendency needed to be strongly opposed by those who valued equality. Critics objected not only to the obligations on individual householders but to the demands placed on local councils, particularly in poorer areas. Christian pacifists agreed on this point, objecting to the fact that ARP would involve a serious restriction of social services that were already overstretched in poor areas.[45] The Communist Party noted that the money available for ARP per head varied widely between rich and poor areas. In Westminster, £16 3s. were available for protection per individual, with the prosperous areas of Holborn and Richmond rating at £9 0.5s. and £4 7s. respectively. In areas such as Walthamstow, Bethnal Green, Camberwell, and Lambeth this amounted to less than £2.[46] The Cambridge Scientists argued that the poorer areas of the East End required more protection than wealthier areas such as Kensington where structures were solidly built and where there were few strategic targets.[47]

Local councils resented the fact that they were forced to fund a national ARP programme that many felt to be of dubious merit and over which they had little control. An editorial in the *New Statesman and Nation* stated that opposition to government ARP demands by local authorities was well founded because they were being asked to foot the bill for a scheme whose general efficiency was much in doubt. In return for increased rates, local leaders believed that the populace deserved more protection.[48] Another editorial on the release of the 1935 circular claimed that it turned 'horrific fantasy into a close and appalling reality' and criticized the government for allowing the costs of shelters to fall on individuals and local councils.[49] Complaints were still voiced after Herbert Morrison and the London County Council (LCC) had negotiated for a higher supplement from the central government. Herbert Morrison was at this time a Labour MP and leader of the LCC and would be appointed Home Secretary in 1940. Many still felt that the only truly equitable solution was a fully subsidized programme that would spread the costs among all citizens, whether they lived in remote Cumbria or in East London. They were convinced that since ARP was vital to the survival of the nation as a whole, it was by default a national and not a piecemeal responsibility.

The Leftist Critics Justify Their ARP Estimates

The monetary figures that J.B.S. Haldane, the Cambridge Scientists, and the Communist Party arrived at for their desired deep shelter scheme were very large indeed. The financial estimates devised by Haldane were the most important to be forwarded, and his ideas were picked up almost verbatim by others, particularly left-leaning councils. He concluded that his two-part scheme would cost approximately £400 million to institute, with a high estimate of £600 million for an even more comprehensive plan.[50] This admittedly startling figure represented slightly more than half of total government expenditure during these years. Haldane envisioned that the cost would be spread over a period of two or three years at a rate of around £11 per head, although the annual figure would still constitute a large percentage of total government spending at peacetime rates.[51] These exorbitant figures did not pass unnoticed by his critics. One such anonymous critic scoffed at the idea that Haldane 'who is neither engineer nor architect' could promise 'absolute protection for a trifle of from £400 million to £600 million'.[52] Haldane proposed a combination of a capital levy on property and a 'civilian defence loan', offered to the public like a war bond to fund his programme, though he did not provide much detail as to how these schemes should work.[53]

The Haldane estimates became the guiding marker for other leftists. The figures proposed by the Cambridge Scientists came in at considerably less than those proposed by Haldane or the Communist Party. They estimated that their recommendations for a modest system of smaller reinforced brick shelters would cost only £2–3 per person, compared with a current rate of less than five shillings per person, if carried out over a period of five years.[54] However, brick shelters proved unpopular with both the majority of critics agitating for deep shelter and with the general population. The Communist Party figure of £11 per head entailed 60-foot deep shelters with entrances no more than 200 yards apart in central urban areas.[55] Their proposals demanded nothing less than tunnels for the entire population of Greater London, which constituted 8 million people. It is worth noting that some architectural professionals took up Haldane's conclusions on the sound economic basis of deep shelters. The *Architects' Journal* commissioned a report on ARP and the possibilities of deep shelters in 1939 and it endorsed the general consensus, stating that 'fully bomb-proof shelters' at a depth of 50 feet could be built at a cost of around £10 per head.[56]

Given the scale of the figures, the critics needed to persuasively argue that these expenditures were not exorbitant for the state, and they suggested possible sources for the funds. The Communist Party literature presented a simplistic class-based argument, calling for increased taxation of business and the very wealthy. The communist publication *A.R.P. for Londoners* ended its proposals with the rhetorical question: 'Is it too much to ask that these wealthy people should find out of their abundance the £11 per head needed to save the people of London and the women and children from horrible death?'.[57] Both the communists and the leftist scientists attempted to rationalize the sums as only a fraction of the combined expenditure on armaments over a period of years. This argument allowed them to access powerful pacifist and antiwar feeling that Britons still shared, even as it became clear that war with fascist powers was both necessary and inevitable. Haldane pointed out that his sum was only a fraction of the amount spent annually on armaments and would average about £10 per head over the duration of his two-part ARP programme, a figure that might seem more palatable than the larger combined figure.[58] The Cambridge Scientists likewise compared the £6 per head that was devoted to armed forces expenditure to the mere shillings that were allocated for civilian defence.[59]

The communist pamphlet writers also pointed to the huge profits of large national businesses, public companies, landlords, and armament manufacturers. These amounted to hundreds of millions per year, and the leftists attempted to make a moral argument about the duty of the rich to assist poorer members of the community. They pointed out that even a tiny tax surcharge on large business – which they believed would hardly be noticeable to such enterprises – would amply provide the resources required for the Haldane project. They also objected to war profiteering. As Communist Party organizers in Hampstead alleged: 'The tax-payer is being sucked dry, while huge profits are piled up. Not a single penny should be made from profiteering. The Government must tax the firms who are pocketing the people's money, and thus get all that is needed for ARP.'[60] By contrast, ARP shelters would be a publicly-constructed amenity, free from the danger of profiteering if constructed through the aegis of government and the trade unions. Haldane even went so far as to speculate that it was because 'no vast fortunes would be made from bomb-proof shelters' that they were not contemplated.[61]

The scientists approached the issue by justifying their proposals on sheer economic grounds. They pointed to the value of scientific standardization, believing that this approach would lower total costs while providing a higher standard of protection. The proponents of alternative ARP also proposed that the preparations should employ thousands of unemployed men at trade union rates, men who were currently drawing money on the dole. Much of ARP would therefore 'pay for itself', and the labour requirements for ARP construction programmes would immediately benefit thousands of presently unemployed men, contributing to the national economy and ameliorating living conditions in poor areas. In the years 1937–8 the numbers eligible for insurance benefits fluctuated from around 600,000 to 1 million.[62] Setting at least some of these men to work on ARP would therefore help to reduce this large social expenditure. Herbert Morrison believed that it was a national scandal that 2 million men were out of work when they could be utilized for these preparations.[63] These arguments were also taken up by the planners of the Finsbury project detailed as the final episode of this book. While deep shelter proposals were at many levels socialistic or at least communal, their professional proponents truly believed that their benefits in cost-efficiency would make them equally appealing to those of a more conservative bent.

Individuals on the opposing side of the political spectrum were not immune to many of the arguments presented by the critics, even those based on equality and fairness. Some non-leftist commentators pointed to the class inequality inherent in ARP recommendations, believing that this was ultimately wrong-headed. H. Montgomery Hyde, secretary to the former Secretary for Air, Lord Londonderry, acknowledged that the lack of resources available to construct gas-proof rooms for the majority of the population constituted a serious social problem. He suggested, somewhat naively, that the wealthy should volunteer to shelter other citizens in their own accommodations.[64] The radical commentators, however, were not content to hold out in hope of such private generosity. The Communist Party demanded that air raid shelters for the rich should be brought under municipal control for the benefit of all citizens and that offices and factories should have gas- and bomb-proof shelters at the owners' expense.[65] One publication put the issue of deep shelters thus: 'surely the British Broadcasting Corporation and the Ministries that will remain in Whitehall in war are not the only elements in national life for which deep shelters can be justified; and they are to go underground.'[66]

Perhaps one measure of the reach of the LBC's ARP campaign was that the Home Office ARP Department catalogued issues of *Left News* in its own library, noting that they were to be read in conjunction with Haldane's *A.R.P.* Home Office records indicate that literature by the Cambridge Scientists along with literature by Haldane and the communist critics constituted at least one-third of the items listed in the catalogue of the ARP Department.[67] This may have been partly following the dictum 'know thy enemy', but it was inevitably the case that to the extent that the government felt obliged to respond to criticisms, they were in fact addressing those critiques brought forward by this group of scientists. Sir John Anderson later accused Haldane of being the instigator of agitation on the issue of deep shelter, and we can only conclude that Haldane's books were widely read by both opponents and supporters. Biographers of J.D. Bernal have likewise noted that the CSAWG's 'intervention in the controversies raised about civil defence was to have immediate and durable effects'.[68] Though public statements by officials tended towards the blithely dismissive, the government was sufficiently worried about the critics to devote a great deal of time to refuting their claims. If criticism did not force an about-face in government plans, officials at least felt to the need to better explain provisions to the public. By 1938 the ground had been set for a clash between radically differing views of society and the civilian relationship to the state. The conflict would force the government to cement and justify its idea of particularly British values as reflected in ARP provisions.

CHAPTER 7

TERROR FROM THE SKIES –
WARTIME AND THE
CHALLENGE TO CIVIL
LIBERTIES

There are only two types of control suitable to the large-scale organization and movement of millions of people which will be required to give the warning, occupy the shelters, maintain observation and make the all-clear arrangements. There can be a military-police control in which people are subject to the dictatorship of officers. Or there can be the democratic method, whereby the people obey, with a voluntary and intelligent discipline, the decisions of their representatives [...] only the democratic form of control would work, because it alone would command the confidence of the people.[1]

–The Communist Party of Great
Britain, *A.R.P. for Londoners*

The functioning of democracy in a time of total war always pushes the extent to which voluntary compliance and representative institutions prove sufficient to the task. This Communist Party statement reflected a fundamental suspicion of government authority and the arbitrary powers that might be granted to air raid precautions (ARP) officials. While most leftists believed that ARP was necessary, they still bristled at the attempts to discipline the citizenry that they saw as evident in air raid drills and in the ARP Bills. Critics were wary of how dissent and freedom of speech would be impacted, citing the example of the Defence of the Realm Act and the prosecution of protestors and pacifists during the First World War. They were particularly concerned with the ill-defined rights to 'prevent public panic' that would be accorded to air raid wardens and other ARP workers and believed that the hierarchical structure of the air raid warden system and its affiliation with the police posed a danger to public freedom.

On the other end of the political spectrum, conservatives also responded to a 'John Bull' eschewing of intrusive authority, as they had since the nineteenth century. The language of patriotism was available to a range of political and social groups.[2] A particular mythology has grown up around the idea of the 'freeborn Englishman' and the sanctity of British liberty. Historian of early industrial Britain E.P. Thompson has detailed how invocations of these liberties informed the actions of crowds and popular protests.[3] On the right, 'cakes and ale' conservatism promised to protect Englishness from meddling liberals, temperance advocates, and reforming individuals viewed as busybodies. On the left, these same notions denoted freedom of the press, freedom to hold heterodox opinions, and concepts such as the right of unionization for workers. This cross-political notion of rights provided a rich tradition on which the critics of the 1930s could draw to formulate their criticisms of censorship and government control.

Although the campaign for alternative ARP called for expanded services and shelter provisions to be provided by the central government, leftist commentators were unwilling to allow the same government to have iron control over these services. It was admittedly something of a contradiction in their philosophy, but the activists did not view it as such and invested a great deal of time and energy into forwarding their ideas of 'democratic defence' – a model of citizen involvement that they had observed in Spain. However, their plans for democratic defence were difficult to articulate, especially given that they acknowledged the inability of local councils to provide for even basic ARP and because they remained inflexible in dealing with the central government. Wartime experience later proved that ARP services would need to be more centralized, rather than less. Indeed, many services, especially in the Greater London area, were necessarily amalgamated in a more hierarchical fashion.

Many of the fears over civil liberties were at some level not entirely without merit. At this time, secret plans were being drawn up to suspend normal government and institute emergency powers should the domestic situation deteriorate in wartime. Though these plans remained secret and were not declassified until recently, contemporary critics rightly suspected that these contingency measures were in place, similar in scope to 'Emergency Scheme L', drafted during the First World War to deal with any serious breakdown in civil order. The new preparations by the Home Office were entitled 'Scheme Y', and civil defence formed a large part of its mandate. Planners were largely concerned with 'making arrangements as necessary for reinforcing the local ARP services in any area where a breakdown is threatened'.[4] Regional commanders would take charge of wide areas, being wholly responsible for civil defence and filtering instructions down a chain of command to individual ARP wardens. Yet, as was the case with other provisions, their actual powers were only defined in brief, general terms.[5] Yet these preparations were worst-case contingency plans and the government was in no way as eager to impose authoritarian control as the left imagined. *The Economist* explained the conundrum in this way:

In one respect it hardly goes far enough: in peacetime the regional structure will remain no more than a 'shadow' framework, with the commissioners and their staffs holding only a watching brief. In another respect it may prove to go too far: in the event of a breakdown in communications during hostilities the regional commissioners, who will be nominated as men of standing and not elected or chosen as democratically popular leaders, will be vested under the Defence of the Realm Regulations with the full powers of His Majesty's Government and will exercise unlimited authority. The need to safeguard the maintenance of law, order and government in emergency is clear; but the rumoured refusal of Mr Herbert Morrison [. . .] to serve as London's 'dictator apparent' is scarcely surprising.[6]

The prospect of unqualified wardens with broad police powers was particularly troubling. The Cambridge Scientists' Anti-War Group (CSAWG) believed that 'air raid wardens armed with ill defined powers to "prevent panic" could also be instructed to prevent any kind of publicly voiced opposition to war as "dangerous to the morale of the public."'[7] During wartime, pacifists such as Vera Brittain did find their activities subtly curtailed. For example, Brittain was denied an exit visa to undertake a speaking tour in the United States – a prospect that would have been potentially embarrassing for the British as they sought aid from the Americans and their eventual entry into the conflict. Her wartime diaries detail many obstacles to campaigns against the course of the war.

The lingering distrust of militarism also filtered into fears about the predicted wartime loss of civil liberties. Some leftists and pacifists refused to condone ARP at all, since they believed that doing so indicated a support of war and an implicit belief in its inevitability. Committed pacifists believed that a principled stand against such measures would demonstrate a public refusal of war and reduce the chances – in the most idyllic world – that governments would resort to war. The Union of Democratic Control and the British Movement Against War and Fascism were ambivalent about the very existence of ARP, believing that such measures would simply encourage war. The Peace Pledge Union professed that 'pacifists should refuse to take part in practice black-outs and gas drill [. . . during peacetime these are] preparations for war, and it is the duty of pacifists to protest, not only in words, but also in actions, against such preparations'.[8] Few phrased their suspicions quite as strongly as Bertrand Russell, who gave a series of peace lectures around England in 1938, during which he stated that ARP was 'sham and lies' and that pacifists should refuse to take part. On another occasion he declared, 'There is, I think, a certain element about air-raids precautions that is extremely sinister.

It is creating a war mentality in the country.'[9] Yet even committed pacifists found it difficult to hold to unmoderated views in a situation where the civilian population would be targeted. For example, Russell acknowledged that in the event of actual war no one would deny gas masks to children or fail to do all that was possible to protect the innocent.[10] Almost all critics did accept that ARP was an unfortunate necessity for the protection of civilians. Many found it impossible to imagine pressing the idea of non-participation in ARP and anti-gas measures, even if they felt that it contravened their beliefs and constituted preparation for war. Indeed, very few pacifists went to the extent of refusing to participate in civil defence during World War II. Although there were some instances of opposition to forced ARP duty, such as fire-watching, most pacifists had decided that strict beliefs were inadequate in the face of the fascist threat and the nature of modern warfare. Yet it did not mean that pacifist attitudes were jettisoned; rather, they were expressed in different terms within the ARP critique.

The issue of civil liberties was not only a concern for the left, although leftist opposition was most vociferous. Many commentators drew on the bitter experiences of the First World War and the institution of the Defence of the Realm Act at the onset of war in 1914, which gave the government wide-ranging powers including the censorship of the press and the stifling of dissent and labour agitation. Critics feared that a similar suppression of pacifist and dissenting opinion would recur under autocratic ARP legislation and that the true extent of restrictions might not be known until after the outbreak of hostilities.[11] The *New Statesman* reflected the belief that ARP was merely a device for public control, stating, 'The only aim of so-called "defence" is to postpone panic until after the war can be won, hence the key of the Circular is the word "discipline".'[12] Many community groups were critical of measures that might lead to the creation of a war mindset that was incompatible with democracy. When gas drills were introduced in Southgate, the Wood Green Women's Arbitration Committee protested that they would 'have a harmful effect upon the plastic minds of children'.[13] The Union for Democratic Control had concluded as early as 1935 that government proposals were, in their analysis, 'deceptive', in that they did not offer true protection.[14]

A prominent theme forwarded by critics was the pacifist-inspired allegation that ARP was not intended actually to protect the population but rather to keep civilians from mass panic while the military waged war.[15] After all, the governmental emphasis on morale and the importance of war production was not exactly hidden in public discourse. The Cambridge Scientists, for example, made a presentation to the Cambridge Borough Council on the subject of democracy and air raids. They claimed that present precautions served only to engender a 'state of war-mindedness', enriching special interests and industry without providing any true protection.[16] In their book they noted that 'fear of panic is the dominant note of all speeches of Air Raid Precautions officials. Seldom do they fail to mention that panic is the greatest danger which they fear.'[17] As has been noted, there was indeed a strong public order element to ARP, alongside the mandate to protect life and property. A doctor commented in the *British Medical Journal* that he had been told his duty would be to prevent panic, reassure gas casualties, and 'to get it into people's heads that whether they have gas-proofed rooms or not the important thing is to be under cover in their own houses'.[18] Editorial writers for the *New Statesman and Nation* believed the Royal Air Force would then be free to destroy enemy cities 'without the embarrassment of panic at home,' if the civilian population were kept docile in their own homes.[19] The Communist Party of Great Britain General Secretary Harry Pollitt believed that the population was being encouraged to place their faith in mechanisms that could not ultimately provide security, but merely gave the illusion of public safety.[20] All these commentators echoed the pacifist critiques familiar in the anti-gas debate.

The British Movement Against War and Fascism published a pamphlet that dealt significantly with dangers to civil liberties, insisting that 'the population is to be kept in a state of continued alarm by propaganda, by constant gas mask drill, mock raids and black-outs. The whole atmosphere of war time is to be made permanent.' They believed that this internalization of 'gas discipline' would inevitably lead to police control, government stifling of criticism, and the imprisonment of pacifists.[21] J.B.S. Haldane even went so far as to suggest that the government, if taken over by rightist elements, might engage in 'Police Bombing' against their own people to subdue revolutionary elements within the population.[22] Haldane and fellow critic John Langdon-Davies called for a clearer government policy on civil policing should persistent raids threaten to shut down the capital.[23] Even 50 years later, some leftist historians would continue to believe that Home Defence measures were simply an arm of civil control to deal with public disorder, strikes, or any insurrection that might occur in wartime.[24]

There were contradictory opinions regarding how this control mechanism would work. Some critics believed that the government would attempt to keep the population in a constant state of fear and panic, and others thought that it was aimed at keeping the population docile. Often the same commentators expressed both opinions, depending on their audience or the subject of their ARP comment. The commonality of these interpretations was the belief that the government sought to manipulate rather than to protect its citizens. These critics were equally concerned with the public ability to internalize the militarism of the state and to activate latent 'warmongering' instincts. Leftists were ever mindful of the supposed patriotic frenzy of 'Mafeking night' during the Boer War and the celebration with which the Great War had been welcomed. By the 1930s, the mythology of the enthusiastic Tommy marching happily off to a war that 'would be over by Christmas', formed the accepted narrative of the First World War. In its 1935 *Air Display Special* leaflet, the CSAWG insisted that the real purpose of the ARP drills was 'to prepare people's minds for war, to regiment the civil population for war'.[25] Consequently, the critics were equally suspicious of the reaction of the general public.

The structural intent of the ARP Bill and its implications for the daily functioning of communities and neighbourhoods was also a subject of grave concern. Communist Party affiliates, including the prominent Hampstead group, insisted that 'democratic control' of all ARP was essential to the success of plans in greater London.[26] Their notion of 'democratic control' corresponded strongly to the way in which Spanish ARP had been organized. In effect, it meant that local councils should control ARP wardens and that those wardens should be carefully chosen on the basis of ability and their potential to cooperate with their fellow citizens, rather than to command them. The critics also argued that decentralized control of volunteers was ultimately a question of national importance for the cooperation of civilians. J.B.S. Haldane was concerned with how resentment against air raid wardens might impact the entire practice of ARP and the morale on the Home Front, both of which were essential to the wartime survival of the country. Believing that raising these questions denoted a justifiable patriotic concern, he stated that:

> The air-raid wardens are being given a duty which may well prove impossible, and for this reason many people are refusing to become wardens. I think this is a mistake. We must do what we can to protect one another. But some Air Raid Wardens actually believe much of the propaganda which is being put over in lectures [...] They are adopting a tone with their neighbours which democratically elected officials would hardly do. It is perfectly clear that after a single air raid such people will lose their authority which they may now possess with their neighbours.[27]

Yet ultimately, Haldane also trusted in the rationality of ordinary British people, believing that the majority of wardens would resist the temptation to take such an attitude. He expressed faith that the people would respond to the idea of 'democratic defence', and he appealed to progressive people to enrol as air raid wardens. Even though existing schemes were inadequate and lectures given to wardens were full of untruths, simplistic thinking, and propaganda, he believed that there was a clear need for intelligent citizens to staff these services.[28] Objecting to the trumpeting of government propaganda without due deliberation, he believed that wardens who openly acknowledged the gaps in official advice and who took a more flexible attitude would be more likely to retain the confidence of their neighbours in wartime than those who simply parroted the official, and sometimes simplistic, government line.[29] By encouraging the constituency represented by the Left Book Club to join the ranks of the air raid wardens, he was attempting to promote left-wing patriotic service and to establish a cadre of volunteers who would represent democratic interests. In this way 'democratic defence' would be ensured by the people themselves, despite the sometimes-faulty (as he deemed) direction the government was taking.

By encouraging active participation, critics such as Haldane hoped to demonstrate that individuals could simultaneously criticize government policies yet remain patriotic and sincerely concerned about the wartime performance of the nation. It was also hoped that the involvement of progressive people in sufficient numbers could result in nation-wide policy changes. Haldane's 1938 pamphlet *How to Be Safe from Air Raids* focused on direct action and called for individuals to contact their MPs, housing estate owners and other relevant officials, demanding full ARP shelters at their workplaces. He believed that 'if the people of Britain knew the facts, they would turn out any Government, regardless of its political views, which did not promise them full protection, and act on the promise'.[30] Calls for local and individual involvement in ARP were an important facet of leftist strategy, especially from 1938 onwards, after it had become clear that neither the example of Spain nor the proposals for deep shelters would move the national government position on their determined policy of self-help regarding ARP.

Yet the far left was often blind to the fact that the notions of 'British freedoms' and 'democracy' did not only appeal to leftists and that others could use the same language to draw opposite conclusions regarding government intentions. A cross-section of the British population were equally opposed to 'meddling', and they could interpret the self-help and volunteerism inherent in government plans as acknowledging that antipathy towards control was commonplace. This sentiment reflects the suspicion of fellow citizens 'getting above themselves', or becoming wardens due to a desire to exert control over others. This fear corresponded to traditional ideas of Britishness, including an intense dislike of manipulation and a suspicion of neighbours wielding undue authority. The records of Mass Observation, the large-scale research organization that meant to ascertain representative opinions from a variety of contributors, provide some evidence that the populace received the general prospect of ARP wardens with a fair degree of scepticism. Some observers even ventured that most wardens would 'cower at home' in the event of an actual raid.[31] In the postwar era, this deep-seated antipathy was brilliantly captured in the television show *Dad's Army*, which portrayed the character of the air raid warden William Hodges in a particularly authoritarian and odious light. Opinion regarding compulsion to perform war duties was mixed and complex, with many respondents agreeing that although the voluntary system was preferable, compulsion was necessary if other attempts at securing war workers were unsuccessful.[32]

While the far left represented a reflexively hostile position towards air warden policy, Parliamentary Labour and the LCC held a more conciliatory attitude towards the central government. The position of Herbert Morrison over a plan to place air raid wardens under the control of the Metropolitan Police emphasized the gap between the rhetoric of vague concepts such as 'democratic defence', and an acknowledgement of how events would actually unfold in practice. The Labour Party was more willing than the Communist Party to accept the reality that the wartime organization of air raid workers needed to be hierarchical. Philip Noel-Baker, for all his criticism of government ARP, also acknowledged that the organization of ARP volunteers was in essence a military one. He did not object to this fact, but insisted that civilian local authorities have control over the process of recruitment and that all volunteers be trained to a central standard.[33]

Under the guidance of Herbert Morrison, the LCC and the Metropolitan Boroughs Standing Joint Committee supported the government plan for the control of air raid volunteers and coordination with the Metropolitan Police. Yet there was still friction between these factions and the 'hard-left' rebel boroughs that objected to the police control provisions.[34] Morrison was among those who tried to smooth over these differences, believing that infighting between the boroughs was unhelpful in achieving their joint goal of improved ARP. Morrison worked with Alderman Charlie Key of the Borough of Poplar to persuade the rebel boroughs that they had no choice but to cooperate. The various parties reached a compromise solution by which local councils recruited and trained their own wardens, but coordination for control of the warden system was centralized under a principal warden appointed by New Scotland Yard.[35] Morrison was politic enough to hold a series of meetings with the rebel boroughs, allowing them to express their concerns, but he was firm in his conviction that the boroughs had nothing to fear by cooperating with the government on the subject of air raid wardens. His conciliatory policies set the tone for the war itself, and his inclusion in Cabinet as a Labour Home Secretary signified the unifying ethos that a wartime Britain wished to project.

Critics would have little choice but to cooperate within an environment that somewhat constrained their customary freedom of expression. But for the most part even far left critics, with the exception of some dyed-in-the-wool communists, took developments in stride. *The Daily Worker* was shut down in early 1941 due to its extreme provocative stance. The credit that might have been due to the communists for warning about fascist aggression was completely erased following the Nazi–Soviet Pact, and the absurd position of being apologists for the Soviet Union's own appeasement of Fascism. The decision was personally overseen by Herbert Morrison, a long-time opponent of the communists, and undertaken with great reluctance. It demonstrated one case of a political party and news outlet pushing the wartime tolerance for dissent too far, but the fact that it only occurred one-and-a-half years into the war is instructive of the endurance of 'British liberty'. But this relative toleration of the Communist Party, and the release of the British Union of Fascists' Oswald Mosley from custody in 1943, also reflects the fact that neither extremist party was viewed as presenting much of a subversive threat.[36]

The repercussions of this debate were of importance to many aspects of war planning and reflected widely based concerns and an antipathy that government services would need to delicately negotiate. As war preparation gave way to wartime itself, much official time was devoted to the question of not only preventing panic but rousing feelings of community and inclusiveness throughout the country. It was vitally important that civilians of all classes and political persuasions continued to feel that democratic institutions represented their needs and responded to their concerns. The many iterations of the People's War were influenced by a number of factors that had their roots in the interwar years, including the example of Spain and how British liberties would be preserved in an atmosphere of total war. While the government was able to quietly sideline most dissent, officials had to simultaneously retain the flexibility to deal with reasonable criticism. We now turn to the question of Britishness in ARP, a concept that the Home Office employed to denote flexibility and the ability to adapt to changing circumstances. The subsequent three chapters reflect the apogee of the complex meanings of national character and myth, duty and belonging, and social obligation.

CHAPTER 8

BRITISHNESS – CIVILIANS ON THE HOME FRONT AND NATIONAL IDENTITY

There are many people who are inclined to say that we with our go-as-you please methods can be at best but a poor match for countries which have at their disposal a close-knit organization, held by authority at every point in an inflexible grip, organizations of whose mechanical efficiency the world has recently had conspicuous and spectacular illustrations. I respectfully decline to accept that view. The elephant is a cumbrous and ungainly creature, and to all appearances singularly ill adapted to the performance of tasks requiring delicacy or precision [. . .] I think that in this country we shall probably never achieve the degree of mechanical efficiency that is possible, for example, in Germany [. . .]. For those who believe in free institutions and in individual liberty, it must be a task of supreme importance to prove that in the pursuit of all worthy aims in life a system based upon those principles can at least hold its own against any rival.[1]

–Sir John Anderson

In this speech to the House of Commons in June 1938, Sir John Anderson laid out in direct and succinct form his view of the contrast between 'mechanized' German plans and a more 'organic' and flexible method of British war preparation. Anderson poetically compared England to a noble elephant, emphasizing the nation's solid and immovable character that existed despite its apparent lack of dexterity and speed in adapting to new circumstances. He went on to state that German plans suited the supposed 'idiosyncrasies' of the German people — at least they were 'idiosyncratic' to British eyes. This clash of stereotypes, so familiar to the modern newspaper reader or viewer of comedy news programmes, set out a definitive contrast in national characters. It furthermore provided a basis for the British government to follow its own path, regardless of continental practice or British commentators who advocated that British practice follow that on the Continent. Anderson further insisted that 'mechanical precision is not everything; it may even be a positive disadvantage in dealing with conditions which cannot be precisely foreseen'.[2]

The more astute critics sought to affirm that they were as concerned as the government with questions of civilian morale and the successful prosecution of a national war. They believed that their ideas were superior both technically and ideologically, but reached an impasse with the government over irreconcilable versions of how British air raid shelters should be provided. Sir John Anderson continued to believe that the people had not been given a fair estimate of why Home Office plans for defence were best suited to British conditions. While 'patchwork' could be interpreted negatively, the writers of one editorial clearly applied this word in a positive light and suggested that the flexibility of multiple schemes served best for national defence.[3] Writers of letters to the editor in *The Times* reflected similar sentiments. One noted that British air raid precautions (ARP) had unfortunately been cast in a negative light due to the 'energy and drive' of European dictatorships, but that it would prove adequate to the task when necessary.[4] The language of the 'British way' could be contorted to fit any number of circumstances.

Many insisted that the war would be lost if the nation's citizens ducked into shelters whenever an air raid siren sounded. The implication was that British people, unlike continentals or foreigners in East London, should not take to 'funk-holes' or neglect essential war work by cowering underground. As a pejorative term, 'funk-hole' referred to culturally-embedded notions of how British people should behave in wartime. The tension continued with how ARP planners suspected the population might actually react. As Home Office files reveal, the 'British way' did not entail much confidence in the performance of the British people. The necessity of continuing war production and keeping the London transport system operational was factored into the policy that forbade the use of Underground stations as civilian shelters. The director of the Underground had reiterated in the 1920s the undesirability of the stations being used as shelters, due partly to the unsanitary condition in which they had been left following such usage in the First World War. As had occurred in 1917, however, this directive was to be quickly rescinded in 1940 due to overwhelming public demand. Residents of London simply purchased the cheapest fares available and refused to vacate stations at night, undertaking a virtual requisition of these places of refuge that the government was all but powerless to stop.

British Identity: Domesticity and Middle-Class Volunteerism

As demonstrated in the previous chapter, the critics were keen to forward their own notions of democratic defence and egalitarianism. They also wished to demonstrate that Britishness encompassed more than a stereotypical and middle-class notion of the nation. These ideas were in opposition to some deep-seated notions regarding national identity and the roles that belonged to different individuals based on class, gender, and status. As Peter Mandler reminds us in *The English National Character*, constructions of Britishness and Englishness were often contradictory and contextually dependent. In *Britishness Since 1870*, Paul Ward also emphasizes that national identity relates to the political, economic, social, cultural and personal factors prevalent at the time any subject chooses to reflect on his or her own 'Britishness'.[5] While one-dimensional notions of British identity could not begin to encompass the wide variety of conceptions of the nation, such ideas were easily employed to bolster political arguments. The Victorian ideal of personal and national character still had strong cultural purchase in the interwar period. Some of these ideas included introspectiveness, modesty, enjoying the quiet pleasures of home, and despising 'alien' zeal and political high-handedness.[6] British people were also popularly depicted as light-hearted, unassertive and lacking driving ambition, yet reliable and dutiful in times of crisis. This was typified by Stanley Baldwin's famous 1924 speech 'On England', when he stated, 'the Englishman is made for a time of crisis, and for a time of emergency'.[7] For the government, popular conceptions of national identity served as comforting images that reassured them of British superiority. As we have seen, Sir John Anderson frequently deployed ideas of a distinct national character in his discussions of government preparations. Characteristics peculiar to the British were thought to be the basis of British resistance to the extremes of both Communism and Fascism, although such a simplistic explanation may not stand up to historical scrutiny.[8] The construction of the stoic Briton was used to praise the ordinary people and proved practically useful to the government.

The government drew on two older notions of British identity – the individualistic and volunteer ethic, and the perceived British preference for home and mistrust of strangers. The individualist basis of government ARP echoed a long tradition of liberal values and notions of self-help that had predominated in British political and social thought since the mid-nineteenth century. The professional ideal was defined by the demands of social duty and altruism. One historian has suggested that the 'pedestrian' virtues of the Victorians, including moral conscience and respectability, shaped ideas about government and the obligations citizens held towards each other and towards the state.[9] This middle-class ideal went virtually unquestioned and was reflected by the myriad of voluntary institutions that sprang up in Britain. Naturally, other nations had similar ideas of civic duty, but the British entwined it directly to national identity. The idea of 'character' was considered a determining factor for both individuals and nations[10] and was evident in the government conceptions of ARP.

The evolution of the debate over ARP reveals interesting developments and contradictions regarding volunteerism. The government and leftist critics praised differing versions of the volunteer ethic in the call for citizens to become involved in ARP. In *The War Come Home*, Deborah Cohen details the extent to which the interwar British state was based on private philanthropy rather than state intervention. Studying the case of war veterans, she concludes that volunteerism was crucial to the stability of interwar Britain. Although this era has been viewed as the genesis of the welfare state, Cohen argues that the continued importance of volunteerism has not been adequately acknowledged.[11] Moving into wartime itself, James Hinton has emphasized the extent to which the volunteer work of 'middle-aged and middle-class' women demonstrates the continuities and endurance of class. The voluntary service of housewives appealed directly to middle- and upper-middle class citizens. Hinton is one of several historians to explore Mass Observation as a source to gauge reception of wartime calls to service and public opinion. Much of this work focuses on gender; Hinton has shown how wartime activities provided outlets for women and opportunities for them to feel vital to the national community. Lucy Noakes has demonstrated similar interactions between national identity and gender.[12] Though facets of these works demonstrate discernable social change, such as expanded roles for women, there are also many continuities: an inherent conservatism, a dislike for drastic change, and comfort taken in the familiar. There are no easy generalizations regarding behaviour, and there are many contradictions in individual motivation. This chapter serves to demonstrate some of these continuities and to show how they mirrored government ideas regarding the 'British way' of ARP and home sheltering. Mass Observation records support the notion that the British people largely endorsed the status quo. Neither denunciation nor great enthusiasm is much in evidence, although the populace on the whole responded to calls for the government's version of active citizenship.

Sir John Anderson believed that 'we must have an organization comprising a hierarchy of officials working in free collaboration with local authorities, voluntary bodies, and with a vast number of individuals giving voluntary service'.[13] Such a system would be more intrinsically home-grown and would also contrast with the 'compulsion' of the authoritarian regimes. *The Times* praised the volunteer basis of ARP, maintaining that the best and most innovative ideas came from individuals – reflecting the cult of the amateur which still dominated the middle- and upper-class view of the nation. The paper's reporters believed that the system of volunteerism could work on a large scale, but that expertise should not be sacrificed to the 'zeal of the civilian'.[14] This represented a fine balance between the competing ethos of professionalism and the amateur, and class played a major role in how this wartime system was envisioned.

There were a variety of practical problems inherent in a volunteer system. To begin with, the recruitment of adequate numbers proceeded slowly before the Munich Crisis, which was perhaps natural given the initial uncertainty over provisions and local obligations and the general lack of urgency about the issue.[15] This lack of enthusiasm prompted the Home Office in turn to prod the local authorities to accelerate recruitment and training at the local level. It expressed concerns about the quality and quantity of volunteers, the level of instruction, and an absence of qualified officers throughout the 1930s.[16] In peacetime, many 'public-spirited volunteers' faced time constraints preventing their participation, although according to a government spokesman, citizens would be only too eager to assist in whatever way possible during wartime.[17] Some commentators even believed that an over-zealous execution of ARP duties was un-British. One brigadier-general was fearful that the rush to distribute gas masks and institute blackout drills imperilled the British qualities of 'coolness and common sense'.[18] Most British people held a range of attitudes that fell between the poles of volunteerism and compulsion. During the early stages of the war, many believed that compulsion was necessary to force everyone to do their part and ensure equality of service.[19] Wartime diarists reflect a complex and mixed picture, but there is strong evidence that stirring patriotic appeals found a receptive audience with many citizens, and perhaps even motivated them to the level of sacrificial duty desired by the authorities.[20]

Wartime voluntary work for women (as opposed to compulsory military service) was primarily under the auspices of the Women's Voluntary Service (WVS) for Civil Defence. Stella, Marchioness of Reading, led the organization that had over 1 million female members by 1942. As early as 1933 she had warned: 'Our job is to look after ourselves, and to have sufficient force to prevent the next sudden German attack on civilization.'[21] Home Secretary Sir Samuel Hoare recognized in the Marchioness the qualities that would allow her to organize women and housewives who were otherwise exempt from compulsory national service. These women were to take on the myriad tasks that were necessary if the official ARP system was to operate efficiently. The WVS, by its very nature, attracted middle- and upper-middle class women who were community-orientated and filled the ranks of its part-time service. Lady Reading was aware that the patronage of titled ladies and the Royal Family was essential to the success of the organization, and she cultivated these contacts. Reading came from a modest background, and she was eager that WVS should become as close to a meritocracy as was possible. The WVS proved particularly useful during the evacuation of children from London in 1939 and also took on more 'manly' duties as the war commenced, with women serving as wardens, fire watchers, drivers and first aid attendants. Volunteers undertook the task of listing the residents of every street so that this information would be available for searchers in bombed areas. They also provided a human touch to the official services that aided victims of bombing, providing meals, practical facilities, helping with incident reports and providing something as simple and cheering as tea and cake. The WVS followed a long tradition of voluntary service but differed in one particular aspect – as a part of the military structure members were under orders to perform whatever tasks were necessary, even dangerous and disagreeable ones. It serves as an example of an organization of civil society that found itself on the cusp of social change. While patronage, charity, and the Victorian model of voluntary service were falling out of favour, the WVS managed to retain an important role in national service even after the war, partly due to relatively meritocratic structure encouraged by the Marchioness when she set up the organization.

The middle-class constituency that responded to the WVS was also receptive to language that confirmed the individualist ethos of ARP plans. Officials from the Home Office would not have gone ahead with the scheme had they not been certain of the support of the middle classes, since the interwar political economy was engineered to serve their interests.[22] Many members of this class lived in the suburbs surrounding London that attempted to recreate a leafy idyll within the confines of the city. Another idea that was stressed particularly strongly was the assumed 'domesticity' of the British and an innate suspicion of strangers.[23] If the Englishman's home was his castle, it was also thought to be most suitable for sheltering during air raids. The Home Office was able to employ the image of the nation's citizens as 'worshippers of home', as described by George Santayana.[24] Since the British and particularly the English were assumed to be highly domestic and private, they were therefore unsuited to mass shelter schemes such as those planned on the continent. This idealization of home and antipathy towards strangers and crowds also evoked a long-standing idealization of rural Britain. Though there has been substantial historiographical debate regarding the extent to which the interwar state could be in any sense classified as 'anti-urban' or 'anti-modern', many of these images were deep-seated.[25] They continued to hold a powerful rhetorical currency, even if most Britons lived in towns and did not wish to return to a pre-industrial past. As was the case with the middle-class basis of volunteer policies, the government may well have assumed that its plans for sheltering would please supporters who owned homes in which to shelter or had gardens in which Anderson shelters could be placed. This constituency was growing in size and influence, and also represented a base of support for 'small c' conservative policies.

Even if only vaguely articulated, the desire for privacy, a preference for home and a dislike of strangers were embedded in a particular view of British national identity. As the engineer Ove Arup noted, these ideas easily overlapped with other deeply held class prejudices. He expressed the opinion that the 'desire for privacy is especially pronounced amongst the people with higher incomes or of certain social strata, and some of these can afford to pay for a more expensive private shelter, or are, at any rate, willing to face an increased risk from bombs to ensure privacy'.[26] Class as well as British identity was implicit in these discussions of privacy, shelter, and the issue of crowds and morale. These issues of privacy as envisioned by the central government, namely their insistence that the appropriate 'British way' was to shelter at home, did find some public resonance. A Mass Observation report in 1940 confirmed that for varying reasons relatively few people utilized public shelters. Only 4 per cent of respondents reported utilizing these shelters, with the majority sleeping in their own homes. The prime reasons for remaining at home or using backyard Anderson shelters were cited as familiarity and comfort. Some wanted to be close to family and neighbours, remarking that they felt more at ease with their 'own people' around. Many expressed a dislike of the lack of privacy in public shelters, fearing both crowds and strangers.[27] There was a notable feeling of 'ownership' associated with the Anderson shelter, confirming the importance to many of staying close to home.[28] A visceral preference for private rather than public shelters, even though such shelters did not offer deep protection, was also evident prior to the outbreak of war.[29] At least some of the government's assumptions about what British people wanted did ring true with the public. As had been observed in Spain, however, people did also appreciate the *choice* of deep shelters. This was closely observable with the public insistence on Underground stations being made available at least on a partial basis for those without any sheltering facilities.

Press Reception of Governmental Plans

The tenor of coverage in the most widely read newspapers reflected an acceptance of the general outlines of ARP as set out by the government. As a rule, the right-of-centre newspapers and populist papers such as the *Daily Mail* and *Daily Mirror* chose not to criticize government schemes in the interwar years in any substantive way. They also tended to conflate civilian defence with questions of offensive strength and aerial tactics.[30] Tabloid newspapers could have plausibly used the lack of shelter preparation as a tool for selling copies. After all, the *Daily Mail* had been prominent in decrying the lack of civilian defence in the First World War and in pressing for reprisal raids against Germany. Yet criticism in the press largely related to the implementation of policies such as gas-mask distribution or the recruitment of ARP wardens. An instructive example is the periodic coverage of the issue in *The Economist*, which criticized the implementation of ARP on some levels, including coordination, inaction by local authorities, squabbling over the financing of schemes, and the 'belatedly burgeoning' schemes for volunteers and shelters. Enthusiastic about the eventual righting of these issues under the capable leadership of Sir John Anderson, the editorial writers nevertheless also tepidly suggested that more underground shelters should be considered. However, it hardly equalled a strong call on the issue: 'and it may well be that, in the new wave of effort, more will be made to provide sufficient accommodation, in trenches and blast-proof steel shelters, for most of the population pending the construction of genuine refuges underground'.[31]

Much of this coverage reflected the confusion that marked public discussion from 1935 onwards, but it was also an acquiescence to the fact that ARP policy was largely fixed. These newspapers represented the bulk of national readership. Even the Labour-controlled *Daily Herald*, which was one of the only left-of-centre papers to rival the *Daily Mail* and *Daily Mirror* in readership, refrained from directly attacking the government on the issue of ARP, tending to cover only superficial aspects of the issue.[32] Their editorials of 1937 and 1938 were concerned with the Spanish Civil War, but also, significantly, with the failure of the Unity Front and the suppression of communists and socialists in the Labour Party. It is not surprising that Labour publications remained extremely wary of association with the far left criticism of government ARP, even as Labour

MPs advocated improved ARP on the floor of the House. Nor were most critics opposed to volunteerism, though their idea of active citizenship differed from the government ideal. The more judicious critics, such as those affiliated with Parliamentary Labour, were aware of the need to choose their ARP battles carefully.

The national newspaper of record, *The Times*, published a three-part series in January 1938 on preparations for air raids. The articles dealt with defence against the bomber, the problems local ARP officers faced, and the vaguely termed topic of 'things that need knowing'. Though admitting that some uncertainties existed, including the lack of preparations for the East End of London, the paper nevertheless praised the 'miracles' that the ARP Department had produced and deemed the basis of government plans to be sound. Striking a partisan tone, it noted: 'that will not satisfy the pacifist, Communist, and critical Left-winger, whose suspicions and gibes have made more impression on the middle-class populations than people think'.[33] The paper therefore seemed to conceive of the 'middle-class populations' as a distinctive group that might be predisposed to accept government recommendations. It also demonstrated that the paper's writers believed that the radical critics wielded some influence. The sole letter to the editor published in reaction to the three-part series in 1938 supported the government's position. It portrayed the policy of dispersal as 'common sense' and insisted that providing mass bomb-proof shelters could 'not [be] capable of economic justification'.[34] The lack of a sustained campaign on the issue in the popular daily press no doubt provided the government with a certain level of proof that their 'British way of ARP' found resonance with the citizenry.

The issue of evacuation was particularly fraught with questions of the rights, obligations, and the expected behaviour of citizens. As previously noted, the act of sheltering during the First World War was coloured by ideas of appropriate behaviour for British people, particularly British men. Plans to evacuate the vulnerable 'non-essential' urban population did not substantively begin to take shape until the late 1930s[35] and were also tied to questions of morale. The government was particularly concerned with the signals that a mass evacuation of the capital would send to enemy nations. The report of the Committee on Evacuation in July 1938 concluded that there should be evacuations of some persons, but not wholesale removals that might hamper the war effort.[36] The general guiding principle was that children, along with some invalids and elderly persons, should be relocated from London to designated evacuation zones. The official historian noted that these principles were established by 1938, though there were 'many details' to be sorted out.[37]

The approach to the question of evacuation suggests that the government did not consider that the population needed to be informed about provisions much in advance of war itself. While the critics insisted that specific procedures should be standardized and publicized for public review, the government believed that a more *ad hoc* British approach would be less alarming. The wartime experience of evacuation, of course, often proved far too *ad hoc*. Many railway transports of children from the cities to the countryside occurred with only the vaguest notion of destination or how and where the children would be housed. Some children were regarded as free farm labourers, leaving them at the mercy of local families and meaning that young, strong-looking boys were often picked first from the ranks of bewildered urban children deposited on train platforms. The whole operation was based on a network of volunteers of uncertain training. In his satire of the Phoney War, *Put Out More Flags*, Evelyn Waugh parodied the system brilliantly. The anti-hero of the piece, Basil Seal, shops around the ghastly 'Connolly children' from one hapless and unsuspecting family to another, pocketing bribes from those desperate to rid themselves of the mischievous urchins.

Preparations for Air Raids in Germany, France, and Views of 'Backward Spain'

Along with Spain, France served as a lodestone of superior planning for critics intent on showing up what they deemed shabby and haphazard preparations on the part of the British government. Highlighting the advanced scientific standards of continental ARP allowed leftist critics to demonstrate the value of a progressive national government, since France was under the direction of the leftist Popular Front government until early 1938. Leftist critics felt that the French approach to ARP ('*La Défense Passive*') represented a rational and equality-based approach, and critics believed that British people would be equally desirous of large shelter plans. They tied comparisons with France to their simultaneous emphasis on left-wing nationalism and its benefits to the entire citizenry.

The case of German ARP provides an interesting contrast with the discussion of France. German preparations were discussed, yet they were treated with a measure of caution by all observers. Parliamentary ARP Committee members went to study French and also German preparations for air raids in early 1938, quite shockingly close to the build-up of tensions with Germany that would come to a head that September. Sir Samuel Hoare praised the 'courtesy' of the host governments and remarked: 'While the different conditions in different countries necessarily result in different methods of dealing with air raid precautions, it will, I think, be agreed that in making our own preparations we should not ignore what can be learnt from methods which are being adopted elsewhere.' The report of the visit provoked Liberal MP Geoffrey Mander to ask sarcastically if the Home Secretary was satisfied that German civilians were adequately protected against British air raids.[38] At this time British diplomats were still attempting to retain positive relations with Germany, and the visit was doubtless an opportunity for valuable information gathering, though the findings remained secret.

Though taking the existence of German preparations into account, most experts were hesitant to compare German preparations to those of the British for political and moral reasons. The Air Raid Protection Institute, for example, investigated the basis of German preparations and noted that homeowners were refunded 60 per cent of the cost of reinforcing household cellars as bomb shelters.[39] The engineer Ove Arup also made a study of a German report called 'Splinter and gas-proof concrete tube shelters' that focused on bomb-proof shelter policy. He felt that in the absence of British technical information, critics had to rely on whatever foreign sources were available.[40] Yet there was no real consensus about what data from Germany actually meant, and details remained vague and contradictory. In addition, very few commentators wished to be seen even slightly praising the war plans of a fascist dictatorship. As has been demonstrated, the government publicly dismissed the 'mechanical' German plans as having little relevance to the British situation. Nor would leftists have been interested in extolling the preparations made by Nazi Germany, even for the purpose of arguing that a free country should protect its citizens better than an authoritarian one. It was certainly more productive for them to point to democratic countries such as Republican Spain and France.

The programme of building air raid shelters in Paris was the most obvious preparatory element to be subjected to foreign scrutiny. Various MPs studied French ARP during the 1930s and spoke of the issue during debates in the Commons. Geoffrey Lloyd travelled to Paris under the auspices of the Parliamentary ARP Committee to observe its air raid precautions, which were completely funded by the central state. The account of the visit published in *The Times* pointed out that 'the average [Parisian] householder pays little, if any, attention to good advice about storing gas-masks [or] shovels [. . .] but is grateful for the address of the nearest shelter, to be sought "without haste but without delay".'[41] Liberal MP Megan Lloyd George praised evacuation policies in Paris and plans to build tube shelters to house 350,000 people as the proper work of 'a free country'.[42] The Conservative MP Oliver Simmonds, Chairman of the Parliamentary ARP Committee proposed that new buildings in Britain should be required to be resistant to air attack, as was the policy in France.[43] Various ARP experts raised this issue, though it was generally agreed that it would do little to accommodate the majority of the population of London who would be using existing structures for shelter. By this point, many in the government were of the opinion that the issue of deep shelters would need to be addressed, and many, such as Simmonds, held more moderate views on the subject than official policy would suggest. Yet they still were unwilling to embrace a Parisian-style programme, and their visits to

France remained of a cursory interest to British policy-makers. From the government's point of view, although French ARP provoked comment, it did little to alter the 'British way' of civil defence that had become entrenched in policy.

Provisions for ARP in Paris also attracted the attention of the experts from the Air Raid Protection Institute who studied both German and French preparations and sent their own representatives on fact-finding trips to France. Jean W. Partridge, Inspector General of Public Works in Paris, read a paper at an Institute general meeting, apparently to great acclaim.[44] The Cement and Concrete Association dispatched members to review the conversion of Metro stations into air raid shelters and reported on their structural soundness and efficiency.[45] The leftist critics also praised the scientifically-advanced approach taken on the Continent and emphasized their opinion that instituting similar provisions in Britain was simply a matter of political will and providing the requisite funds. They had concluded that Britain lagged five years behind the Continent in technical innovation.[46]

Critics also contrasted British and French policies for evacuation, with the latter receiving praise for foresighted planning. The Cambridge Scientists made a study of French preparations for their second book and found that evacuation from populated areas formed the core of French air raid preparedness. They noted that by the mid 1930s 'the partial evacuation of Paris in case of war is a settled matter of policy in France. Plans for orderly evacuation of two and a half to four and a half million population in the first few weeks of mobilization have been drawn up, and it is not expected that the efficiency of either industry or defence should suffer.'[47] In contrast to the vague public assurances of the British government that contingencies were in place to remove vulnerable persons from London, French policy on evacuation was depicted as an orderly and rationally-planned scheme. Summarizing their opinion of French preparations, the Cambridge Scientists stated 'there can be no doubt that foreign methods, relying largely on bomb-proof shelters, by paying more attention to the dangers of high explosives, and by supplying a relatively efficient, if expensive, mask, are likely to be more effective than the British'.[48]

These commentators, however, had no first-hand knowledge of the details or feasibility of plans on the Continent. As historians of interwar France have pointed out, there were multiple contradictions in French planning, which emphasized a 'pro-evacuation' policy, perhaps to the detriment of shelters and gas-proofing measures in cities. British commentators may have thought Parisian attempts wholly superior to those contemplated in London, but many Parisians saw it differently.[49] The Cambridge Scientists often cited the superior properties of German, French, Swiss and Russian gas masks, although they do not appear to have carried out tests on these models. Nor did they acknowledge that foreign plans could also be aimed at assuaging the civilian morale of their own populations. In their haste to point out gaps and contradictions in Home Office plans, these scientists may have taken the claims of foreign governments too closely at face value. After all, critics argued that the British provision of gas masks and paste-and-paper refuge rooms were simply reassuring gestures. In their eagerness to praise foreign preparations, the leftist observers did not always take an adequately critical perspective on the information they espoused. The proclamations of the mayor of Barcelona or the ARP officials in Paris aimed to please their own worried citizenry as much as they were for the consumption of foreign journalists. The vaunted French evacuation plans did not, in the final analysis, work as well as had been hoped before the war.[50] Many problems emerged with the immediate and long-term issues of the evacuees, much as occurred in Britain. The demands of total war, civilian suffering, and aerial bombardment offered no easy solutions for any European nation.

As demonstrated, critics of government plans put great stock in the brave undertakings of Spanish civilians to construct shelters in the midst of wartime, holding this up as a model for citizen-run air raid preparations. The use of nationalist language allowed these critics to make a financial appeal to the British government to increase ARP funding based on the example of 'backward Spain'. Participants and activists interpreted the Spanish conflict through the lenses that best suited their goals. They were able to contrast the national resources of Spain and Britain to forward class-based accusations against the British government. Civil defence comparisons served as a means of shaming the British government into providing more resources for civilian protection. By emphasizing that Spain was much less advanced, the commentators hoped both to inspire local authorities to build shelters and to demand improved funding from the central government. They invoked an image of the 'impoverished Spanish people' who nevertheless mustered the resources and manpower to construct underground shelters during wartime. There were multiple uses for this rhetoric. For example, commenting on the 'laughable' recommendations by Sir John Anderson for two-foot-deep garden shelters – the Anderson Shelter. The Communist Party commented, 'If the Impoverished [sic] Spanish people, in the middle of war, could in a short time build tunnel shelters which give adequate protection, is it impossible for us to do the same in Britain?'.[51] Haldane characterized the shelters in Spain as 'crude', but noted they were nevertheless effective, and he expressed the belief that 'if Spain, a poor nation, can protect her people in time of war, then Britain, a rich nation, can do so in time of peace'.[52] The Cambridge Scientists similarly wrote a letter to *The Times* claiming that:

> the experience of Spain has shown that it is perfectly possible, even in a poor country in the midst of war, to build effective shelters for the civil population. With the resources and time at our disposal we should be able to do far better. We feel that unless this is done all who support air raid precautions in their present form are effectively perpetuating a tragic deception on the people of this country.[53]

Comparing Spain and Britain was a tactic that the Cambridge Scientists continued to use unapologetically. In the early years of the war the group contributed to a Cambridge ARP Exhibition in which they answered the question of whether improved shelter protection was possible in wartime by pointing to the example of Spain: 'If poverty-stricken Spain could build bomb-proof shelters in the midst of civil war, there is surely every reason why a country as rich as this one should do so now.'[54] In 1938, Philip Noel-Baker praised the will of the population of Barcelona to construct 400 shelters and their plans for building an additional 800, which would be able to house almost a million people. He said, 'They are spending, at a time when, Heaven knows, they have not much money to spare, great sums upon these shelters [. . .]. If war should ever strike us we should do it, too. But we should be far wiser to do it now.'[55]

Emphasizing the relative wealth of Britain and the 'poverty' of Spain allowed these critics to avoid a contradiction. They extolled the ability of the local Spanish citizens and communities to build their own shelters without funding or support from the central government, yet at the same time insisted that the British government's partial ARP subsidy for local authorities was inadequate. By pointing to the far greater wealth of the British state, their very high estimates for deep shelters could be portrayed as less exorbitant. Critics argued that if the cash-strapped Spanish government could commit to constructing such shelters in wartime, certainly the far wealthier British government could entertain the notion while the nation was at peace. One of the critics' strongest uses of Britishness had little to do with Britain itself, but rather evoked a distant country. Ultimately, these debates regarding the role of the British state and Britishness operated in contradictory and complex ways. We now turn to the final episode in these discussions and the official implementation of the government's notion of practical preparations for war.

CHAPTER 9

ARCHITECTURE AND IDEALISM – THE FINSBURY DEEP SHELTER PROJECT

[ARP] cannot be solved by haphazard and unco-ordinated measures. Only a body of scientific workers and technicians is capable of formulating proposals that will satisfactorily meet all the difficulties we are likely to encounter [. . .] But to achieve all this we require the systematized help of a whole array of statisticians, surveyors, architects, town-planners, engineers, chemists, hospital authorities, physiologists, and so forth.[1]
–Serge Chermayeff, *Plan for A.R.P.*

As a case study, the project proposed by the Borough of Finsbury represents practically all the political and technical issues that surrounded 'the British way' of air raid precautions (ARP). Joseph Meisel, who has written on the Finsbury project, portrays the episode as a conflict between the political imperatives of the government on one hand and the scientists' and architects' views of activist citizenship and social commitment on the other.[2] The architectural firm of Tecton, headed by the architect Berthold Lubetkin, was commissioned by the Finsbury Borough Council to design underground shelters that could house up to 13,000 people each. The council and central government disagreed over the degree of protection that urban Londoners should expect, with the latter promoting their particular 'British' protection schemes involving a preference for home and familiar surroundings. Finsbury was intended to serve as a model of a mass scientific scheme instituted by local councils for the urban working class. The council emphasized the economic value of its plans and the willingness of ordinary residents to pay for the scheme — a prime example of citizen activism. Finsbury also represented a clash of ideals between the narrow dictates of bureaucracy and rebel critics who were outside the circles of expertise consulted by Whitehall, critics whom they considered 'amateur at best'.[3] Tecton presented the council's plan for Finsbury as scientific and standardized, thus providing the most efficient use of national resources. The architects also emphasized the postwar utility of the plans. The shelters were designed to be easily converted to underground car parks. Such bold plans were a natural outgrowth of the ethos of these progressive planners, and they were equally at odds with the predominant conservative notions of the city.

The events of Finsbury thus demonstrate a conflict between self-consciously modernist ideas of architecture and urban planning and more conservative, *laissez-faire* attitudes of physical space. Ideas surrounding progressive architecture and urban planning played a central role in the conception of communal shelters. The architects involved with the plan held distinct ideas about national civil society and the role of professionals in ameliorating the ills of modern life. Many saw twentieth-century planning as a way to remedy the evils of the nineteenth-century industrial city,[4] those blights on urban existence that had been the legacy of Victorian capitalism despite the counter-efforts of Victorian utopianism and urban reform. English planners reflected long-standing fears of the metropolis, the spectre of the 'satanic mills', and the desire to create new and modern forms.[5] Many important modernist projects were undertaken in interwar Britain, even if the modernism of London did not correspond to continental notions of the Bauhaus masters or Le Corbusier. Architectural historian Gavin Stamp argues that views of 1930s architecture have tended to follow the stark dichotomies of the age — fascist or communist, modernist or traditionalist, old or young. Yet there were far more connections between British and continental design than have often been assumed by later commentators.[6] Many landmark modernist British buildings were designed in the 1930s, from the De La Warr Pavilion in Bexhill-on-Sea, East Sussex, to the Peter Jones department store in Sloane Square and the Art Deco masterpiece that still houses BBC Broadcasting House in Portland Place.

But while British interwar architecture may not have been completely aesthetically conservative, it was certainly too politically conservative for the tastes of many progressive and activist architects. Consequently, British left-wing architects imagined themselves as rebellious and heroic figures battling an unfriendly architectural establishment. Many of these modernist architects were European émigrés who had come to practice their profession in England from the early twentieth century onwards. Their status as foreigners and outsiders and their infusion of continental dash exerted an important influence on British architecture. Much like their colleagues on the scientific left, they formulated their goals with social planning in mind, believing in slogans like the 'architect was a planner and the planner was a socialist'.[7]

The vision of the Tecton architectural firm and its allies was as important to the Finsbury project as was that of the council. The firm was founded in 1931 by émigré Berthold Lubetkin, whose aesthetic sense was shaped in post-revolutionary Russia. Having apprenticed in Berlin, he worked in Warsaw and Paris, where he studied under Auguste Perret, an early master of the reinforced concrete building, a staple of modernist design. As an émigré, Lubetkin greatly admired British toleration but disliked the moderate political status quo which, as he saw it, had replaced the radical promise of the 1920s. He believed that his role as an outsider in the British architectural scene afforded him the opportunity to help bring about social reform.[8] Other contributors to the project shared Lubetkin's background, though they did not necessarily share the full extent of his political views. One of these individuals was architect Serge Chermayeff, who collaborated on both the De La Warr Pavilion and BBC Broadcasting House. Chermayeff was a fellow

Russian émigré who viewed modernist architecture as 'the expression of an earnest desire of intelligent and highly trained people to change the living conditions in proportion to the immense strides made in general education, medicine, and applied technique'.[9] The renowned engineer Ove Arup also contributed to the plans, although he was not entirely in agreement with the political motives of his fellow architects. He was much less tolerant of left-wing politicking and was somewhat critical of the Tecton architects for not taking as 'sober' a line in their pronouncements as he would have liked.[10] Unlike Lubetkin, he was wary of making statements on politics, and at times he seemed less certain of himself among the British. Nevertheless, he cooperated with Tecton in a professional capacity and shared a warm relationship with Lubetkin.

Tecton contributed many important designs to British interwar modernist architecture, including the famous Penguin Pool at the London Zoo, the Highpoint housing towers, a tuberculosis patient housing project in East Ham, and the groundbreaking Finsbury Health Centre, which was completed in 1938. The Health Centre was renowned for its design that combined social medicine with slogans such as 'fresh air night and day'.[11] As such, the centre was not merely a modernist triumph but also a precursor of wellness thinking in architecture. It was developed under the Town and Country Planning Act of 1932, which enabled local councils to exercise aesthetic control over development projects. Fred Skinner, an activist architect, later remarked to Haldane that the Health Centre prepared Tecton for the task of deep shelter design. He explained that 'although it was not designed with ARP in mind, it is nevertheless a very interesting building, architecturally, constructionally, [sic] and sociologically'.[12] The social and civic aspects of architecture were of primary importance to the Tecton architects and their early projects led almost inexorably to their involvement with Finsbury.

The architects clustered around several research organizations and unions that backed their high-minded and politically-active goals. One such entity was the Modern Architectural Research Group (MARS), a group that was founded in 1934. With Berthold Lubetkin as a founding member, the group was convened to represent Britain at international design events, and its stated goal was to unite those in the architectural professions by the 'common realization of the necessity for a new conception of architecture and its relation to the structure of society today'.[13] Their bold and hubristic proposals had their apogee in their 'Plan for London', a scheme based on 'garden city' planning ideals which advocated razing much of the city and replacing the old road patterns with 'rationalized' radial roads.[14] In the age of high-minded and earnest political statements and manifestos, this assortment of British-based architects, engineers and planners believed in their mission to challenge the professional establishment. The group organized a West End exhibition in 1938 to showcase some of their ideas for civic planning in London. The exhibition attracted over 7,000 visitors in two weeks. Yet for the most part the group lacked significant financial resources,[15] and consequently the architects concentrated their activities on small discussion groups and committees to address specific areas of concern, such as legislation, schools, propaganda, and housing.[16]

As a union, the Architects' and Technicians' Organisation (ATO) was more overtly politicized than MARS. Individuals such as Lubetkin and Fred Skinner, who believed that the profession must be seen in a more radical context, joined the ATO in the mid-1930s.[17] Lubetkin was involved with the ATO housing exhibition that was held in 1936 with the goal of recruiting fellow architects to participate in social architectural projects. Members of the union included engineers, surveyors, clerks, construction workers, and others who were enlisted for specific projects, such as Harold Laski and the communist intellectual Rajani Palme Dutt.[18] Bernal and Haldane were consulted on ARP and war preparation; thus some members of Tecton might have been exposed to their civil defence ideas prior to the Finsbury project. The ATO was closely identified with the Popular Front and was involved in the *Aid for Spain* campaign, but it refrained from an official political party affiliation. Lubetkin felt that the Communist Party of Great Britain was too doctrinaire and he himself was a 'non-joiner', even if a committed socialist, so this progressive but non-partisan union likely suited him politically.[19] The Association of Architects, Surveyors and Technical

Assistants (AASTA), another professional union, became a centre of mild activism by the late 1930s. It was less political than the ATO. AASTA had been established in 1919 and was represented on many professional committees of the Royal Institute of British Architects. Fred Skinner was sent to Barcelona under its auspices, and the union's call for improved ARP did much to make the subject respectable in professional circles.[20]

The link between modernist architecture and 'radicalism' was a tenuous one, since these individuals represented a minority of professionals in the field, and their actual political radicalism was more a matter of conjecture than fact.[21] In addition, for all their self-conscious representation as rebellious iconoclasts, the modernists associated with MARS, the ATO, and Tecton were remarkably integrated into the mainstream of their professions and were hardly marginalized radicals. Nevertheless, they formed a coterie of experts who forwarded a 'progressivist ideology' of urban planning and design.[22] In the words of one architectural historian, 'they had the confidence to think that an advanced industrial society could create an urban environment worthy of its highest values'.[23] Form and design were invested with the power to express and encourage progress. Such ideas not only contributed to their aesthetic values but also to the philosophy of projects, such as health and community centres, and they would contribute to air raid shelters.

Finsbury and the Tecton Survey

The Borough of Finsbury was one of the 'rebel Boroughs' that battled with Herbert Morrison over cooperation with the government on the 'coercive' elements of ARP. As a local authority, it was also responsible for drafting its own ARP plan, and its leadership intended to reflect the 'democratic defence' model. The Finsbury Council appointed an ARP committee as early as 1935, and its representatives were party to the frustrating and inconclusive ongoing government discussions with local authorities. At the time, the Borough of Finsbury included areas that now comprise parts of Islington and Clerkenwell. The area had an extremely high population density, and it contained only one Underground station, Farringdon, a shallow Circle Line station that was not even wholly underground. This put the area in sharp contrast to surrounding boroughs that had deep Underground stations within close reach. The borough was dominated by Labour, and the mayor, most commonly referred to as 'Alderman' Harold Riley, was predominantly concerned with improving social and living conditions in his Borough. Along with the London County Council, local authorities such as Finsbury were in charge of administrating many social programmes on their own. This system allowed many reform-minded local politicians to practice progressive public policy on a small scale, and the Finsbury Council believed strongly in this ethic. The councillors had also had prior dealings with the Tecton firm, having employed them in constructing the Finsbury Health Centre.

The decision to investigate mass shelter possibilities seriously was a direct product of the Munich Crisis of September 1938 and the unpreparedness that came to light as a result. Alderman Riley later recalled that 'with the crisis over, the Council immediately concentrated on methods to be adopted for protection of the whole of the population in the event of war'.[24] Members had grown increasingly concerned over the lack of public ARP facilities and the fact that existing – and in their view ineffectual – ARP requirements added significant costs to the already overstrained budget. In light of the casualties that were expected, the council found it more sensible to attempt to prevent death rather than fund mortuaries. At the outset Alderman Riley also sought to reframe the issue of deep shelter as one of true protection rather than temporary and low-level shielding from blast and splinter. He believed that the proposed project would be the first comprehensive analysis of the 'relative protective value for money spent' for mass deep shelters *versus* backyard and individual schemes.[25] Riley believed that government shelter provisions would serve only a small percentage of the population 'and that in such a congested area as Finsbury, to provide trench shelter for all would be impossible'.[26] The council was also troubled that its area had been classified as receiving only 65 per cent central funding in the ARP Bill of 1937, along with boroughs such as Hammersmith and Lambeth, while nearby boroughs such as Islington and Hackney were to receive 70 per cent.[27] The minutes of Finsbury Council meetings note that on 4 October 1938 it voted to employ 'Messrs. Tecton' at an estimated cost of £250 to conduct a survey of the boroughs, with a view to build deep shelters for residents.[28] The Tecton firm was well placed to draft air raid shelter plans, given its affiliation with the ATO and the AATSA, both of which had studied civil defence questions and Spanish ARP. Their previous social and community projects also reflected their philosophy that design should serve the welfare of the citizenry.

Finsbury was hardly alone in attempting to expand ARP services beyond what the Home Office was already prepared to provide. Simultaneous plans for deep tunnels were proposed by the London Federation of Peace Councils and were being considered in Marylebone, Lambeth and St Pancras.[29] Hackney and St Pancras had both set up ARP sub-committees in the mid 1930s. St Pancras made a survey of cellars in 1938, although experts such as Haldane were advising against the conversion of basements and cellars into shelters.[30] By May 1938 at least 21 boroughs had lodged ARP schemes with the Home Office, but the bureaucratic system proved slow in approving proposed plans.[31] In the House of Commons Labour MPs questioned the government over the glacial speed of approving council applications. The Labour MP for Finsbury, George Woods, also supported the idea of deep shelters for the people of his constituency, arguing that a shelter policy that did not encompass the majority of the population could not form the basis of a sound ARP plan.

The official Tecton report was presented with great anticipation to the council on 1 February 1939, and members expressed satisfaction with its contents. The estimated cost of the proposed measures was £1,388,860, and the estimates were quickly forwarded to the Home Office for approval. Aware that the cost did appear prohibitive, the council determined to discuss issues of finance with the central government, relying on its self-funding argument to carry the day.[32] Finsbury Council had already made provision for the theoretical shortfall in funding from the government subsidy to be financed through a 4*d*. rate increase,[33] which most believed would be overwhelmingly accepted by ratepayers. Tecton's findings were published in a book that accompanied a public exhibition at the Town Hall. As it proved, financial issues were of relatively little concern to the Home Office in contrast to the predominant issue of morale and the potential of setting a troubling new precedent for other boroughs. The architects remained in the background of the project, for the most part refraining from making political statements on the nature of the project. Lubetkin was particularly careful with his public comments, limiting himself to the advocacy of the technical merits of professionally-designed deep shelters while Alderman Riley dealt with the press and questions of Home Office policy.

The final recommendations forwarded by Tecton were bold in scope, involving circular structures and concentric circles super-imposed on a map of the borough. The physical study entailed two areas of investigation. First, the architects conducted a full statistical survey of the area, including 20 individual maps that detailed data such as day and night population densities, business distribution, existing basements and open spaces, heights and structures of buildings, geological formations, surface water, tunnels, telephone wires, sewage and gas, and electricity. This work was coordinated by A.L. Downey, the borough engineer,[34] and was more extensive than any such previous study undertaken in the borough. This sound 'scientific' basis for the Finsbury plans was the primary point emphasized by the architects and Finsbury officials. The professional outlook of the Tecton firm also reflected Haldane's famous dictum that 'the problem of ARP is three-quarters technical and one-quarter administrative'.[35] Secondly, Tecton architects, with the assistance of concrete engineer Ove Arup, made a detailed report of the effects of direct hits by large bombs on various types of shelters including basements, tunnels, steel shelters, trenches and surface shelters. This study bore many similarities to, and borrowed heavily from, the work of Fred Skinner for the AASTA and some of the mathematical calculations devised by Haldane from observations in Spain. Tecton's Finsbury report suggests that the firm had already accepted Haldane's conclusion that the shallow steel shelters proposed by the government would merely increase casualty figures.[36] Serge Chermayeff believed that his Tecton colleagues had effectively disproved dispersal as a serious professional theory, calculating the effect of a blast radius in reference to various patterns of population distribution.[37] The architects therefore felt justified in ignoring the official government publication for contractors that advised that no more than 50 persons should be in any given building used as a shelter, or purpose-built shelter, during an air raid.[38]

The massive scale was designed to accommodate the entire population of the borough, ensuring that most residents were only 100 to 300 yards from the nearest shelter and could reach the shelter within seven minutes, which was the accepted warning time before a raid. This necessitated multiple entrances for the shelters and the construction of at least four tunnels to allow underground movement and relieve congestion in areas that were likely to experience large amounts of foot traffic during the day.[39] Alderman Riley explained that the design provisions of the shelter would ensure against panic: 'The shelters are approached by two wide roads, allowing 40 people a second to enter a shelter. There is no possibility of people trampling one another to death in a panic.'[40] The shelters themselves were circular in shape, with a wide spiral ramp that would allow many people to move downwards towards lower levels, filling the shelter quickly and safely. Reinforced on the surface with concrete, each shelter could house between 7,000 and 15,000 people, and a total of 15 shelters were proposed for the borough.[41] The architects were careful to frame their plans as representing efficiency and practicality, contextualizing their financial figures in terms of cost-effectiveness.

They also addressed the psychological basis of the government's dispersal principle, believing that it was a diversion to preclude debate on the shelter issue. As they stated in their book *Planned A.R.P.*:

To screen oneself behind such ambiguous phrases as 'maintenance of productive efficiency' and worries over 'mob psychology' is merely to evade the issue. All these mysterious and terrifying conceptions may well be found to melt away in the light of dispassionate technical analysis.[42]

Tecton made further claims for the patriotic value of their plan, noting that the government's reaction to the crisis of September 1938 had done absolutely nothing to help the situation of civilian morale; in fact, the 'haphazard' nature of ARP services had undermined public confidence to a great extent. They believed that 'the civilian morale [issue] was so seriously endangered that nothing short of a complete technical clarification of the situation will now have any value in restoring it'.[43] The architects argued that the national embarrassment of the ARP crisis of September 1938 demonstrated that the nation did not have a 'rational policy' for ARP. They charged that: 'The present chaotic state of this country's ARP is due to the fact that there has been no planned policy, but rather a spontaneous growth.'[44]

The Response of the Popular and Professional Press

Newspapers across the political spectrum gave the plan extensive coverage, at the very least believing Tecton's massive borough survey to be a valuable exercise and worthy of careful consideration. Like all revolutionary ideas, a certain level of pressure and activism would need to be brought to bear, and there was little question that a protracted conflict between the borough and the Home Office would ensue. Ove Arup worked quietly in the background to persuade officials to consider the Finsbury scheme. General G.S. Collins, Director of Fortifications and Works, thought the proposals worth pursuing and offered to intercede with Sir John Anderson, although it is uncertain how much influence he actually had. Arup apparently also received supportive responses from Dr. Oscar Faber, a prominent concrete engineer, Sir Henry Japp, director of the John Mowlem civil engineering firm and, unsurprisingly, J.D. Bernal.[45] Alderman Riley produced a press release to drum up excitement for the plan and its importance to dense urban areas such as Finsbury.

A variety of newspapers deemed the Tecton efforts worthy of study and consideration, and none openly attacked either the idea behind mass, bomb-proof shelters, or suggested that the technical basis of the plans was unsound. Reception of the plans gave Finsbury Council reason for optimism that its proposals could not simply be summarily rejected. There was, however, an important distinction between positive press attention, and the conversion of the public or professional colleagues to the cause of pressuring the government for deep shelters. General interest did not necessarily denote support to undertake the practical or sacrificial steps necessary if the shelter plans were to be realized.

The radical left press, including the *Daily Worker* and the *Finsbury Citizen*, unsurprisingly, proved the exception. Each devoted a great deal of column space to the events in Finsbury. The *Daily Worker* proclaimed that the council had provided a 'lead to Britain', and that Finsbury proved that 'you can get 100 per cent protection; you can get it in the form of deep shelters, useable as car parks in peace time; you cannot get it by way of Sir John Anderson's hoax schemes'.[46] The monthly socialist *Finsbury Citizen* featured prominent reports throughout the spring and summer of 1939 on the progress of talks with the Home Office. Its February 1939 issue featured full details of the plan, dismissing official blast and splinter-proof bomb shelter specifications as 'futile'. The *Finsbury Citizen* also emphasized that although the cost of the shelter scheme was large, the borough's ratepayers were prepared to shoulder a disproportionate tax burden, which would amount to £340,000, to see the shelter constructed.[47]

Mainstream and broadly liberal newspapers, such as the *News Chronicle*, which had backed the Popular Front to aid Spain, also supported the Finsbury scheme. Immediately after the presentation to the council, the paper declared to its readers: 'You ought to know about Finsbury,' arguing that the borough represented the ideal of local ARP initiative. Its correspondent believed that 'the scheme is vigorous, scientific, exciting. You should see [the exhibition]. And I sincerely hope Sir John Anderson will pop out of his steel shelters and examine it very thoroughly.'[48] The paper later claimed that the strength of the Tecton plans demanded an alteration of the present 'haphazard' policy, and believed that there existed 'an overwhelming vote in favour of deep shelter'.[49] The *Manchester Guardian* also supported the Finsbury plans, stating that the survey was notable for its thoroughness.[50] Centrist and right-leaning newspapers also found some merit in the Finsbury plan, even demonstrating mild enthusiasm. The *Daily Telegraph* reported that the scheme would provide 'uniform protection for all'. Their architectural correspondent analysed the technical and economic aspects of the plan and deemed them to be sound.[51] The *Evening Standard*'s reporter similarly defended the principle, cost, and technical merits of the Tecton plan. Citing the truism currently circulating that steel shelters had been fully condemned in Spain, the writers claimed that Whitehall 'has never shown the imagination needed to deal with the problem'.[52]

The architectural press represented a secondary forum in which the Tecton plans were debated. It immediately became evident that the work done by the firm was serious and well-researched. Berthold Lubetkin had berated his colleagues for being slow to study ARP shelters,[53] but this professional indifference changed suddenly in 1938 when the issue became more publicly prominent. The Royal Institute of British Architects organized a special conference on ARP in June 1938 and reported extensively on the proceedings in its official journal.[54] To this end, many architects and engineers contributed to the Air Raid Protection Institute, which tasked itself with filling the 'serious gaps' in knowledge regarding ARP shelters.[55] Given the potentially vast and lucrative private market in air raid shelter construction, the subject flourished in the architectural press. A glance through any architectural publication from that period reveals a plethora of advertisements for suppliers and designers of air raid shelters. Between the Munich Crisis and the start of World War II between one-third and one-half of advertisements in *The Architects' Journal* addressed some aspect of ARP.[56] Many of these plans were of dubious quality, though some effort was made to address the problem of regulating industrial standards in the professional press.[57]

Following the Munich Crisis, the editors of *The Architect and Building News* argued that the problem of ARP could not be shelved, and that the 'ludicrous inadequacy of the eleventh hour scramble,' did not bode well for the future.[58] This publication also featured extensive coverage of the Finsbury Town Hall exhibition, including long extracts from the Tecton report and maps of the proposed shelter. Giving professional sanction to the technical findings of Tecton and their refutation of government principles, the publication's editors endorsed the Finsbury ARP exhibit's 'scientifically planned scheme of permanent structural shelters'.[59] The writers of an ARP supplement to *Architectural Design and Construction* used Tecton's arguments extensively in their own findings. They agreed that the architects had proven the government's policy of dispersal to be a 'mathematically demonstrable fallacy'.[60] The publication's editorial board was also uncertain that the 'blast and splinter' protection code being so forcefully pushed by the government was a technically sound course of action. They published and endorsed the view of the AASTA on the subject: 'Adequate protection against possible air attack is fast being recognized as an urgent national necessity [... professionals] have a particularly important part to play in this work in applying their technical knowledge to the solutions of problems upon which there is as yet all too little information available.'[61]

The Institution of Structural Engineers also endorsed the opinion that basements, whether reinforced or not, were likely to be the most dangerous type of shelter to advocate.[62] *The Architects' Journal*, in one of its regular reports on ARP, stated that the Finsbury Council was taking its defence responsibilities seriously to 'protect the civil population, as much as the civil population can be protected'.[63] Another journal's editors claimed that the Finsbury scheme constituted a challenge that could not be ignored. The publication also declared that if good reasons for opposing the construction of deep shelters could not be proven, the Tecton policy 'should have the force of Government co-ordination, authority and action behind it'.[64]

The response of the architectural press to the Tecton proposal was supportive on the whole, and as had been the case in the popular press, no architect or publication published any technical criticisms of the plan. Yet, to the chagrin of Finsbury supporters, much of the architectural establishment remained suspicious of their political motives. Despite praise for the Tecton plan itself, professional resentment of the AASTA and left-leaning architects manifested behind closed doors. Associations such as MARS and the ATO had been formed as a reaction of younger progressive architects to feelings of exclusion from a professional ethos that was still Edwardian in many respects. As such, many 'acrimonious arguments' over the subject of deep shelters raged within the profession, although these rows were not reflected in the professional press.[65] As architectural historian David Dean puts it, some older architects had their feathers somewhat ruffled by what they regarded as a young and brash 'motley crew with unattractive political motives'.[66] Fred Skinner had indeed bluntly informed Haldane that: '[Finsbury] is probably a very important development politically speaking, as the Borough intends to publish the scheme and demand grants from the government for putting it into effect.'[67] The political point that Skinner was referring to was that the leftist critics wished to provoke a public clash with the Home Office, forcing the government either to acquiesce, or publicly to reject deep shelter plans. Whatever the official outcome, they felt that members of the public would be persuaded to support the left on the subject of deep shelters.

Within the profession there was consequently some support for the technical merits of the Tecton plan, though many held reservations over the political bias of Tecton and the Finsbury Council. In addition, there may have been unexpressed indifference within the profession to the Finsbury plan and the implications of advocating deep shelters. Although the government did not disclose the names of most of its technical experts, including architects, there were certainly many who felt that Tecton may have been using their professional credentials to create public unrest and harm national morale. While no substantial professional criticism of the Tecton plans appeared in the press, a close reading of press reaction demonstrates that an expressed desire for deep shelter was not the same thing as active campaigning on the issue. There was consequently a recurrent tension between enthusiasm and indifference which did not bode well for a movement which required broad-based demand that shelters be made a national priority.

CHAPTER 10

DISSENT, PATRIOTISM AND THE FINAL SHOWDOWN OVER DEEP SHELTER POLICY

Sir John displayed a quite unreasonable suspicion of technical innovations, such as the Finsbury scheme, which he seemed to regard as a patent medicine. This stubborn opposition to scientific research and to new ideas in engineering and architecture seems to be widespread not only in the cabinet but among official experts.[1]

—*New Statesman and Nation*, March 1939

[We must not] abandon all hope that even advocates of the extreme policy, many of whom were well disposed but misguided, would modify their views when all the relevant considerations were placed before them.[2]

—Sir John Anderson, Committee of Imperial Defence,
Civil Defence (Policy) Sub-Committee

The Hailey Commission (or Conference) was convened to address the Borough of Finsbury's plan in particular, but also to settle the general agitation for deep shelters on the part of activists and an anxious public. All the previous issues regarding political activism, Britishness and the role of the state came together just prior to the war in a struggle of vision, ideology and competing notions of scientific and moral authority. An underlying issue was the extent to which patriotism equalled acquiescence to government dictates. The architects' ideals of communal shelters and scientific precision were in sharp contrast to the Home Office view of the vaguely defined and individualistic 'British way' of civil defence. Finsbury Council members were initially optimistic regarding the approval of, and funding for, their scheme. Councillors might have felt that the tide of public opinion was swinging in their favour. In January 1939 Sir John Anderson had been forced to defend the Home Office against charges that they were merely 'muddling' ARP plans and lacked clear direction, especially on the question of shelters. Even moderate commentators expressed guarded concerns that ARP plans were not coming together as efficiently as they should. *The Economist* cited both the Finsbury Plan and the Air Defence League in stating:

> ... the backing of people from every walk of public life and every political group [will] impress upon the people the urgency of the present ARP position and to focus attention on the steps that ought to be taken. Already the Government has been pushed well beyond its first obstinate entrenchments by widespread pressure. Further forced retreats will be a victory for commonsense and public safety.[3]

At the time, Sir John Anderson had to concede that production and installation of steel surface shelters (the Anderson shelter) should be speeded up.[4] Although it does not necessarily indicate a potentially mutinous dissatisfaction with proposed arrangements for civil defence, the Home Office consideration of some deep shelter implementation did represent acquiescence to public demand. It was also a reflection of the vulnerability to public dissatisfaction in the minds of Home Office officials, an important factor that led to the Hailey Commission. The official historian of civil defence believed that public pressure over the question of deep shelters weighed heavily on the mind of government planners. This was especially true following the Munich Crisis, given the fact that the Labour and Liberal parties had both adopted deep shelters as a long-term policy goal.[5]

Alderman Riley suspected early on that the Home Office might try to stall the Finsbury Council plans, as was proved the case. Even before the Tecton report had been officially released, government officials informed the borough that the gist of their proposals went beyond anything as yet contemplated and consequently an answer would be some time in coming. It gave no guidance or indication of what level of cooperation the borough might expect to eventually receive. Riley later remarked that he hoped 'the Home Office will jerk itself out of its dictatorial sulks in time to make some comment before war actually breaks out'.[6] Delaying their response gave the Home Office time to allow the initial furor to die down, to marshal their own experts to poke holes in the technical plans, and to convene the Hailey Commission. At the end of March Sir John Anderson himself responded, claiming that 'the scheme has been found to require very close examination in its technical aspects,' but there would be no 'avoidable delay in completing the examination'. Due to the 'revolutionary' engineering proposition, the Home Office needed to gather the best advice before sanctioning the plans – decisions could not be made 'without proper consideration'.[7] Despite the frustrations of the local councils, such a position by the Home Office was not unreasonable, given that its assent to any project would hold it at least partially liable for mistakes or disasters. Even prior to the outbreak of war, an accident or cave-in of an officially sanctioned shelter would be politically disastrous for a government and would not help to shore up civilian morale.

Some background to the Hailey Commission is necessary to understand the government's mindset in the months immediately following the Munich Crisis. Throughout early 1939 the Civil Defence (Policy) Sub-Committee of the Committee of Imperial Defence met to discuss the handling of the deep shelter issue. The sub-committee, chaired by the Lord Privy Seal, included members such as the Hon. Oliver Stanley, President of the Board of Trade, Sir Samuel Hoare, the Home Secretary, Sir Horace Wilson, Earl De la Warr, and the MP Geoffrey Lloyd, Under-Secretary of State for

Home, who had been responsible for refuting the claims of the Cambridge Scientists. It is clear from Cabinet papers that Anderson and air raid precautions (ARP) officials were never really open to considering the deep shelter plans of any local authority on their own merits. Less than two weeks before the public unveiling of the Tecton plans for Finsbury, the sub-committee met to discuss what it believed to be 'growing restlessness' on the part of the public for deep shelters. Anderson continued to insist that those who demanded deep shelters could not have 'taken account of the relevant considerations' and must have been misled by critics such as Haldane who 'had no real knowledge of the problem'.[8]

The Hailey Commission was presented as an impartial technical survey, but a memo penned by Anderson, even before the public appearance of the Tecton plans, confirms that he was already planning a public relations event to convene 'a body of representative outside opinion' to tout government conclusions. He perhaps had in mind something along the lines of the Air Raid Defence League, a non-governmental voluntary association, which posited the same conclusions as the government. Anderson believed that the League's public statements were 'written in a constructive and helpful spirit,' in contrast to the extreme platform offered by the leftist critics.[9] His draft memorandum for the conference included a number of individuals who would lend credence to the proceedings. They were to be representative figures of the 'nation', and enforce the conclusion that British ARP policy represented a consensus that all reasonable persons should accept. These participants were to include an engineer, a scientist (both noted in the singular though many were consulted), an accountant, a representative of commerce and industry, a representative of Labour, and 'a woman', preferably a medical doctor.[10] These individuals were meant to affirm a broad-based liberal ideal of citizenship, consensus and professionalism.

Exactly one month following the memo from the Lord Privy Seal, the Hailey Commission was convened on 24 February 1939 and reported to the government on the unfeasibility of deep shelters. There was really no illusion that Lord Hailey, a retired colonial administrator and chairman of the Air Raid Defence League, and the government scientists and experts were independent of the Home Office. Lord Hailey reported to Sir John Anderson personally, who then endorsed and submitted the report. Along with the representative middle-class individuals, the conference also included members of the Air Staff, technical advisors to the Home Office, and other 'distinguished engineers, scientists, and public men'.[11] Tellingly, it also included commissioners of police, underlining the public control aspects of ARP policy – the very aspect the critics feared.

Dispersal, Psychological Fears and Technical Detail

During these meetings the Hailey Committee voiced the customary fears that had been part and parcel of the government's position for some time. The main points of fixation included the principle of dispersal, the concern over inadvertently creating a 'shelter mentality', and the ultimate fear that mass shelters had multiple technical weak points. The Hailey Committee decided that a policy of deep shelters for all persons at risk, the principle behind Finsbury, was unjustified due to the impracticability and scale of such provisions. Winston Churchill was among those who dismissed the rationale behind the Tecton plans, telling his private secretary that the proposals were inherently political in nature and that they 'wish to exaggerate the danger of air attack and to emphasise [sic] the futility of basement protection in the interests of some particular scheme'.[12] Sir John Anderson ruminated that the issue was already 'prejudged in the public mind'. As he saw it, only one side of the argument – the side of the critics – was being aired in the press. He believed that supporters of the government policy simply 'did not display the same zeal' as the highly motivated and vocal critics. The critics, he charged, 'write for the most part as if the problems of underground shelters were essentially an engineering problem. Actually, a balanced view must take into consideration *mass psychology* [author's emphasis] and the probable strategy of enemy air attack.'[13]

The overriding concerns regarding wartime patriotism and morale were evident in the discussions over shelter protection for critical

works. One contemporary critic, writing in *Time and Tide*, believed
that the government was most concerned about the 'massive
dislocation of civil life' that would result from the provision of deep
shelters.[14] Indeed, the report's authors were not reticent in pointing
to psychological fears as the basis of their philosophy, stating at the
outset that the government's first priority was to safeguard activities
essential to the successful prosecution of the war. Primarily concerned
with the maintenance of the nation's industries and services, they
believed that widespread public provisions 'might involve dangers
such as those of creating a shelter mentality, of interrupting the
process of essential production, or of unduly diverting national effort
from other measures of defence'.[15]

The Home Office decided that shelters could be provided for
'essential employees' of government and industry to stem the tide of
public criticism. The tone of these discussions, however, simply
demonstrated the degree to which issues of morale and maintaining
war production weighed on the minds of officials. The purpose of
'critical works' shelters was to ensure that these employees remained
at work, rather than fleeing to the (relative) safety of household or
community shelters.[16] The Hailey Committee bluntly stated that
such shelters would be provided not so much for protection of the
physical person as to relieve employees from 'strain' and thus enable
them to perform their work more effectively. This policy was in
keeping with Anderson's intent that the main purpose of protection
'must be reconciled with a paramount necessity of maintaining the
productive efficiency of the nation in time of war'.[17]

The Hailey Commission also made arguments regarding the
prioritization of national resources and the patriotic duties of
citizens. The authors of the report felt that civilians were not entitled
to demand additional measures that might shift labour and materials
from military preparedness. In this vein, they felt justified in
recommending that stronger protection should only be made for vital
industrial undertakings but not for the protection of the general
public. The availability of resources was a legitimate government
concern, especially by 1939, when many feared that a general war
could not be far off. Previous experience in the construction of the

London Underground demonstrated that it would take approximately two years to build 16 miles of tunnel, and this amount of tunnel would protect only 160,000 people.[18] In fact, this fear did turn out to have a solid basis. Air raid shelter tunnels excavated in Northeast London during the war took much longer to construct and cost more than had been anticipated.[19] The leftist critics, on the other hand, believed ARP to be an essential component of national readiness that should have been given a significant portion of the government's military budget since the mid-1930s. They were therefore not inclined to be swayed by arguments of national resources, since they believed these to have been chronically mismanaged.

Secondary to the worries over morale – but directly related – the Hailey Commission endorsed the theory of dispersal. The familiar objections were once again raised, including the possibility of mass deaths if a single bomb were to breach a large shelter, and the potential for a stampede among panicked civilians attempting to reach these shelters. Lord Hailey stated that 'mass catastrophes have a far greater effect upon the public mind than a similar number of isolated casualties'.[20] In other words, the government acknowledged that surface shelters and other ARP recommendations might not necessarily prevent more loss of civilian life than deep shelters, but at least those deaths would be dispersed and thus less likely to garner sensational public attention than one notable and tragic large-scale incident. The members of the Hailey Commission further sought to demonstrate that mass centralized shelters were simply unworkable and that dispersed household shelters had the advantage of providing protection that was readily at hand in a moment's notice. Time would be of the essence during an air attack, especially given that people were likely to fall prey to some degree of panic and hence be unable to perform many otherwise ordinary tasks to normal standards. They outlined the practical steps necessary for individuals to reach these shelters in the short time offered by air raid sirens. For example, a night-time air raid would necessitate awakening family members in the night, finding and putting on clothing, jostling on the street in the blackout to find the shelter, and then efficiently entering the shelter night after night. All of these steps would need to be completed within seven to ten minutes, and those who successfully reached the shelters would be 'packed amongst a mass of strangers, some of whom will be temperamentally less stable than others'.[21] These were not unreasonable arguments, given the logistics of thousands of people attempting to converge on a single location in darkness. The Home Office consequently believed that any policy that encouraged the removal of large numbers of people from their homes was fundamentally unsound.

Lastly, the Hailey Commission functioned as a public relations exercise in conveying to the public the justifications for the 'British way' of ARP. The tone of the final report and the technical criticisms of the Tecton plans revealed contrasting ideas of what the government and critics expected a national ARP plan to provide. The arguments surrounding critical works, dispersal, mass psychology and the proclivities of the British citizenry all reflected a certain view of how ordinary people should comport themselves, and the limits of the provisions they should expect from government. The Committee of Imperial Defence, unsurprisingly, endorsed the recommendations as 'highly satisfactory' and claimed that the report provided the 'strongest justification for present Government policy'.[22] Following the publishing of the Hailey Commission, report the Home Office did not forward any further technical information to the Borough of Finsbury, because it no longer felt the need to deal with the local councils on the issue of shelters. It was safe in the knowledge that the boroughs would have little recourse to pursue their claims.

The Hailey Commission further considered the question of how British people would ideally choose to shelter, if they were even inclined to leave their homes at all. The report, citing the presumed preference of the British for home and hearth to justify their policy of home shelters, implied that the decision not to build deep mass shelters reflected the inherent preferences of the British people, especially their antipathy towards strangers and physical crowding.[23] The authors of the report stated:

But we believe that most British citizens would prefer to count upon a less effective protection at their homes, even though this may make no pretence of warding off direct or near hits of bombs, if they can be safeguarded against the one danger which must loom largest in their minds, namely that of being themselves, or seeing their families, buried under fallen roofs or masonry. We believe that if they pause to reflect that on occasion they may fail to hear the warning signal, and that the first indication of a raid in progress may be the dropping of bombs within earshot, the advantages of having some shelter close at hand will be still more apparent to them.[24]

The clear implication was that proponents of mass air raid shelters did not understand the English or British national character or the probable reaction of Londoners to being forced out of their homes. As we have seen, these ideas also subtly reflected the notion that deep shelters were un-British and cowardly. This was despite the observations of MPs such as George Woods, who had observed the provisions of air raid shelters in Spain and who fully believed that the British people wished for their widespread availability and would use them responsibly.[25]

Once again, Mass Observation records provide one means of accessing the complexities of the public reception to sheltering. A survey of attitudes towards shelters before the war revealed that, while there was *some* demand for deep shelters, respondents felt most comfortable with backyard Anderson shelters, which were thought to be familiar and close at hand. Brick shelters, the goal of the smaller shelter-building schemes launched by many local authorities, prompted a great deal of hostility and there was an evident unwillingness to use these structures.[26] One of the subjects detailed in *Nine Wartime Lives*, Matthew Walton, found that his enthusiasm for communal shelters as a committee secretary dissipated with the disinterest of residents to maintain the shelter.[27] A report into efforts to construct brick shelters in Hampstead in the first year of the war emphasized this antipathy and the ambivalence with which campaigners were treated. It noted that opposition to government

ARP was 'middle-class intellectual' at its base. This was a true representation of the background of the prominent critics, although they believed that they spoke on behalf of the working class, in opposition to perceived middle-class bias in government plans. The Mass Observation report writers believed that:

> At sporadic intervals, these undercurrents have broken out into organized local campaigns: the response to which was almost invariably one of polite sympathy: enlivened something by the tripping over of some local red tape, and the resulting squabbles. On no occasion has there been any thing that could be described as a real mass response, with real drive and feeling behind it.[28]

The report mentioned J.B.S. Haldane's campaign in Hampstead and the mixed reaction to it, concluding that the gathering of a requisite number of signatures calling for increased shelter provision did not indicate that any real enthusiasm had been roused. Residents may have been too polite to turn down the earnest campaigners' requests for signatures, but at the same time felt no attachment to these shelters and did little to maintain them once they were built or improve their amenities. They lacked sanitary facilities and so were not fit for long-term use; citizens baulked at sheltering in them. The public therefore remained aloof from the campaign to build additional brick shelters. Another reason for ambivalence was that local officials appeared in 'a manner hurried, confused, and bristling with impersonal officialdom'.[29] These ambiguous feelings towards shelters made it difficult for the leftists to stir real emotion on the issue and doubly hard for both the government and the campaigners to differentiate between polemic and real dissatisfaction with present arrangements. Mass Observation noted that the *feeling* of safety was important to the general public, but there were other points to consider such as to what extent the public was willing to pay higher tax rates or leave the comforts of home to utilize these shelters.[30] It remained unclear in the pre-war period whether citizens would be prepared not only to institute mass public schemes but also commit to their staffing and upkeep for an indefinite period of time.

Public Relations and Sensitivity to Public Opinion

Subtly hidden in the public statements, though patently obvious in the Home Office records, is the extraordinary attention that officials paid to the public relations measures of their policies. The government did not wish to appear hard-hearted in face of the dangers that civilians would be exposed to in wartime. Politicians and civil servants gave a great deal of thought to the appearance and wording of certain statements, demonstrating that they were not immune to public reception. An urgent need was felt to put relations with the civilian population on a good footing before the outbreak of hostilities. One question that exercised the Hailey Committee, for example, was how they should delicately indicate that some 'essential workers' would be eligible for deeper and better shelters while others were not.[31] Because civilian casualties would cause grave demoralization, particular care needed to be taken to disguise any inequality of protection. They believed that morale would suffer if it became clear that an area that had suffered high casualties had been afforded an inferior standard of protection.[32] Members of the Committee of Imperial Defence were consequently concerned about maintaining the appearance of equality, an acknowledgement that they understood that it was an important consideration for the general public. Oliver Stanley, Conservative MP for Westmorland, believed that a clear and definitive refutation of deep shelters should have been made in early 1938, before the Munich Crisis caused greater agitation for them. He believed that it was most unfortunate that 'the idea had been allowed to grow that bomb-proof shelters were both desirable and practicable, and public opinion had now got completely out of hand'.[33] While he believed it was important to not appear too intransigent on the issue, it was equally important 'not to use words which would commit the Government to any general extension of the more limited policy,' that is, to provide only a few shelters for critical workers.[34]

The Hailey report claimed that Tecton had reduced official policy
to two simple principles – that the level of congestion in the area
made steel backyard shelters unfeasible, and that the principle of
strengthened basements was unsound. Tecton replied that the
government's own figures showed that only 3 per cent of houses in
the area could be equipped with the proposed steel (Anderson)
shelters. On the second point, the architects believed that the Hailey
Commission had been deliberately evasive. By highlighting the
many unknowns of aerial bombardment, the government experts
placed the architects in an impossible position since there was no
means by which to 'prove' that any bomb shelter was entirely bomb-
proof. The architects maintained that such arguments were
completely irrational coming from a government that continued to
advocate haphazard steel and trench shelters that had actually been
proven fatal in Spanish cities. At any rate, it was well known that
they were distinctly *not* bomb-proof. The best refutation Tecton
could muster was that the shelters could be made to resist any
specified bomb weight by altering the thickness of concrete. They
also pointed out that they had appealed for assistance from the Home
Office in determining such technical figures – claiming to be able to
meet *any* set of standards – but had received no guidance
whatsoever.[35]

The majority of the Hailey Commission criticism focused on the
short warning time for civilians to reach the safety of the shelter,
and the problem of preventing panic at its entrance. The Hailey
Commission commented on the width of the entry ramps and their
ability to deal with the volume of people expected to be hurriedly
rushing to the doors, pointing out that several thousand people
would need to move into the shelter within minutes. The
government believed that panicked citizens would stop their
descent into the shelter upon reaching a position of safety, creating a
bottleneck and endangering those behind them. Tecton's architects
replied that they had previously worked out all these mathematical
calculations, and had taken into account these factors given a
'warning time' of ten minutes before an air raid. The series of
tunnels and shelters would help the greatest number of people to

reach shelter in the least amount of time by, for example, eliminating the need to cross major thoroughfares.

The Tecton architects and the Finsbury Council also engaged in retaliatory public relations endeavours. The Tecton architects responded to each of the technical points raised by the government experts, and their response was presented to the Finsbury Borough Council on 25 April 1939.[36] Berthold Lubetkin also wrote a letter to the editor of *The Times* on behalf of Tecton. He refrained from any direct attack on the Home Office or Sir John Anderson, and indeed simply proposed that his firm would be able to comply with any standard which the government laid down for shelter construction.[37] Lubetkin was careful not to leave himself or his firm open to charges of political radicalism or undermining national morale at a sensitive time. Supporters of the Tecton plans believed that they had demonstrated the economic superiority of underground shelters and the efficiency of modern British design. The Finsbury Council stated that 'none of the criticisms of the Home Office and their advisors has been directed to fundamental principles'.[38] The plans emphasized the principle of 'uniformity', arguing that it was necessary to keep all shelters as standardized as possible in terms of their protective value. A scheme that provided protection for 50 per cent of the population while leaving the other 50 per cent with no protection, or a mixture of shelter types, would not reduce casualties in proportion to expenditure per head.[39] The architects believed that the case for their shelters was so strong 'that it cannot be swept aside by such light-hearted and ill-considered interpretations of the truth'.[40] They were, therefore, hardly heartened by Sir John Anderson's letter in which he declared the hope that the Finsbury Council:

> would not regard these unfavourable conclusions as implying that the work [was wasted]. The survey which was carried out will be of great value in the formulation of further proposals, and in addition the report has served a valuable purpose in assembling and focusing issues, even though its conclusions cannot be regarded as acceptable.[41]

Architectural historian John Allan believes that Berthold
Lubetkin and Tecton answered all the Home Office criticisms
sufficiently.[42] Lubetkin also pushed for the Home Office to publish
the technical evidence for their counter-claims, yet no response was
forthcoming. The deep shelter question had been concluded in the
minds of officials, and there was therefore no requirement to put
themselves at extra pains to satisfy the press and the 'misguided
critics'. The Association of Architects, Surveyors and Technical
Assistants continued to support deep shelters, and defended the
Tecton plan with a pamphlet attacking the official shelter policy for
its mistaken principle of dispersal.[43] Cyril Helsby, a 'technical man'
writing to *The Times*, was a structural engineer who had studied
precautions in Spain. Helsby also disputed the notion that deep
shelters were unfeasible and that problems such as multiple
entrances and depth requirements could not be solved through
diligent study. He believed that Sir John Anderson was ill-advised
in summarily rejecting plans that could, in essence, negate the peril
from the air, which was the cause of most war planning concern.[44]

Local Activism: Finsbury and the Aftermath of the Hailey Commission

The deflating effect of the Hailey Commission findings undoubtedly
left many struggling councils with an inescapable 'where do we go
from here?' feeling. Many were determined to proceed with the
'democratic defence' model of Spanish ARP in which the people had
provided for their own shelters, even in light of central government
opposition. George Woods wrote in the *Finsbury Citizen* that Sir John
Anderson had inadvertently let slip that the Tecton shelters were 'too
good for the people', stoking the nagging class resentment that
leftists felt over ARP.[45] The *Finsbury Citizen* reported on the
continued efforts of the council to institute deep shelters,
emphasizing class issues. Alderman Riley was quoted as saying:
'Finsbury is determined to see that bomb-proof shelter accommodation is forthcoming, whether the Government likes it, or whether
they do not.'[46]

Finsbury Council was consequently unwilling to concede defeat and investigated several means of building multiple mass shelters regardless of government objections, including dual-use structures that would be built by private companies. In what was deemed an 'ingenious scheme' in the press,[47] the Council negotiated a temporary lease of an underground shelter that was to be constructed by a local company. Cooperating with private business was quite a turn of strategy for a council that advocated socialist principles. The shelter, amended from their original plans, became known as the 'Busaco Street' project. The company pledged to build the space for dual-purpose use, as the architects had originally intended, and there were plans to construct two more underground rental shelters in commercial areas such as the Finsbury and Charterhouse Squares.[48] The government had contemplated such an eventuality, and was prepared to do its utmost to prevent such privately owned dual-use spaces being used as mass public shelters. To this end, the Hailey report had concluded that the same concerns voiced over the technical flaws of single-use deep shelters would apply to dual-use shelters.[49] This provision put yet another obstacle in the path of innovative local councils.

For a period of weeks the project appeared to be fully feasible. On the eve of war in August 1939, the socialist newspaper *Finsbury Citizen* published an article on the borough's mass shelter project with the headline 'Borough Council Defeats the Government: Finsbury's Sensational Victory'. Alderman Harold Riley declared, 'There is nothing the Government can now do to stop us building [our deep shelter]. We have not even got to ask the Government whether we may build it, or in any way seek its opinion.' Yet, unfortunately for the Finsbury Council, plans for the Busaco Street shelter had barely begun when the private company contracted to build it invoked the war clause to sever their obligations. The Council was even levied a surcharge for the monies already expended on the project. Finsbury's rejoicing over finding a means of 'driving an express train through the law' was therefore short-lived.[50] The events of September 1939 overran its efforts, and wartime ARP provision in Finsbury was limited to providing smaller surface and shallow underground shelters on an *ad hoc* basis. Alderman Riley believed that if the government was entitled to build elite 'funk-holes' for its own officials, Finsbury was entitled to provide protection for the people. The rhetoric of the 'funk-hole', along with being a charge of sedition, was also a mutable epithet and a criticism that both government and critics used against their political opponents. The government believed that mass shelters were funk-holes that would damage national morale, while the leftist critics maintained that elite shelters were indicative of the preferential treatment that the privileged would enjoy in wartime. The leftist critics believed they had successfully linked nationalism with the goal of equality, particularly equality in wartime.

Wartime experience demonstrated the importance of the ability of local councils to provide rudimentary ARP, though the grand ideas acquired by leftists from Spain had to be dramatically downsized. Following the official Home Office rejection of deep shelter plans, the relationship between the central government and local councils was characterized by inertia and a certain amount of 'muddling through'.[51] Alderman Riley had further offended the Home Office through his vitriolic attacks on the ARP Department in the *Finsbury Citizen* and his ostentatious boycott of a national flag ceremony,[52] meaning that no *rapprochement* between the warring levels of government would be forthcoming. In light of the failed mass shelter scheme, three days after the outbreak of war the Finsbury Council planned to construct rather more modest 'surface shelters' and trench systems in King Square, Spa Fields, and Spa Green – some of the scant few spaces available in the crowded borough.[53] Tecton's original study had encompassed the possibility of surface 'wall shelters' with reinforced concrete on the sides, protecting against blast damage and debris, although not direct hits.[54]

In this spirit, other local Labour leaders were galvanized on the question of deep shelters following the drafting of the Finsbury plans and their attempt to provide alternative shelters for the populace. These individuals emphasized the continued importance of equality and standardization in ARP provisions. Herbert Morrison called the official shelter provisions 'a collection of odds and ends' falling short of a comprehensive policy, especially for the chief danger zones.[55] Finsbury's plans directly inspired the Hampstead Council to employ Dr Oscar Faber, who had been in communication with Ove Arup, to make a report on the provision of deep shelters.[56] Hackney was another borough that took a proactive approach to ARP, yet at the same time its members had a more conciliatory relationship with the central government. This was largely due to the influence of Dr Richard Tee, who was appointed to his position when Herbert Morrison was mayor of the borough, and who was invited to assist the Committee of Imperial Defence on the subject of gas decontamination. He was consequently well-situated to draft local plans for ARP, and Hackney was the first local authority to file a draft scheme with the Home Office in early 1938. E.J. Hodsoll of the ARP Department praised Tee's work and his political savvy in dealing with opposition and dissent on the issue of ARP. Tee's work, as he saw it, ensured that the borough proved reasonably well-prepared for aerial attack.[57] There were doubtless many other unsung versions of Dr Tee spread among local authorities throughout Britain who made the best they could of the small, piecemeal plans for ARP that they were able to construct. Most officials involved with the issue came to accept the proposal of the Air Raid Defence League, which stated that not everything could be done in true equality to protect the whole population: 'What we require is not something for everybody, but a great deal for some of the people – that is, for those who are most likely to be attacked.'[58]

Joseph Meisel notes that the Hailey Commission's endorsement of government policy ultimately relied on argumentation rather than scientific or engineering principles.[59] The events of Finsbury had a particularly 1930s tinge, with high-minded moral pronouncements and extreme positions claimed by duelling sides. The borough planners were wholly convinced of the justness of their proposals and saw no reason why they should give up their principles just as civilians would actually require wartime advocacy. The Tecton plans were thus based not only on moral imperatives, but also on the conviction that standardized deep shelter plans could provide far greater protection than the same resources being spread in a haphazard way. As Lord Baker, a government engineer, noted decades later, the bureaucratic process ensured that the 'technician armed with new knowledge' was unable to introduce new ideas.[60] The government held steadfastly to its concept of dispersal, and the belief that no shelter could ever be 'bomb-proof'. Therefore, they too could call on experts and scientists who would affirm the justness of governmental policy. In the end, the terms of discussion came down to questions of patriotism, morale, and British national character, rather than simply those of technical feasibility. The Hailey Commission, with its cross-section of British expertise, was aimed to confirm a national consensus regarding appropriate ARP. It served as the final expression of the government's idea of national character and the 'British way' of civil defence.

CONCLUSIONS

VIOLENCE AND TERROR – REFLECTIONS ON PERPETUAL FEARS

Considering the paucity of facts about air attack at the time, Sir John had produced a pretty clear resume of the possible situation.[1]

−Herbert Morrison, on his immediate predecessor as Home Secretary

Unlike the First World War, World War II was greeted with quiet resignation due to the expectation of aerial attack against civilians, including poison gas, and the grim memories of soldiering in the trenches on the Western Front. There was little stomach to undertake the depressing years of warfare that most knew lay ahead, but acceptance of the final inevitability of conflict was nearly universal. The final entry in George Orwell's pre-war diary captures this ambiguous feeling well:

Air-raid practice this morning immediately after the proclamation of state of war. Seems to have gone off satisfactorily [...] believed of many people to be real raid. There are now great numbers of public air-raid shelters, though most of them will take another day or two to complete [...] no panic, on the other hand no enthusiasm, and in fact not much interest.[2]

The inaction of the Phoney War proved something of an anticlimatic let-down. Some observers even expressed relief following the first air raid, feeling that the worst had finally arrived after the tension of expectancy and the hyperbolic rhetoric of the doomsayers. Initial raids produced a great deal of confusion, although they did not cause very much destruction – false air raids sounded and ARP wardens were unsure of how to perform their duties. Much 'muddling' occurred in these first months, though evidence suggests that people quickly learned how to act during a raid.[3]

As suggested in Chapter 5 of this book, previous experience of the psychology of populations under bombardment proved that most people were more resilient than authorities feared. The medicalization of anxieties and panic is reflected in psychiatry records, one prime source for analysing wartime emotion. As Amy Bell has pointed out, our impression that there was an overall lack of psychological trauma among civilians in Britain is largely based on an *absence* of sources, particularly among psychiatrists and doctors. Case notes reveal few examples of civilian fear. There is a great deal of evidence for a surge in other medical complaints related to stress, such as insomnia, ulcers, and gastric conditions, but not of overtly expressed psychological distress. There may be specific, institutional reasons why this material was either unrecorded or not preserved, but it appears that psychological trauma may have been lightly swept under the rug by authorities, the media, and perhaps even victims themselves.[4] Whatever the truth regarding these medical records, it is nevertheless true that the population did not revolt, retreat into 'funk-holes', or demand that the government sue for peace. Indeed, feelings of mutual suffering and deprivation elicited a type of solidarity – an element that is extremely common in nostalgic remembrances of wartime. One analysis of workplace morale in World War II has demonstrated that social cohesion prevented mass panic through the feeling of mutual aid.[5] The feeling, that 'we are all in this together,' naturally bolstered by government and the press, was a powerful boost to morale.

The Blitz and the official account of civilian fortitude, whether propagandistic or not, requires little accounting here. Once it had ended there was a general perception that the worst of aerial attack had been squarely met. Consequently the attacks by V-1 and V-2 (*Vergeltungswaffe* in German, meaning 'revenge weapon') unmanned rockets against London, beginning in 1944, brought some civilians close to the breaking point. The British population had endured the Blitz and had fought through three more years of war, rationing, and great hardship on the Home Front. Glimpsing the end of hostilities in sight and believing that Germany was close to ruination, the rocket attacks proved too much for some. Unlike the bombers, they came virtually without warning and seemed entirely purposeless. No attempt to lighten the situation by nicknaming the weapons 'doodlebugs' or calling them 'flying bombs' could mitigate the devastating effect they had on morale. Expressed fears about these weapons appear in personal diaries but have largely been expunged from collective memory; the nature of attack did not meet the same triumphal narrative as that of the Blitz.[6] Scenes of individual attacks were haunting, including at Croydon, Aldwych, Kensington High Street, and the market at Lewisham. Within the first three days of V-1 attacks, 647 bombs fell, killing 499 people. As Home Secretary Herbert Morrison wrote, 'after five years of war the civilian population were not as capable of standing the strains of air attacks as they had been during the winter of 1940–41. I will do everything to hold up their courage and spirit – but there is a limit, and the limit will come.'[7] Fortunately for the state of civilian morale, the V-1 and V-2 attacks proved to be relatively short-run. Yet, from the governmental point of view, they demonstrated the knife-edged balance between fortitude and despair on which the nation's wartime efforts rested.

Apart from the dedicated pacifists, the infliction of suffering on *enemy* civilians was not a question many wished to dwell on, then or now. Many Royal Air Force officials were disappointed that the

First World War ended before they were able to 'prove' what the force could accomplish with an attack on a city such as Berlin.[8] During World War II they would get their wish, and the practice of area bombing and the deliberate terrorizing of civilians in German cities advocated from 1942 onwards, particularly by Air Marshall Arthur 'Bomber' Harris, has provoked a great deal of controversy then and since. Only more recently have historians attempted to come to terms with the policy of area bombing and firebombing. This aspect of the Allied war effort is discomforting to our preferred collective memory of the war. A.C. Grayling's landmark work *Among the Dead Cities* is among the preliminary attempts to acknowledge the suffering of German and Japanese civilians in the narrative of the war, without diminishing the atrocities of the Axis powers. Jörg Friedrich's *The Fire* represents a German attempt to both give voice to civilian victims and divorce that voice from far-right politics.[9]

The contemporary writer Vera Brittain, a staunch pacifist since the First World War, penned a renunciation of the practice in *Seed of Chaos: What Mass Bombing Really Means* in 1944. Combining humanitarian concerns for human suffering with strategic arguments, she contended that there was no evidence that the war would be shortened by such destruction – the victims were likely to simply seek revenge. This observation was one of those derived from Spain for careful students of air raids. Contemporary critics in Britain, particularly clergymen and pacifists, argued that this practice was morally indefensible, no matter what crimes the Nazi regime had committed. They felt that intensified bombing raids as the war was drawing to a close were especially reprehensible. These raids culminated in the devastating firebombing of Dresden on 13 February 1945. Many prominent clergy who voiced reservations if not open opposition to such raids were, like Brittain, exposed to vociferous attacks and anger by a war-weary population who were themselves prone to the desire for revenge. As occurred during the First World War, the terror of air raids provoked complex emotional reactions, but a collapse of morale or an insistence on ending the war were not among them.

The Performance of Government Plans

We have seen how Mass Observation demonstrates public reception to various sheltering provisions and how urban residents responded to communal shelters in contrast to privately owned structures. Diaries also provide particular insight into how the psychological aspects of air raid sheltering and government dictates were manifested. The suspicion expressed towards air raid wardens and the regulation of local air raid precautions (ARP) demonstrates that, as the critics had predicted, voluntary action and not compulsion proved to be the only means of proceeding.[10] There were certainly complaints about many measures, including the inaccessibility of Underground stations for sheltering. Yet as James Hinton points out in his analysis of wartime Mass Observation diaries, there are no easy generalizations about the wartime populace. Grumbling did not necessarily equal widespread opposition, and Mass Observation also suggests that feelings of unjust compulsion or displeasure with war measures were negligible.[11]

Following the war, Geoffrey Lloyd, who had been Under-Secretary of State for the Home Department and who held important ministerial positions in the wartime Cabinet, defended the planning and wartime performance of the ARP and civil defence services. He argued that by taking a calm and measured approach and conducting research and training, the government alighted on the correct methods of defence. From its point of view, decisions regarding ARP were neither insensible nor insensitive, for they aimed to preserve the very survival of the nation if widespread panic should ensue. While government officials such as those who wrote the Hailey report could be accused of using panic as a mere excuse to dismiss the plans forwarded by Finsbury and other councils, they felt that their policies reflected a truly rational estimate of the threat. Anticipating hundreds of thousands of dead civilians and millions of refugees and psychological casualties, it was not inconceivable that society could break down, rendering expensive 'rationalized' shelters all but unusable and ripe for transformation into a lawless subterranean world.[12] The specifics of advice to householders were also seen to have had a sound basis. The Home Office had been mocked for its 'sand bucket and shovel' advice regarding the extinguishing of incendiary bombs. The official suggestion was to fill at least two buckets of water and have two corresponding buckets of sand readily available 'if there should be a threat of war'.[13] Lloyd recalled that jokes were 'spread over the country when all the clever gentlemen found it wise to make fun of Sir Samuel Hoare and Sir John Anderson when they first proposed that the incendiary bomb could be dealt with [. . .] with the aid of buckets, sand and shovels'. Yet he believed that when the war commenced these plans proved their value.[14]

In addition, the evacuations of the Phoney War period did run relatively smoothly, given the scale of removals. One-and-a-half million people were relocated from cities to 'reception areas', including half the schoolchildren in cities designated as evacuation areas. Angus Calder suggests that problems that arose with the evacuation of London schoolchildren to the countryside tended to be the result of existing social tensions rather than the scheme itself.[15] The historian Sir Keith Hancock, responding to drafts of *Problems of Social Policy*, stated curtly that insinuations of ARP Department negligence or lack of planning on subjects such as evacuation were unfair and that plans did unfold as well as could be expected.[16] As has been explored, the much-praised evacuation plans of the French government were also fraught with difficulties.

Official policy continued to emphasize dispersal and household protection, highlighted by the scale of the Anderson shelter programme. The outbreak of war hastened the production of corrugated steel Anderson shelters and later the Morrison indoor cage-like shelter, providing evidence that the government was forced to address questions of inequality and demands for at least rudimentary shelters. The income cut-off for free shelters was £250 per annum for the Anderson shelter and £350 per annum for the Morrison, which excluded many middle-class and lower-middle-class families from the scheme.[17] Yet the means test figures were set to respond to the class-based criticism of official plans. The programme demonstrates that the Home Office was willing to make adjustments to address concerns of poorer families, but that officials firmly believed that the principle of dispersal remained the soundest. By the start of the war in September 1939, 1.5 million Anderson models had been delivered, estimated to hold up to 6 million people, and the rate of production had reached 50,000 per week.[18] The Anderson shelter had profound psychological benefits for the families who installed them. Jospeh Meisel notes that the shelter provided families with an 'illusion' that they could be protected against the effects of modern war.[19] This statement mirrors the Mass Observation findings that the feeling of safety was important to respondents who favoured the provision of Anderson shelters.[20]

Deep mass shelter was another point on which the Home Office was forced partially to recant. The use of London Underground stations as shelters was a concession to public demand, as had occurred during the First World War. Members of the Hailey Commission had stated in April 1939 that 'a number of individuals' might obtain protection in the Tubes. They did believe, however, that the practice should be limited as much as possible and Sir John Anderson also thought that it was wisest to attempt to practice a policy of deterrence. Thus the number of people actively seeking shelter might be limited, even if some individuals forcibly contravened official policy.[21] By 1940, however, Anderson's refusal to provide deep shelters was thrown into question, although the War Cabinet initially backed him. For critics, the popular action demanding some sort of sheltering system was illustrative of the people acting democratically in obtaining their own civil defence, with or without the approval of the Home Office. Although perhaps only 4 per cent of the population of London used Underground stations as a frequent venue for sheltering, the demand was high enough to force the government's hand.

As a concession to the new orthodoxy that there was a limited role for deep underground shelters within official policy, especially in the crowded areas of Central and East London, attempts were made to regulate the use of tunnels and the London Underground. The government appointed Dr David Anderson, Joint Consulting Engineer of the London Passenger Transport Board, to provide advice on deep shelters and constructing extended tunnels to accommodate additional persons. Government officials were also forced to accept the inevitable and provide sanitation, water, and canteen food for those sheltering underground.[22] Despite these new measures, Anderson's handling of ARP became increasingly unpopular. In the words of one Mass Observation report, 'probably no Cabinet Minister has a lower public appeal, as far as our investigations show. His rather formal and uncompromising manner has never infused into the machinery for which he is responsible any warmth, humour or general sympathy likely to appeal to the many.'[23]

The appointment of Herbert Morrison as replacement Home Secretary was one way for the government to stem this tide of criticism, given Morrison's long record of ARP advocacy as a Labour politician. He continued to espouse a moderate approach to questions of ARP after he entered the Cabinet. In 1940 for example, he refuted the notion that complete bomb-proof protection was a feasible goal, stating, 'We have to beware of looking for 100 per cent safety for the civil population [...]. If we hide ourselves and are unwilling to take any risks [...] the striking force of the enemy will be increased and we will be whacked.'[24] Morrison took over the enormous task of reorganizing civil defence services, which was completed only in the summer of 1941. Recognizing that there was not enough steel and cement available for deep shelter construction, he nevertheless believed that a public announcement of at least limited shelter construction would serve as an important morale booster. Cooperative efforts with local councils were likely an outgrowth of Morrison's continued belief in the value of local government and the London County Council. As Home Secretary he was insistent that the structure of local democratic government should be maintained to the greatest extent possible during wartime, an opinion that was especially vital because the nation was fighting to protect those very values.[25]

Under his aegis, the boroughs of Hampstead, Holborn and St Pancras all benefited from the decision to grant requests for the construction of new tunnels. By the end of 1940, Morrison was able to boast of accommodation for 200,000 persons in well-organized shelters.[26] Even those who had an Anderson or other household shelter admitted that they would be at greater ease knowing that public shelters were available if they were caught away from home during a raid. The government made plans to adapt eight underground shelters throughout London to facilitate public sheltering, although seven of these shelters – some of which could hold up to 14,000 people – did not open until 1944, at which point few people took shelter in them. These structures took longer than expected to construct, and surpassed their original budget, partially justifying the Hailey Commission's conclusion that the 'time factor' for constructing deep shelters precluded the commencement of a mass scheme when war appeared imminent.

The question of deep shelters overlapped with the mandate of local authorities to provide air raid accommodation, and as demonstrated, the attempt to build brick shelters was met with a mixed reaction since people did not believe they provided an adequate level of safety. Indeed, some of the first bombs that fell in Finsbury destroyed a Farringdon Road brick shelter. Other authorities in Islington, Richmond, Brentford, Chiswick, and Ramsgate took steps to initiate deep shelter plans though these areas were also only able to provide the unpopular brick shelters to residents.[27] One local councillor, who expressed a personal dislike of public shelters, affirmed that people desired some provision of both personal and communal shelters to be available for their use. He believed that citizens felt safer knowing that shelters were in close proximity, and were proud of corporate efforts made to install shelters. He had witnessed a rush for shelters following the first raids, and felt that further raids would doubtless increase demand.[28]

As a consequence of public pressure, increasing efforts to blunt the lack of provisions for crowded areas was evidenced by the belated construction of small public shelters, the distribution of Anderson shelters to lower income earners, and the toleration of limited sheltering in Underground stations. Yet reactions to public shelters and the experience of taking refuge demonstrate a wide range of emotional responses to the physical circumstances involved, perhaps justifying many of the government's principles regarding dispersed shelters. For example, it is doubtful whether thousands of Finsbury residents would have actually continued to use the mass shelters night after night. It is also not known how mass usage would have played out sociologically. For a number of reasons, many people preferred to stay close to home, whether in home shelters or simply braving the danger of sleeping in their own beds – taking a rather fatalistic 'if there is a bomb with your name on it then you are done for' attitude. The numbers of those habitually using shelters remained small, and those who turned into avid 'Tube Dwellers' were even smaller. The records kept by Mass Observation put the number at several thousand individuals who had to some extent taken to virtual night-time living on the platforms of Tube stations, and continued this activity until at least 1943.[29]

There were some instances of panic arising at mass shelters, most particularly the Bethnal Green Tube stampede disaster of 3 March 1943 in which 173 people perished, 62 of them children. After the air raid warning sounded, an anti-aircraft battery at nearby Victoria Park went off, startling those approaching the shelter of the Tube into thinking that bombs had started to fall. As the crowd surged, someone possibly tripped on the stairs – initial reports claimed that it was a woman with a baby carriage, but what actually occurred still remains unknown. It provides one example of a true mob panic, since it did not even occur during an actual raid but due to fright, and it turned into the worst single civilian disaster of World War II. At the same time, the fact of the tragedy having occurred on steep and narrow stairs might validate the arguments of Tecton, the Finsbury Council, and the leftist critics in favour of scientific purpose-built shelters. This incident occurred in the East End in the area of London thought to be in the greatest danger of mob panic. At the same time officials were quick to quell rumours that the incident was caused by 'foreign', namely Jewish, residents. They were equally eager to paper over the incident in general, at least partially censoring it from memory of the war. Even if an event such as the Bethnal Green disaster was, thankfully, a tragic anomaly, it highlighted the unpredictable nature of crowds and morale.

Critics and Government Service

Although the government largely failed to adopt suggestions proffered by the leftist critics in the interwar period, the critics themselves were invited to advise the wartime state on ARP. In addition, at least some of the major reorganization by Herbert Morrison of the civil defence services was based on the critics' pre-war suggestions. Joseph Needham's claim that the ARP experiments conducted by the scientific left had posed 'a challenge to people in high places'[30] provides an indication of how these scientists and critics perceived their role as being to question received opinion, challenge authority, and forward their ideas of social democracy. Despite their numerous dust-ups with the Home Office in the 1930s, these critics were respected for their base of technical knowledge. In fact, most had been well-integrated into professional and academic life already, and minor concerns over radical politics were highly unlikely to have jeopardized these positions of influence. Naturally, the new Home Secretary Herbert Morrison rose to be the highest of the interwar ARP advocates. He managed to somewhat bypass political squabbles in the spirit of wartime coalition and cooperation. But the primary contribution of the critics to wartime governance was in the deployment of their technical skills. As Serge Chermayeff had stated in the architectural press, all facets of ARP, including evacuation and shelter construction, were part of an 'organically whole problem' that was primarily a technical issue.[31] The scientific left served as advisors and consultants to multiple government committees, an acknowledgment of their observational expertise from Spain and study of the ARP issue.

In 1939, J.B.S. Haldane was asked to stand as a Labour MP for Cambridge but turned down the offer due to the fact that both his political work and his technical expertise were required for imminent war.[32] His war work was indeed prodigious, and he acted as a private consultant on ARP, fielding professional enquiries, including some from the private manufacturers of protective equipment such as gas masks. He also served with the Labour Party's Air Raid Protection Committee and with a similar body consisting of fellow professionals who shared his leftist ideology. The group advocated tunnels and heavy protection air raid shelters for small groups similar to those that had been constructed in Spain, but their efforts on that particular front were of little effect. Under the conservative coalition, Haldane was an important advisor to the National ARP Coordinating Committee and official groups pertaining to public morale. Having publically shelved some of his more overtly partisan rhetoric 'for the duration', he insisted that only a national movement on non-party lines would save Britain.

Ove Arup of the Finsbury project also remained as a consultant on ARP, while his colleague Berthold Lubetkin drew back following the rejection of the Tecton plans for Finsbury by the Home Office. Lubetkin's sense of frustration over missed opportunities was long lasting — looking back on the 1930s from the perspective of the late 1970s, he expressed the view that 'these buildings [Tecton's projects] cry for a world which has never come into existence'.[33] Arup continued to believe in strong public demand for shelters, bringing this issue to press attention throughout 1940. He lamented official policy in a letter to his friend Lubetkin in 1940, stating that 'there seems to be no question of increasing the standard of safety. On the contrary, they are now prepared to lower the standard and have expressly said so in Circulars issued to the Boroughs.'[34] Arup designed over 80 private and civic shelters and aided 'Red' Ellen Wilkinson, the Labour MP for Jarrow who worked with Herbert Morrison and the Home Office and held special responsibilities for shelters. Unlike many leftists, however, she defended the policy of dispersal and was instrumental in the distribution of Morrison shelters to individual householders.[35] Morrison shelters were essentially small, steel cage-like structures of seven by four feet with a 'table top' and room for a mattress to be placed underneath. These shelters were to be used within rooms to protect from falling debris, or the partial collapse of a two-storey house. Unlike the Anderson shelter, they neither required a garden nor involved the resulting cold, damp, and outdoor discomfort. By the end of 1941, around 500,000 Morrison shelters had been distributed free to lower-income householders.

The Cambridge Scientists likewise continued their air raid shelter advocacy in somewhat altered form – for one thing, the 'anti-war' portion of the Cambridge Scientists' Anti-War Group's moniker no longer applied. The locus of the scientific left shifted from Cambridge to London, with many of its members having been drafted in to perform war work. Those who remained in Cambridge continued to work for local ARP, producing pamphlets and organizing an exhibition in 1941.[36] J.D. Bernal, who had reconciled himself to the inevitability of war against Fascism by the late 1930s, sought to establish 'the means by which the most useful contribution of science and the work of scientists can be made to national defence'.[37] He believed that 'the full utilization of scientific workers' for war aims and ARP was desirable, and following the war he was proud that British scientists 'were more fully employed and with greater success than in any other combatant country'.[38] Some objections were raised to Bernal working in an official capacity due to his radical political connections, but Sir John Anderson personally approved his appointment, citing the urgency of present circumstances.[39] As argued by Gary Werskey, the inclusion of the leftist critics into government planning demonstrated not only the astuteness of politicians such as Anderson but also the success of the scientific left in the ARP debate.[40]

The 'People's War'

The primary theme running throughout this book has been the claims to British popular identity inherent in both governmental plans and the alternative proposals of the critics. The ultimate expression of Britishness was that of the People's War, a conflict in which all participated and which also promised equality of benefits when peace came. Ultimately the People's War was both a reflection of popular sentiment and a conscious creation on the part of government, newspapers, broadcasters, and filmmakers, including American media personalities such as Edward R. Murrow and his famed 'This Is London' radio broadcasts. J.B. Priestley and George Orwell served as the most popular articulators of Britishness.

Orwell's ode to the 'national character' in *The Lion and the Unicorn* (1941) produced a hyperbolic vision of the nation. Orwell himself described the book as an attempt to 'reconcile patriotism with intelligence'.[41] As Orwell wrote to Victor Gollancz, 'when the pinch comes the common people will turn out to be more intelligent than the clever ones'.[42] J.B. Priestley wrote the working class into the national narrative in a largely depoliticized context, serving as the 'voice of the nation' in wartime and confirming the innate goodness of the masses.[43] His words on Dunkirk are among his best known, including his praise of 'the ordinary British folk [. . .] whose courage, patience and humour stand like a rock above the dark morass of treachery, cowardice and panic'.[44] These contributions to national morale were notable for their affability, upbeat temper and inclusiveness – all characteristics of the People's War itself.

I have suggested that a specific view of national character underlay government plans – a depiction that was at times contradictory. Despite the reservations of historians as to actual cause and effect, the People's War is invariably bound up in the public imagination with the birth of the welfare state. Susan Grayzel has proffered the argument that the welfare state was intertwined with David Edgerton's notion of the 'warfare state'.[45] This is to say that the erasure of the line between combatant and civilian under the conditions of total war necessarily refashioned a more inclusive model of citizenship. It has been the goal of this narrative to demonstrate the tensions inherent in the debate over these questions from the 1930s onwards. The role of ARP and the fear of aerial warfare are both crucial to understanding these issues and how wartime social identities were constituted.

In the pre-war period the British government was of two minds concerning the rationality and stoicism of its citizens, illustrating the difficulty of using this rhetoric to explain any true state of national identity. It is clear that many officials held only a tenuous confidence in the performance of the British people, and they held even less trust in the working classes who populated the areas that would be subject to the full force of enemy bombing raids. The ultimate meanings of national identity and belonging are diverse and highly fraught.

Joanna Bourke has noted that many preferred to 'wallow in fanciful notions of "British bulldog courage".[46] The idea of 'muddling through' was in some measure a source of pride to ordinary Britons during the war and a reflection of the People's War. Images of the democratic and resourceful citizen served as an antidote to the pre-war malaise represented by the downtrodden 'little man in the suburbs'.[47] The evacuation of Dunkirk was depicted in this heroic light, and the stoicism of Londoners during the Blitz was used as another affirmation of British exceptionalism. Angus Calder maintains that the much-vaunted stoicism of World War II demonstrates 'the myth of British or English moral pre-eminence' as an essential national trait.[48] The war served as an education for those in power. Nothing turned out as badly as they had feared, least of all in the realm of public morale.

Individuals such as Haldane and his colleagues continued to advocate a specific version of volunteerism, bolstering their view of citizen-driven ARP, such as that observed in Spain. The Home Guard was one way to involve the civilians in war – a 'People's Army', based on the model of the Spanish militias. Orwell's involvement in the Home Guard despite his declining health was his lived expression of these ideals. Leftist ARP critic John Langdon-Davies made his farm in Sussex available to the government for training purposes. The Marxist military theorist, T.H. Wintringham, who had been an officer in the British Battalion in Spain and who directed training of the Home Guard, expounded the theory that 'free men will often overcome in battle, even against considerable odds, men relatively less free'.[49] He argued that the British army needed to develop a 'democratic' military model that prized individual initiative rather than the blind obedience and was inclusive of different members of society.

Efforts at inclusiveness and a form of vaguely-termed 'democratic defence' bore much fruit. To a fair extent, national identity expanded in wartime to encompass individuals who may not previously have felt the pull of these appeals,[50] and the volunteer ethic continued to cross left–right political boundaries. Mass Observation records indicate that individuals who joined up as ARP wardens or volunteers did so for a variety of reasons. Class and political identification caused subtle differences in the reasons given for volunteering. A sense of duty and patriotism were most commonly cited as the primary motives of the upper class and readers of right-wing newspapers. Among other classes and the readers of left-wing newspapers, a desire to 'help' was cited as a primary motive.[51] The desire to 'help' echoes some of the ideas of popular cooperation and community action that the leftist ARP critics had advocated. Yet there may be a mere semantic difference between the two motivations; it is safe to say that most citizens saw themselves as 'active' participants in the wartime state.

As emphasized by the ARP Committee, which included J.B.S. Haldane, repetition of the idea that it was truly a People's War was intended to strengthen morale and to minimize the danger of mob revolt. The Home Office advised the ARP Committee that the population should be constantly informed that 'this is a civilian's war'. If people felt that they were being 'taken into the Government's confidence as never before,' they would better understand and participate in war activities.[52] Taking the people into the government's confidence required treating all citizens with at least rhetorical equality, the position that the leftists had always favoured. It was also an admission that an active model of citizenship was required for the duration of the war and that citizens needed to feel that their interests and contributions were vital. It is not coincidental that many of the enduring images of cooperation and stoicism in the face of the Blitz came from London's East End, the very area that had provoked so much concern over mass chaos. For the purpose of public consumption and public memory fear had been decisively conquered, and the anxious individual of the 1930s had given way to the confident and capable citizen.

NOTES

Introduction

1. Parliamentary Debates, *Commons*, 5th series, CCLXXV (1933), col. 1816.
2. Tami Davis Biddle, *Rhetoric and Reality in Air Warfare: The Evolution of British and American Ideas about Strategic Bombing, 1914–1945* (Princeton, 2002), p. 102.
3. Quoted in Robert Graves and Alan Hodge, *The Long Weekend: A Social History of Great Britain* (London, 1995 [1940]), p. 326.
4. Amy Bell, 'Landscapes of fear: wartime London, 1939–1945,' *Journal of British Studies* IIL (January 2009), pp. 153–175.
5. Edward Glover, Chairman of the British Psycho-Analytical Society, cited in Juliet Gardiner, *The Blitz: The British Under Attack* (London, 2010), p. 177.
6. Richard Overy, *The Morbid Age: Britain Between the Wars* (London, 2009), p. 175.
7. Roxanne Panchasi, *Future Tense: The Culture of Anticipation in France Between the Wars* (Ithaca, 2009), pp. 2–6.
8. Corey Robin, *Fear: The History of a Political Idea* (Oxford, 2004), p. 13.
9. Dan Gardner, *Risk: The Science and Politics of Fear* (Toronto, 2008). See also Nick Pidgeon, Roger E. Kasperson and Paul Slovic, (eds), *The Social Amplification of Risk* (Cambridge, 2003).
10. Adriana Cavarero, William McCuaig, (trans), *Horrorism: Naming Contemporary Violence* (New York, 2009), pp. 66–77.
11. Joanna Bourke, 'Fear and anxiety: writing about emotion in history' *History Workshop Journal* LV (Spring 2003), p. 114.
12. William Reddy, *The Navigation of Feeling: A Framework for the History of Emotions* (Cambridge, 2001). For a good overview of current theory in emotional history, see Jan Plamper, 'The History of Emotions: An Interview with William Reddy, Barbara Rosenwein, and Peter Stearns,' *History and Theory* IL (May 2010), pp. 237–265.

13. Joanna Bourke, *Fear: A Cultural History* (London, 2005) and Bourke: 'Fear and anxiety.'

14. Bourke: 'Fear and anxiety,' p. 115.

15. Michael Roper, 'Between manliness and masculinity: The "war generation" and the psychology of fear in Britain, 1914–1950,' *Journal of British Studies* XXXXIV (April 2006), pp. 343–362 and Martin Francis, *The Flyer: British Culture and the Royal Air Force, 1939–1945* (Oxford, 2008). See also Martin Francis, 'Tears, Tantrums, and Bared Teeth: The Emotional Economy of Three Conservative Prime Ministers, 1951–1963,' *Journal of British Studies* XXXXI, no. 3 (2002), pp. 354–387.

16. Panchasi: *Future Tense*, p. 2.

17. Bourke: 'Fear and anxiety,' pp. 123–126.

18. Richard Titmuss, *Problems of Social Policy* (London: HMSO, 1950) and Terence O'Brien, *Civil Defence* (London: HMSO, 1955).

19. Robin Woolven, 'Civil defence in London 1935–1945: The formation and implementation of the policy for, and the performance of, the A.R.P. (later C.D.) services in London' (PhD. Diss., University of London, 2002), pp. 22–23.

20. Joseph S. Meisel, 'Air raid shelter policy and its critics in Britain before the Second World War,' *Twentieth Century British History*, V, no. 3 (1994).

21. Robin Woolven, 'London, Munich, and ARP,' *Journal of the Royal United Services Institute*, XXXXIII (1998); 'Air Raid Precautions in St Pancras, 1935–45: The Borough Against the German Air Force,' *Camden History Review*, XVI (1989), and 'First in the Country: Dr Richard Tee and Air Raid Precautions,' *Hackney History*, VI (2000).

22. Robert Mackay, *Half the Battle: Civilian Morale in Britain during the Second World War* (Manchester, 2001), p. 1

23. Angus Calder, *The Myth of the Blitz* (London, 1992); John Gregg, *The Shelter of The Tubes: Tube Sheltering in London* (Harrow Weald, 2001); Philip Ziegler, *London at War, 1939–1945* (London, 1995), and Helen Jones, *British Civilians in the Front Line: Air Raids, Productivity and Wartime Culture, 1939–45* (Manchester, 2006).

24. Susan Grayzel, *At Home and Under Fire: Air Raids and Culture in Britain from the Great War to the Blitz* (Cambridge, 2012), pp. 16, 22.

25. Angus Calder, *The Myth of the Blitz* (London, 1992).

26. Steven Fielding, 'What did 'the people' want?: The meaning of the 1945 general election,' *The Historical Journal*, XXXV, no. 3 (1992), pp. 623–639 and Steven Fielding, Peter Thompson, and Nick Tiratsoo, *'England Arise!': The Labour Party and Popular Politics in 1940s Britain.* (Manchester, 1995).

27. Mackay: *Half the Battle*.

28. Sonya O. Rose, *Which People's War? National Identity and Citizenship in Britain 1939–1945* (Oxford, 2003), pp. 14, 20.

29. Lucy Noakes, *War and the British: Gender, Memory and National Identity* (London, 1998) and Grayzel: *At Home and Under Fire*.

30. Marjorie Morgan, *National Identities and Travel in Victorian Britain* (New York, 2001).

31. Krishan Kumar, *The Making of English National Identity* (Cambridge, 2003) and Linda Colley, *Britons: Forging the Nation, 1707–1837* (New Haven, 1992) offer interpretations on the formulation of a common 'Britishness'.

Chapter 1   Situating Moods – Aviation Enthusiasts and Fear

1. Cecil Beaton, *Winged Squadrons* (London, 1942), pp. 6, 46.

2. Martin Pugh, *'We Danced All Night': A Social History of Britain Between the Wars* (London, 2008), p. 304.

3. Roy Hattersley, *The Edwardians* (London, 2004), p. 429.

4. Pugh: *'We Danced All Night'*, p. 303.

5. 'War aces who cheated death.' *Flying*, 14 May 1938.

6. Linda R. Robertson, *The Dream of Civilized Warfare* (Minneapolis, 2003), pp. 3–4, and also see Chapters 6 and 8.

7. Henry Newbolt, *Tales of the Great War* (London, 1916), pp. 248–49.

8. Francis: *The Flyer*, Chapter 2.

9. Tom Mitford from a letter to his mother in August 1930 about an aerial outing with Clementine and Winston Churchill, Sir Samuel Hoare and his wife, and 'Aircraftsman Shaw': 'I am a little disappointed with Shaw. He looks just like any other private in the air-force, is very short and has in his five years of service become quite hardened [. . .]. It is curious that he should enjoy such a life, with no responsibilities, after being almost king in Arabia. Some say it is inverted vanity: he would have accepted a kingship, but as he didn't get it, he preferred to bury himself and hide away.' Deborah Mitford, *Wait for Me!* (New York, 2010), p. 57.

10. Francis: *The Flyer*, Chapter 5. Martin details a variety of techniques used to manage fear, pp. 106–130.

11. David Edgerton, *England and the Aeroplane: An Essay on a Militant and Technological Nation* (London, 1991) and Robert Wohl, *The Spectacle of Flight: Aviation and the Western Imagination: 1920–1950* (New Haven, 2005).

12. Azar Gat argues that Jules Verne and his ilk represent a high tide of optimistic democratic-liberalism. Gat, *Fascist and Liberal Visions of War: Fuller, Liddell Hart, Douhet, and Other Modernists* (Oxford, 1998), p. 6.

13. Ian Patterson, *Guernica and Total War* (Cambridge, 2007), p. 132.

14. *Daily Telegraph*, 7 November 1933, p. 13. The ubiquitous Basil Liddell Hart was not always respected within government circles. As Duff Cooper noted, 'his name stinks at the War Office'. Duff Cooper (John Julius Norwich, ed), *The Duff Cooper Diaries: 1915–1951* (London, 2005), p. 226. Duff Cooper also admitted in his diaries that he had a personal reason to dislike Liddell Hart, who had given his book *Haig* Vol. 1 a detrimental review.

15. J.F.C. Fuller, *The Reformation of Warfare* (New York, 1923), p. 150.

16. T.H. Wintringham, *The Coming World War* (New York, 1935), pp. 34–39.

17. Tom Harrisson and Charles Madge, (eds) *War Begins at Home: By Mass Observation* (London, 1940), p. 40.

18. Neville Jones, *The Beginnings of Strategic Air Power: A History of the British Bomber Force 1923–1939* (London, 1987), pp. 34–35.

19. Graves and Hodge: *The Long Weekend*, see Chapter 26.

20. Phrase used by Alison Light in *Femininity, Literature and Conservatism between the Wars* (London, 1991).

21. John Lucas, *The Radical Twenties: Writing, Politics and Culture* (New Brunswick, 1999), p. 137.

22. Roy Hattersley, *Borrowed Time: The Story of Britain Between the Wars* (London, 2007). Also see Ronald Blythe, *The Age of Illusion: England in the Twenties and Thirties, 1919–1940* (London, 1963).

23. Overy: *The Morbid Age.*

24. Laurence Goldstein, *The Flying Machine and Modern Literature* (London, 1986), p. 64.

25. Ignatius Frederick Clarke, *Voices Prophesying War, 1763–1984* (Oxford, 1966). Also see John Gooch, *The Prospect of War: Studies in British Defence Policy, 1847–1942* (London, 1981).

26. Daniel Pick, *War Machine: The Rationalization of Slaughter in the Modern Age* (New Haven, 1993).

27. Martin Ceadel, 'Popular fiction and the next war, 1918–39,' in Frank Gloversmith, (ed) *Class, Culture and Social Change: A New View of the 1930s* (Sussex, 1980). Ceadel and Clarke are the major works on 'next war' fiction. See also Grayzel: *At Home and Under Fire*, Chapter 4.

28. Michael Paris, *Winged Warfare: The Literature and Theory of Aerial Warfare in Britain, 1859–1917* (Manchester, 1992), p. 167.

29. George Orwell, *Keep the Aspidistra Flying* (London, 1936) and *Coming Up for Air* (London, 1939).

30. James W. Hammond, *Poison Gas: The Myth Versus Reality* (Westport, 1999), p. 14.

31. Earl Halsbury, *1944* (London, 1926), p. 7.

32. Neville Jones, *The Beginnings of Strategic Air Power: A History of the British Bomber Force 1923–1939* (London, 1987), p. 41, and Edward M. Spiers, *Chemical Warfare* (Urbana and Chicago, 1986), p. 52.

33. Ceadel: 'Popular fiction and the next war,' p. 171.

34. Wohl: *The Spectacle of Flight*, p. 308.

35. Sebastian Faulks, *The Fatal Englishman: Three Short Lives* (London, 1996), p. 198.

36. Christopher Caudwell, *Studies in a Dying Culture; with an Introduction by John Strachey* (London, 1938), pp. 38–39. Born Christopher St John Sprigg, he was killed in action in Spain in 1937, fighting in the International Brigades for the Republican cause.

37. Patterson: *Guernica and Total War*, p. 117.

38. Wohl: *The Spectacle of Flight*, p. 51.

39. Michael Paris, *Warrior Nation: Images of War in British Popular Culture* (London, 1999), p. 157.
40. Colin Cook, 'A Fascist memory: Oswald Mosley and the myth of the airman,' *European Review of History*, IV, no. 2 (1997), p. 149.
41. Wohl: *The Spectacle of Flight*, p. 49.
42. Peter Fritzsche, *A Nation of Fliers: German Aviation and the Popular Imagination* (Cambridge, 1994).
43. Wohl: *The Spectacle of Flight*, p. 277.
44. Patterson: *Guernica and Total War*, pp. 115–116.
45. Peter Mandler, 'Against 'Englishness': English culture and the limits to rural nostalgia, 1850–1940,' *Transactions of the Royal Historical Society*, 6th Series, vol. 7, (1997).
46. Martin Pugh, *'Hurrah for the Blackshirts!': Fascists and Fascism in Britain Between the Wars* (London, 2005), p. 316.
47. Edgerton: *England and the Aeroplane*, pp. 47–48.
48. Robert Skidelsky, *Oswald Mosley* (New York, 1975), p. 320.
49. Edgerton: *England and the Aeroplane*, p. 49.
50. Richard Griffiths, *Fellow Travellers of the Right: British Enthusiasts for Nazi Germany, 1933–9* (London, 1980).
51. Robert Benewick, *The Fascist Movement in Britain* (London, 1969), p. 95.
52. Griffiths: *Fellow Travellers of the Right*, p. 138.
53. Bernard Rieger, 'From "Duels in the clouds" to "exterminating attacks": legitimizing aerial warfare in Britain and Germany, 1914–5,' in Stuart Carroll, (ed) *Cultures of Violence: Interpersonal Violence in Historical Perspective* (London, 2007), pp. 247–249. For a contemporary source, see B. Wherry Anderson, *The Romance of Air-Fighting* (London, 1917).
54. Cook: 'A Fascist memory.'

Chapter 2 Anticipating New Weapons and Theorizing Aerial Warfare

1. Goldstein: *The Flying Machine and Modern Literature*, p. 73, quoting a 1915 letter by D.H. Lawrence.
2. Davis Biddle: *Rhetoric and Reality in Air Warfare*, p. 22
3. NA, AIR 9/69, September 1922 report, citing 1916 sources. See also Brock Millman, 'British home defence planning and civil dissent, 1917–1918,' *War in History*, V/2, (April 1998), p. 220.
4. O'Brien: *Civil Defence*, p. 19.
5. Michael S. Sherry, *The Rise of American Air Power: The Creation of Armageddon* (New Haven, 1987), p. 3, and Robin Neillands, *The Bomber War: Arthur Harris and the Allied Bomber Offensive 1939–1945* (London, 2001), p. 23. The title of one biography captures the image of the man: Andrew Boyle, *Trenchard: Man of Vision* (London, 1962).

6. Davis Biddle: *Rhetoric and Reality in Air Warfare*, p. 80, and Neillands: *The Bomber War*, p.14.
7. Gat: *Fascist and Liberal Visions of War: Fuller, Liddell Hart, Douhet, and Other Modernists*, p. 56.
8. Malcolm Smith, '"A matter of faith": British strategic air doctrine before 1939,' *Journal of Contemporary History*, V (1980), pp. 423–5. The term 'knock-out' blow was used in a general military sense throughout the First World War. Throughout the 1920s it started to refer solely to air power capabilities. See Bialer: *The Shadow of the Bomber*, pp. 39–46, 129.
9. *Manchester Guardian*, 10 March 1916, p. 5.
10. Barry D. Powers, *Strategy Without Slide-Rule: British Air Strategy 1914–1939* (London, 1976), pp. 55–59. Demands for reprisal air raids were also featured in letters to the editor in *The Times*, 16 June 1917, p. 7.
11. Davis Biddle: *Rhetoric and Reality in Air Warfare*, p. 22.
12. Sherry: *The Rise of American Air Power*, p. 15, and *Scot Robertson, The Development of RAF Strategic Bombing Doctrine, 1919–1939* (London, 1995), pp. 16–18.
13. Stephen Budiansky, *Air Power: The Men, Machines, and Ideas that Revolutionized War, From Kitty Hawk to Gulf War II* (New York, 2004), p. 97.
14. Bell: 'Landscapes of fear,' p. 154.
15. London School of Economics, Richard Titmuss Papers, Titmuss_Add_1/1, June 1946 memorandum.
16. Grayzel: *At Home and Under Fire*, pp. 131–133.
17. O'Brien: *Civil Defence*, p. 12–15.
18. Cornelli Barnett, *The Collapse of British Power* (London, 1972), p. 437.
19. Sherry: *The Rise of American Air Power*, p. x.
20. Priya Satia, 'The defense of inhumanity: Air control and the British idea of Arabia,' *American Historical Review*, III (2006), pp. 16–51, and *Spies in Arabia: The Great War and the Cultural Foundations of Britain's Covert Empire in the Middle East* (Oxford, 2008).
21. T.E. Lawrence to H.M. Trenchard in David Garnett, (ed), *Letters of T.E. Lawrence* (London, 1938), pp. 662–663.
22. Powers: *Strategy Without Slide-Rule*, pp. 138–140.
23. Brian Bond, *British Military Policy Between the Two World Wars* (Oxford, 1980), p. 85.
24. David E. Omissi, *Air Power and Colonial Control, The Royal Air Force, 1919–1939* (Manchester, 1990), pp. 16, 37.
25. King's College London, Liddell Hart Military Archives, PRC Groves Files, 3(f), citing a secret memo from the Chief of Air Staff, 18 November 1918.
26. David Edgerton, *Warfare State: Britain, 1920–1970* (Cambridge, 2006), p. 43. Also see Edgerton's *Britain's War Machine: Weapons, Resources and Experts in the Second World War* (London, 2011).
27. Elizabeth Kier, *Imagining War: French and British Military Doctrine Between the Wars* (Princeton, 1997), p. 16.

28. For example, P.R.C. Groves, 'Our disastrous air policy; A defenceless country, neglect of civil aviation,' *The Times*, 6 June 1922, p. 15.
29. P.R.C. Groves, *Behind the Smoke-Screen* (London, 1934).
30. J.M. Spaight, *Air Power and the Next War* (London, 1938). Earlier in the decade he had also published *Air Power and the Cities* (London, 1930).
31. The most popular of these were L.E.O. Charlton, *War Over England* (London, 1936) and *The Menace of the Clouds* (London, 1937). Also penned by a retired RAF Major: C.C. Turner, *Britain's Air Peril: The Danger of Neglect, Together with Considerations on the Role of An Air Force* (London, [nd]).
32. H. Montgomery Hyde, *British Air Policy Between the Wars 1918–1939* (London, 1976), p. 491.
33. NA, AIR 9/76, File 1, Air Staff memo, 10 September 1937.
34. T.H. O'Brien, 'Hodsoll, Sir (Eric) John (1894–1971),' in *Oxford Dictionary of National Biography*, H.C.G. Matthew and B. Harrison, (eds), (Oxford, 2004); online ed. Lawrence Goldman, May 2006.
35. Central Office of Information, *The Aircraft Builders: An Account of British Aircraft Production 1935–1945* (London, 1947), p. 9.
36. Powers: *Strategy Without Slide-Rule*, p. 123.
37. For example, Sir Norman Brook was concerned that drafts of Richard Titmuss' *Problems of Social Policy* (London, 1950) were unnecessarily critical of the Air Staff, heads of the ministries, and the civil servants in the Home Office. Richard Titmuss Papers, Titmuss_Add1 7/44, File 4. Terence O'Brien notes that the ARP Department began very small, and did not expand until early 1938, when headquarters staff numbered 120 people, with 240 working outside London. O'Brien: *Civil Defence*, p. 112.
38. Home Office, *Personal Protection Against Gas* (London, 1937) and *The Duties of Air Raid Wardens* (London, 1938). Other handbooks included *Anti-Gas Precautions and First Aid for Air Raid Casualties* (London, 1935) and *Incendiary Bombs and Fire Precautions* (London, 1939).
39. Home Office, *Anti-Gas Precautions and First Aid for Air Raid Casualties* (London, 1935) sold 86,350 copies. This was 'Handbook No.2' in the Home Office series. The handbooks were numbered according to when they were planned, not the date of publishing, occasioning some confusion. Handbook No. 1 was initially titled *Air Raid Precautions in the Home* but it was published in 1936 as *Personal Protection Against Gas*. Joseph S. Meisel, 'Air raid shelter policy and its critics in Britain before the Second World War' *Twentieth Century British History*, V/3 (1994), p. 304. Home Office records indicate that by 1939, with the threat of war imminent, 700,000 copies had been printed of Handbook Nos. 1–4, and that 15.5 million copies of No. 5, *Fire precautions in war time*, were due to be printed for mass distribution. NA, HO 45/18207, 1939 Memorandum, ARP Department.
40. NA, HO 45/17196, Draft memo from the Treasury to the House of Lords on the cost of civilian respirators.

41. Norman Hammer, *A Catechism of Air Raid Precautions*, 5th edn (London, 1939), pp. 11–12.
42. *Parliamentary Debates*, Commons, 5th series, CCCXXIX (1937), col. 1937.
43. Home Office, *The Protection of Your Home Against Air Raids* (London, 1938).
44. *Parliamentary Debates*, Commons, 5th series, CCCXXXV (1938), cols. 1698–1702.
45. NA, HO 45/18802, Memorandum by Admiral Taylor, 16 July 1938, pp. 1–3.
46. *Parliamentary Debates*, Commons, 5th series, CCXXIV (1938), col. 181.
47. Robin Woolven, 'London, Munich, and ARP,' *Journal of the Royal United Services Institute*, XXXXIII (1998), p. 56.
48. *Eastern Evening News*, 18 March 1938, p. 1.
49. NA, CAB 16/197, The Committee of Imperial Defence Civil Defence (Policy) Sub-Committee decided, with Sir Samuel Hoare, that employers should take 'reasonable' steps to make safe shelters for their employees, with the Lord Privy Seal serving as the arbiter of what was 'reasonable'. Minutes of the first meeting of the sub-committee, 12 December 1938, pp. 1–12.
50. *Time and Tide*, XVIII/47 (20 November 1937), p. 1539, XIX, no. 40 (1 October 1938), p. 1334, and XIX/7 (12 February 1938).
51. O'Brien: *Civil Defence*, p. 191.
52. John Gregg, *The Shelter of the Tubes: Tube Sheltering in London* (Harrow Weald, 2001), p. 10.
53. House of Commons Parliamentary Papers, 1938–39, Cmd. 6055, Sectional steel shelters: investigation of the standard of protection afforded, pp. 2–8.
54. NA, CAB 16/197, CID Civil Defence (Policy) Sub-Committee, Minutes of the fifth meeting of the sub-committee, 14 April 1939, p. 93.

Chapter 3   'The Dew of Death' – Duelling Perspectives on Poison Gas

1. B.H. Liddell Hart, *Paris: or the Future of War* (New York, 1925), p. 45.
2. Miles D. Wyndham 'The idea of chemical warfare in modern times,' *Journal of the History of Ideas*, XXXI/2 (April-June 1970), pp. 297–304.
3. Joel A. Vilensky, *Dew of Death: The Story of Lewisite, America's World War I Weapon of Mass Destruction* (Bloomington and Indianapolis, 2005), Chapter 8.
4. See particularly Richard M. Price, *The Chemical Weapons Taboo* (Ithaca, 1997), and Hammond, James W., Jr. *Poison Gas: The Myth Versus Reality.* (Westport, 1999).
5. Marion Girard, *A Strange and Formidable Weapon: British Responses to World War I Poison Gas* (Lincoln, 2008).
6. Price: *The Chemical Weapons Taboo*, pp. 1–3, 15–16.
7. Price: *The Chemical Weapons Taboo*, p. 71.

8. F.L. Haber, *The Poisonous Cloud: Chemical Warfare in the First World War* (Oxford, 1986), p. 295.
9. Spiers: *Chemical Warfare*, p. 47.
10. Robert Harris and Jeremy Paxman, *A Higher Form of Killing: The Secret Story of Gas and Germ Warfare* (London, 1982).
11. Haber: *The Poisonous Cloud*, p. 291.
12. Spiers: *Chemical Warfare*, p. 40.
13. Werskey, *The Visible College* (London, 1978), p. 59.
14. Donald Richter, *Chemical Soldiers: British Gas Warfare in World War I* (Lawrence, 1992), pp. 10, 226.
15. J.B.S. Haldane, *Callinicus: A Defence of Chemical Warfare* (London, 1925), p. 34.
16. Girard: *A Strange and Formidable Weapon*, p. 167.
17. Vilensky: *Dew of Death*, pp. 90–91.
18. Union of Democratic Control, *Poison Gas* (London, 1935), pp. 29, 39.
19. F.R. Leavis, *Mass Civilization and Minority Culture (Minority Pamphlets no. 1)* (Cambridge, 1930), p. 11, citing D.H. Lawrence's *Fantasia of the Unconscious and Psychoanalysis*.
20. Haber: *The Poisonous Cloud*, p. 297.
21. Union of Democratic Control, *The Secret International: Armament Firms at Work* (London, 1932) and *An Exposure of the War Machine* (London, 1933).
22. London School of Economics, Papers of the Fabian Society, J36/5, Item 1, S.45, Verbatim report to the Royal Commission on the Private Manufacture of and Trading in Arms.
23. Papers of the Fabian Society, J36/5, Item 1, S.45.
24. Labour Party, *The Sky's The Limit! Plain Words on Plane Profits* (London, c. 1934) and *Who's Who in Arms* (London, 1935). These publications were part of the Union of Democratic Control's presentation to the Royal Commission on Arms in 1935. Papers of the Fabian Society, J37/1. Philip Noel-Baker, *Hawkers of Death: The Private Manufacture and Trade in Arms* (London, 1935).
25. Girard: *A Strange and Formidable Weapon*, p. 160.
26. *New Statesman and Nation*, X/228 (July 6 1935), pp. 4–6.
27. *Time and Tide*, XVII/14 (4 April 1936), p. 462. Other press accounts included, William Harris 'The Poison-Gas Campaign' in *The Spectator*, who concluded that: 'The citizens of this and other countries have read for 6 months and more with sickened disgust of Italian military successes owed to the aeroplanes.' *The Spectator*, 10 April 1936. *The Times* also included eye-witness accounts from 1 March 1936.
28. Grayzel: *At Home and Under Fire*, pp. 181–182.
29. Socialist Medical Association, *Gas Attacks: Is There any Protection?* (London, 1936).
30. Brett Holman, 'World police for world peace: British internationalism and the threat of a knock-out blow from the air, 1919–1945,' *War in History* XVII/3 (2010), pp. 313–332.

31. Norman Angell, *The Menace to Our National Defence* (London, 1934), pp. 61–64, 160.

32. Heinz Liepmann, *Death From the Skies: A Study of Gas and Microbial Warfare* (London, 1937), p. 232.

33. Aldous Huxley, (ed) *An Encyclopaedia of Pacifism* (London, 1937), p. 53.

34. Dr G. Woker 'Chemical and bacteriological warfare' in Geneva Inter-Parliamentary Union, *What Would Be the Character of a New War?* (London, 1933), p. 355.

35. Storm Jameson, *In the Second Year* (London, 1936).

36. Gerald Heard, 'And suppose we fail? After the next war' in Storm Jameson, (ed), *Challenge to Death* (London, 1934), pp. 166–167.

37. Girard: *A Strange and Formidable Weapon*, p. 159.

38. National Archives, HO 45/17591, Letters were dispatched to the Air ministry over Professor Lindemann's conviction that German was building a sodium/potassium alloy bomb.

39. Otto Lehmann-Russbuett, *Germany's Air Force*, (London, 1935) (With an Introduction by Wickham Steed and an Appendix).

40. Haber: *The Poisonous Cloud*, p. 304. Haber maintains that the gas masks 'uselessness against arsenicals remained a well-kept secret. The citizenry, with their little respirators, had no idea what arsenicals were and remained blissfully ignorant of the most elementary precautions to be taken [against mustard gas].'

41. Vilensky: *Dew of Death*, pp. 80–85, 98–99. Mysterious 'explosions' at the testing station are also recorded in Home Office documents. HO 45/17591.

42. Maj-Gen Sir Henry Thuillier, *Gas in the Next War* (London, 1939), pp. 105–120.

43. Thuillier: *Gas in the Next War*, pp. 88, 138.

44. See H. Montgomery Hyde and G. R. Falkiner Nuttall, *Air Defence and the Civil Population* (London 1937).

45. B.C. Dening, *Modern War: Armies, not Air Forces, Decide Wars* (Hampshire, 1937).

46. E.L. Spears, 'The War of the Future,' *The Spectator*, 25 October 1930, pp. 573–574.

47. 'Nonsense About Poison Gas: How Danger To Life IS Prevented, A Chemist's Assurance,' *The Times*, 27 January 1934, p. 7.

48. One example is Alan Brooksbank, *Traps for Young Soldiers and Civilians in Chemical (Gas) Warfare* (Sydney, 1937), p. 5. An Australian anti-gas NCO in World War I, he wrote several books on the subject.

49. F.N. Pickett, *Don't Be Afraid of Poison Gas: Hints for Civilians in the Event of a Poison Gas Attack* (London, 1934), p. 11. Pickett was praised as an expert and friend by Sir Malcolm Campbell: *The Peril From the Air* (London, 1937).

50. James Kendall, *Breathe Freely! The Truth About Poison Gas* (London, 1938). Kendall is said to have advocated a peaceful settlement with fascists powers in the 1930s. Werskey: *The Visible College*, p. 227.

51. Augustin M. Prentiss, *Chemicals in War: A Treatise on Chemical Warfare* (New York, 1937), pp. vii–viii. There is evidence that the two men read each other's work, with Kendall citing the 'sound' findings of Colonel Prentiss on the question of whether a 'supergas' could ever be invented.

52. Werksey: *The Visible College*, p. 227. And see J. Davidson Pratt, *Gas Defence* (London, 1935).

53. C.H. Foulkes, *'Gas!' The Story of the Special Brigade* (London, 1934) critiqued in Richter: *Chemical Soldiers*. Following the First World War, Foulkes advocated using gas against Afghan rebels, believing that gas was now accepted as a fair weapon, and that tribesmen were not covered by Hague Conventions. (Liddell Hart Centre for Military Archives, Foulkes Papers, J-60.)

54. C.H. Foulkes, *Commonsense and ARP: A Practical Guide for Householders and Business Managers* (London, 1939).

Chapter 4   C.G. Grey and J.B.S. Haldane – Two Professional Men, Two Ideologies

1. *Journal of the Air Raid Protection Institute*, I/2 (February 1939), pp. 126–29.

2. Harald Penrose, quoted in Edgerton: *England and the Aeroplane*, pp. 57–58.

3. Griffiths: *Fellow Travellers of the Right*, pp. 124–125.

4. See Thurston James, 'Charles Grey and his pungent pen: personal recollections of a great aeronautical journalist' *Journal of the Royal Aeronautical Society* LXXIII/706, (October 1969), pp. 839–846.

5. Harald Penrose, *British Aviation: The Adventuring Years, 1920–1929* (London, 1973), p. 2.

6. *The Times*, 23 December 1953, p. 9.

7. Edgerton: *England and the Aeroplane*, p. 57.

8. Errol W. Martyn, 'Grey, Charles Grey (1875–1953),' in *Oxford Dictionary of National Biography*, H.C.G. Matthew and Brian Harrison (ed) (Oxford, 2004), online ed.

9. Cook: 'A Fascist Memory,' p. 148.

10. Skidelsky: *Oswald Mosley*, p. 320.

11. *Sunday Express*, 23 July 1939, p. 1.

12. Sir Walter Raleigh, *The War in the Air* (vol.1) cited in Edgerton: *England and the Aeroplane*, p. 50.

13. C.G. Grey, *British Fighter Planes* (London, 1941).

14. Robertson: *The Dream of Civilized Warfare*, p. 183.

15. Manfred Freiherr von Richthofen, *The Red Air Fighter*. (London, 1918), pp. 10–11. With Preface and Explanatory Notes by C.G. Grey.

16. Grey Papers, File 10, R. Winninger to Grey, 20 April 1936.

17. Captain Jose Larios, *Combat Over Spain: Memoirs of a Nationalist Fighter Pilot, 1936–1939* (London, 1968), p. 277. A similar volume was Jesús Salas

Larrazábal, trans. (Margaret A. Kelley, trans, David Mondey, ed) *Air War Over Spain* (London, 1969).

18. Patterson: *Guernica and Total War*, pp. 35–46.
19. *The Aeroplane*, 20 January 1937, pp. 62–64, 29 March 1938, p. 392, and 18 May 1938.
20. James: 'Charles Grey and his Pungent Pen,' quoting C.G. Grey from 1931, p. 848.
21. Pugh: '*We Danced All Night*', p. 311.
22. Pugh: '*We Danced All Night*', p. 309.
23. C.G. Grey Papers, Royal Aeronautical Society (National Aerospace Library), File 9, Samuel Hoare to C.G. Grey, 13 June 1929. Sir Eric Geddes headed a Committee on National Expenditure convened in 1921 to reduce governmental commitments.
24. Thurston: 'Charles Grey and his pungent pen,' p. 850.
25. Thurston: 'Charles Grey and his pungent pen,' p. 849.
26. *The Aeroplane*, 29 December 1937, pp. 811–812.
27. *The Aeroplane* 15 June 1938, pp. 737–738.
28. Peter Berresford Ellis and Jennifer Schofield, *Biggles! The Life Story of Captain W.E. Johns, Creator of Biggles, Worruls, Gimlet and Steeley* (London, 1993), p. 149.
29. *Flight*, 31 August 1939, p. 200.
30. Pugh: '*We Danced All Night*', p. 312.
31. Juliet Gardiner, *The Thirties: An Intimate History* (London, 2010), p. 193.
32. J.D. Bernal, *The Social Function of Science* (London, 1939).
33. Werskey: *The Visible College*, pp. 139–161.
34. J.B.S. Haldane, *A.R.P.* (London, 1938), pp. 66–76. The communist military man T.H. Wintringham also felt that offensive air policy would lead to an escalated arms race and a European war. T.H. Wintringham, *Air Raid Warning! Why the Royal Air Force is to be Doubled* (London, 1934), p. 4.
35. Ronald Clark, *J.B.S.: The Life and Work of J.B.S. Haldane* (Oxford, 1984), p. 126.
36. BBC Newscast, 'Civil War From Both Sides,' 15 January 1937, cited in Shelmerdine, *British Representations of the Spanish Civil War* (Manchester, 2006), p. 126.
37. *Hampstead and Highgate Express*, 20 February 1937, p. 7.
38. Neal Wood, *Communism and British Intellectuals* (New York, 1959), p. 54.
39. Haldane Papers, Box 30 1/a, J.B.S. Haldane to Lt. Col Harry M. Balfour, 3 November, 1939.
40. Communist Party of Great Britain, *A.R.P. for Hampstead* (London, 1938), p. 2.
41. Haldane Papers, Box 30, 1/b, M.S. Wilde to Victor Gollancz, 30 March 1938.
42. *Left News*, no. XXVI (May 1938), p. 836. Victor Gollancz explicitly warned Haldane of the potential difficulty of publishing his scientific findings on ARP, suspecting that booksellers had an unofficial barrier to carrying 'leftist' material. Gollancz assured Haldane of a minimum print run of 50,000 copies. Haldane Papers, Box 30, 1/b, Victor Gollancz to J.B.S. Haldane, 31 March 1938.
43. Home Office: *The Protection of Your Home Against Air Raids*.

44. Haldane: *A.R.P.*, 77.
45. A reviewer in *The Times* referred to this as 'jeering and [with] a pervading flavour of political generalization'. *The Times*, 20 September 1938, p. 7.
46. Both quotations, Haldane: *A.R.P.*, pp 117–118, 119.
47. Needham Papers, K.38, Needham typescript on ARP, c. 1938.
48. Haldane: *A.R.P.*, p. 125.
49. Haldane: *A.R.P.*, p. 173.
50. Haldane: *A.R.P.*, p. 254.
51. Haldane: *How to be Safe from Air Raids* (London, 1938), pp. 38–39.
52. Haldane Papers, Box 30/4 Clipping of *Keystone* article, October/November 1938. It is unclear whether Haldane consulted with engineers when writing *A.R.P.* In his Left Book Club pamphlet *How to be Safe From Air Raids*, he noted that 'my own scheme is probably not so good as the others [he cites the plan by the AASTA]. I am not an engineer.' Haldane: *How to Be Safe From Air Raids*, p. 37.
53. *The Aeroplane*, 8 April 1936, p. 430.
54. Kendall: *Breathe Freely! The Truth About Poison Gas*.
55. *Journal of the Air Raid Protection Institute*, I/1 (December 1938), p. 1. The Institute was founded in 1938, working closely with the Home Office but also consulting a variety of experts from the Royal Institute of British Architects, the Institution of Civil Engineers, and continental experts.
56. Communist Party of Great Britain, London District Committee, *A.R.P. for Londoners: In the Opinion of the Experts only the Tunnel Scheme Can Give Real Protection* (London, 1938).
57. *Labour Monthly*, XX (1938), p. 711.
58. Communist Party of Great Britain: *A.R.P. for Hampstead*.
59. Haldane: *A.R.P.*, pp. 202–210.
60. *The Times*, 20 September 1938, p. 7.

Chapter 5   The Psychology of the Terror Victim in Spain – Morale and Defiance

1. Angela Jackson, *British Women and the Spanish Civil War* (London, 2002), p. 199.
2. *Finsbury Citizen*, April 1939, p. 1.
3. Sherry: *The Rise of American Air Power*, p. 14.
4. Goldstein: *The Flying Machine and Modern Literature*, p. 76.
5. O'Brien: *Civil Defence*, p. 18.
6. Davis Biddle: *Rhetoric and Reality in Air Warfare*, p. 23, and Powers: *Strategy Without Slide-Rule*, pp. 61–63.
7. Titmuss: *Problems of Social Policy*, p. 22.
8. Bourke: *Fear*, p. 8.
9. Bell: 'Landscapes of fear,' pp. 155–159, 175.
10. See Chapter 3, 'Civilians under attack,' in Bourke: *Fear*, pp. 222–254.

11. Peter Stansky and William Abrahams, *Journey to the Frontier: Julian Bell and John Cornford: Their Lives and the 1930s* (London, 1966), p. 313.
12. Shelmerdine: *British Representations of the Spanish Civil War*, p. 3. This reflects the English bias apparent in most accounts of the British in Spain, despite the fact that Welsh and Scottish workers were strongly represented in the British Battalion of the International Brigade.
13. The primary accounts of British involvement in Spain are from Tom Buchanan, *Britain and the Spanish Civil War* (Cambridge, 1997) and *The Impact of the Spanish Civil War on Britain: War, Loss and Memory* (Brighton, 2007). Classics of 1960s scholarship include Stanley Weintraub, *The Last Great Cause: The Intellectuals and the Spanish Civil War* (New York, 1968) and Frederick R. Benson, *Writers in Arms: The Literary Impact of the Spanish Civil War* (New York, 1967). For a compilation and commentary on famous Spanish Civil War writing, see Valentine Cunningham, *Spanish Front, Writers on the Civil War* (Oxford, 1986); *The Penguin Book of Spanish Civil War Verse* (Harmondsworth, 1980), and Hugh Ford, *A Poets' War: British Poets and the Spanish Civil War* (Philadelphia, 1965).
14. The famous *Left Review* Pamphlet 'Authors Takes Sides on the Spanish Civil War' is indicative of the general mood, even if the results were dictated by the highly leading questions: 'Are you for or against the Legal Government and the people of Republican Spain? Are you for or against Franco and Fascism? For it is impossible any longer to take no side.' Given such phrasing, it is highly unlikely that any author would wish to publicly identify against 'Legal Government' and for 'Fascism'. The published results: 127 writers 'FOR the Government', five 'AGAINST the Government', and 17 classified as neutral.
15. At least one poet, Louis MacNeice, admitted that some participants travelled to Spain for 'egotistical' motives or 'sensation-hunting'. Valentine Cunningham, *British Writers of the Thirties* (Oxford, 1989), p. 444.
16. See my 'Writers in Arms and the Just War: The Spanish Civil War, Literary Activism, and Leftist Masculinity,' *Left History*, X/2 (2005), pp. 33–52.
17. Budiansky: *Air Power*, p. 208.
18. Shelmerdine: *British Representations of the Spanish Civil War*, p. 155.
19. Patterson: *Guernica and Total War*, Chapter 1.
20. W.E. Johns, 'Seeing Spain Slaughtered,' *Popular Flying*, March 1939, Cunningham: *Spanish Front*, pp. 76–77.
21. Budiansky: *Air Power*, pp. 202–203.
22. Haldane: *A.R.P.*, p. 51.
23. John Langdon-Davies, *Air Raid: The Technique of Silent Approach, High Explosive, Panic* (London, 1938).
24. G.L. Steer, *The Tree of Gernika: A Field Study of Modern War* (London, 1938), p. 258.
25. Henry Blythe, *Spain Over Britain: A Study of the Strategical Effect of Italian Intervention on the Defence of the British Empire* (London, 1937).
26. Budiansky: *Air Power*, pp. 205–208.
27. Esmond Romilly, *Boadilla* (London, 1937), p. 194.

28. *The Times*, 17 February 1938, p. 8.
29. *Parliamentary Debates*, Commons, 5th series, CCCXXXVI (1938), col. 2105.
30. Budiansky: *Air Power*, p. 208.
31. Haldane: *A.R.P.*, p. 48.
32. Haldane: *A.R.P.*, p. 55.
33. G.B. Shirlaw, *Casualty: Training, Organisation and Administration of Civil Defence Casualty Services* (London, 1940), p. 3. Shirlaw was also an Associate Fellow of the ARP Institute.
34. Louis MacNeice, *The Strings are False: An Unfinished Autobiography* (London, 1965), p. 180.
35. Diary of Charles Ritchie in Penelope Middelboe, Donald Fry and Christopher Grace, (eds), *We Shall Never Surrender: Wartime Diaries 1939–1945* (London, 2011), p. 92.
36. George Orwell, *Homage to Catalonia*, cited in Peter Davison, (ed) *Orwell in Spain: The Full Text of Homage to Catalonia with Associated Articles, Reviews and Letters from the Complete Works of George Orwell* (London, 2001), p. 139.
37. *Parliamentary Debates*, Commons, 5th series, CCCXXXIII (1938), col. 1354.
38. *Architects' Journal*, 7 July 1939, p. 17. Haldane noted that as a conservative, Sandys was 'unlikely to exaggerate facts in such a way as to discredit the value of the precautions taken or proposed by the present Government'. Haldane: *A.R.P*, p. 54.
39. *The Times*, 17 February 1938, p. 8.
40. Letter to the editor, J.N. Fletcher, 'A.R.P. Dispersion In Family Groups,' *The Times*, 15 February 1938, p. 10. Fletcher prefaced his letter by disputing the claim of the leftist critics – derived from Spain – that public shelters could be feasibly constructed in wartime.
41. Office of the Lord Privy Seal, *Air Raid Shelters: Report of the Lord Privy Seal's Conference* (London, 1939), p. 24.
42. Grayzel: *At Home and Under Fire*, p. 188.
43. See Mark Peattie, Edward J. Drea, and Hans van de Ven, (eds), *The Battle for China: Essays on the Military History of the Sino-Japanese War of 1937–1945* (Stanford, 2011).
44. *Evening Standard*, 8 February 1939, p. 6.
45. Peter Jones, *Ove Arup: Masterbuilder of the Twentieth Century* (New Haven, 2006), p. 68.
46. *The Times*, 23 December 1938, p. 9.
47. Haldane: *A.R.P.* p. 52. Haldane discounted the value of basement and cellar shelters, though this is likely to be the shelter provided 'under homes'.
48. Parliamentary Debates, Commons, 5th series, CCCXXXVI (1938), col. 2117.
49. Haldane: *A.R.P.*, p. 52.
50. Shirlaw: *Casualty*.
51. Noel de P. MacRoberts, *ARP Lessons from Barcelona – Some Hints for Local Authorities and for the Private Citizen* (London, 1938), p. 31.
52. Serge Chermayeff, Plan for *A.R.P: A Practical Policy for Air-Raid Precautions* (London, 1939), pp. 34–35.

53. 'Special ARP supplement,' *Architectural Design and Construction*, May 1939, p. 14.
54. *The Times*, 18 March 1938, p. 16.
55. Dening: *Modern War*, p. 19.
56. Tom Harrisson, one of the instigators of Mass Observation, made the same point in 1940, noting that the effect of raids on most people's minds is 'very slight after the first shock'. Mass Observation Digitized Archive, File Report 313, Civilians in Air-Raids, Tom Harrisson for *Picture Post*, 1 August 1940, p. 1.

Chapter 6   Criticism from the Left – Gas Masks, Refuge Rooms, and Deep Shelters

1. Communist Party of Great Britain, *London District Congress 1938 Discussion Statement* (London, 1938).
2. *Daily Worker*, 14 July 1938, p. 3.
3. Cambridge Scientists' Anti-War Group, *The Protection of the Public From Aerial Attack: Being A Critical Examination of the Recommendations put Forward by the Air Raid Precautions Department of the Home Office* (London, 1937).
4. *The Times*, 13 June 1936, p. 11 and Home Office: *Anti-Gas Precautions and First Aid for Air Raid Casualties*.
5. Brenda Swann and Francis Aprahamian, *J.D. Bernal: A Life in Science and Politics* (London, 1999), p. 141, and Cambridge Scientists' Anti-War Group: *The Protection of the Public From Aerial Attack*, p. 9. A few years prior, Bernal and Joseph Needham had helped to revive the Association of Scientific Workers, a trade union which had been originally founded in 1918 but faltered in the 1920s.
6. Gary Werskey defines 'pure scientists' as those attached to labs specializing in biology, chemistry and physics, thereby excluding engineers, agricultural scientists and medical personnel. More than half of the 'pure scientists' who signed the letter were drawn from only two labs, representing less than a fifth of scientists working at Cambridge – a total of 423 post-graduates and faculty members. Only one reader in pure science (Joseph Needham) signed, and there were no full professors on the list. Werskey: *The Visible College*, pp. 219–220, 339–342.
7. Werskey: *The Visible College*, 231. One of Bernal's biographers seems to suggest that it was he who had the idea for the gas mask test. Andrew Brown, *J.D. Bernal: The Sage of Science* (Oxford, 2005), p. 130.
8. The Socialist Medical Association: *Gas Attacks* (London, 1936), and the Union of Democratic Control: *Poison Gas*, pp. 29, 39.
9. Cambridge Scientists' Anti-War Group: *The Protection of the Public From Aerial Attack*, p. 70.
10. O'Brien: *Civil Defence*, p. 81.

11. Cambridge Scientists' Anti-War Group: *The Protection of the Public From Aerial Attack*, pp. 39–52.
12. Cambridge Scientists' Anti-War Group, *Air Raid Protection: The Facts* (London, 1938), pp. 41, 66–8.
13. *The Financial Times*, 15 July 1936, p. 9.
14. Communist Party of Great Britain, *A.R.P.: The Practical Air Raid Protection Britain Needs* (London, 1938).
15. Werskey: *The Visible College*, pp. 230, 236. By 1939 the Association of Scientific Workers had 1,319 members, and had been refashioned in light of the Cambridge Scientific movement under the guidance of J.D. Bernal.
16. To a private gas manufacturer who wished him to recommend their mask to the Cambridge Scientists' Group he wrote, 'I am not a member of the Cambridge Scientists' Anti-War Group, and, as you see if you read my book '*A.R.P.*', am not in complete agreement with their conclusions'. University College London, Haldane Papers, Haldane Box 30 1/a, J.B.S. Haldane to British Draeger Co. Ltd, 12 July 1939.
17. Cambridge University Library, Joseph Needham Papers, K.30, clipping of the *Daily Mail*, 26 February 1937.
18. *Parliamentary Debates*, Commons, 5th series, CCCXX (1937), col. 843.
19. *Parliamentary Debates*, Commons, 5th series, CCCXXI (1937), col. 527.
20. Kendall: *Breathe Freely! The Truth About Poison Gas*.
21. NA, HO 45/18802, Report of Meeting of Gas Sub-Committee of the Parliamentary Committee, pp. 7–8.
22. Needham Papers, K.38, undated typescript and notes.
23. Joseph Needham Papers, K.38, Joseph Needham's notes citing House of Commons Debates of 18 February 1937 and 16 November 1937.
24. Cambridge Scientists' Anti-War Group: *Air Raid Protection*, citing a House of Commons Debate of 16 November 1937, pp. 21–22. It is unclear what 'Anti-War movement' condemnation by Labour that Lloyd was referring to. This author is unaware of any direct Labour judgment on the Cambridge Scientists.
25. Cambridge Scientists' Anti-War Group: *Air Raid Protection*, pp. 19–20.
26. O'Brien: *Civil Defence*, p. 81.
27. Cambridge Scientists' Anti-War Group response, 'Air Raid Precautions,' *Nature*, CXXXIX/239 (1 May 1937), p. 760.
28. *New Statesman and Nation*, XIV/345 (2 October 1937), pp. 485–6. The notice listed Joseph Needham as the treasurer, and was signed by Bernal, Waddington, and Needham. This author has not been able to find evidence that the film was ever made.
29. King's College, London, Liddell Hart Military Archives, LH 1/65/1, 6 February 1937. J.D. Bernal to Basil Liddell Hart. Liddell Hart gave Bernal vague assurances that he would read the manuscript, but there is no record of further support.
30. *Parliamentary Debates*, Commons, 5th series, CCCXXIX (1937), cols. 1906, 1910.
31. Cambridge Scientists' Anti-War Group: *Air Raid Protection*, p. 36.

32. J.D. Bernal et al, Letter to the editor, *The Times*, 11 February 1938, p. 10.
33. Robin Woolven, 'First in the country: Dr Richard Tee and Air Raid Precautions,' *Hackney History*, VI (2000), pp. 51–56.
34. *Left News*, XIII (May 1937). The fact that they were called 'Peace Councils' reflected the continued resonance of pacifist thought in leftist reader circles.
35. *Left News*, 'Special A.R.P. Number,' XXVIII (September 1938), p. 967.
36. Left Book Club, *This Month's Book: A.R.P.* (London, 1938).
37. Reported in *Reynolds News*, April 1938, cited in Gregg: *The Shelter of the Tubes*. In light of the special preparations made for the Royal Family, members of the House of Lords in February 1939 asked whether the public should not be allowed to shelter in the Tubes. Jones: *Ove Arup*, p. 70.
38. British Movement Against War and Fascism, *Behind the Gas Mask: An Exposure of the Proposed Air Defence Measures* (London, c. 1935), pp. 5–6, and Union of Democratic Control: *Poison Gas*, p. 193.
39. Haldane: *A.R.P.*, p. 228.
40. Cambridge Scientists' Anti-War Group: *Air Raid Protection*, p. 18.
41. Cambridge Scientists' Anti-War Group: *Air Raid Protection*, p. 35.
42. *Daily Worker*, 8 January 1938, p. 1.
43. Cambridge University Library, J.D. Bernal Papers, B.3.21, clipping of J.D. Bernal, review of *Air Defence and the Civil Population* by Hyde and Nuttall, *Reynold's News*, 29 August 1937.
44. Haldane: *A.R.P.*, p. 243.
45. E. Leighton Yates, *A Christian Attitude Towards Air-Raid Precautions* (London, c. 1938), pp. 7–8.
46. Communist Party of Great Britain, *A.R.P. For Londoners* (London, 1938), p. 15.
47. Cambridge Scientists' Anti-War Group: *Air Raid Protection*, pp. 57–59.
48. *New Statesman and Nation*, XIII/321 (17 April 1937), p. 623.
49. *New Statesman and Nation*, X/234 (17 August 1935), p. 211.
50. The review of *A.R.P.* in *The Times* noted that this figure was slightly below the 'present scale of rearmament expenditure'. *The Times*, 20 September 1938, p. 7.
51. Stephen Broadberry and Peter Howlett put the government expenditure for 1938 and 1939 at £781,000,000 and £1,261,000,000 respectively. 'The United Kingdom: 'Victory at All Costs'' in Mark Harrison, (ed), *The Economics of WWII: Six Powers in International Comparison* (Cambridge, 1998). Of the total figure, around one-third constituted defence expenditure, which was around £254,000,000 in 1938–9. If instituted over two years, the Haldane ARP plan would have equalled the amount spent on all rearmament during this period. See figures in Edgerton: *Warfare State*, p. 67.
52. 'Martian,' *A.R.P.: A Reply to Professor J.B.S. Haldane, F.R.S., The Royal Institute of British Architects and Some Others, Including the British Government* (London, 1938).
53. Haldane: *How to Be Safe From Air Raids*, p. 51.
54. Cambridge Scientists' Anti-War Group: *Air Raid Protection*, p. 82.
55. Communist Party of Great Britain: *A.R.P. for Hampstead*, p. 11.

56. *The Architects' Journal*, 7 July 1939, p. 15. Haldane was asked to write the forward to the article and he noted, 'I confess that [I would] willingly pay £12 to be at a depth of 60 feet, instead of 50'.

57. Communist Party of Great Britain: *A.R.P. for Londoners*, p. 15.

58. Haldane: *A.R.P.*, pp. 251–254. In his pamphlet *How to Be Safe from Air Raids*, he estimated the cost at £480 million, or £12 per head.

59. Cambridge Scientists' Anti-War Group, *Air Raid Protection*, p. 82.

60. CPGB: *A.R.P. for Hampstead*, p. 15.

61. Haldane: *How to be Safe from Air Raids*, p. 44.

62. Noreen Branson and Margot Heinemann, *Britain in the Nineteen-Thirties* (New York, 1971), p. 341.

63. Bernard Donoughue and G.W. Jones, *Herbert Morrison: Portrait of a Politician* (London, 1973), p. 261.

64. Hyde and Nuttal: *Air Defence and the Civil Population*.

65. This provision was actually the official policy of the government, though there remained little regulatory power to enforce these laws, even after the ARP Acts of 1937 and 1939 were passed. See Donald Hamilton, *The Civil Defence Act 1939 as it Affects Employers and Property Owners* (London, 1939). Policy makers were cautious not to offend business interests by implying that business should be made to pay for ARP provisions that might 'assume astronomical proportions'. NA, CAB 16/197, Minutes of the first meeting of the Committee of Imperial Defence Civil Defence (Policy) Sub-Committee, 12 December 1938, comment by Sir Samuel Hoare, pp. 16–18. It was agreed that large employers should take 'reasonable steps' to assure ARP, leaving companies with wide latitude to interpret these regulations.

66. *The Economist*, 22 April 1939, p. 189.

67. NA, HO 45/18194, 'A.R.P. Department Catalogue of Books, Publications, etc.' [no date].

68. Swann and Aprahamian: *J.D. Bernal*, p. 162.

Chapter 7   Terror From the Skies – Wartime and the Challenge to Civil Liberties

1. CPGB: *A.R.P. for Londoners*, p. 11.

2. See Miles Taylor, 'John Bull and the iconography of public opinion in England c. 1712–1929,' *Past and Present* LXXXIV (1992), pp. 93–128.

3. E.P. Thompson, *Customs in Common* (New York, 1993).

4. NA, HO 45/18124 details Scheme 'Y', the contingency plan to impose military rule in wartime. It involved two stages, a 'precautionary stage' and a 'war stage.' Also NA, HO 45/18152, August 1938 report for the Committee of Imperial Defence.

5. John W. Wheeler-Bennett, *John Anderson: Viscount Waverly* (London, 1962), pp. 204–205.

6. *The Economist*, 11 February 1939, p. 291.
7. Cambridge Scientists' Anti-War Group: *Air Raid Protection,* p. 19.
8. Peace Pledge Union, *Are You Prepared to Support or Sanction Another War? If you are, do you Realise that 'Modern War Means War from the Air.'* (London, 1937).
9. *Yorkshire Observer*, 18 May 1938, p. 5.
10. *Yorkshire Observer Budget*, 21 May 1938, p. 21.
11. Cambridge Scientists' Anti-War Group: *Air Raid Protection*, p. 52–57.
12. *New Statesman and Nation*, X/234 (17 August 1935), p. 211.
13. Philip Ziegler, *London at War, 1939–1945* (London, 1995), p. 12.
14. Union of Democratic Control: *Poison Gas.*
15. Yates: *A Christian Attitude Towards Air-Raid Precautions*, p. 7–8.
16. Needham Papers, K.32 Draft for CSAWG presentation to the Cambridge Borough Council (c. 1939).
17. Cambridge Scientists' Anti-War Group: *The Protection of the Public from Aerial Attack*, pp. 37–8.
18. Dr Duncan Leys, letter to the *British Medical Journal*, 22 May 1937, quoted in Cambridge Scientists' Anti-War Group: *Air Protection*, p. 60.
19. *New Statesman and Nation*, XIV/352 (20 November 1937), p. 823.
20. Communist Party of Great Britain, *Defence of the People* (London, 1939). Harry Pollitt voiced similar sentiments in his pamphlet *I Accuse Baldwin* (London, c. 1938).
21. British Movement Against War and Fascism: *Behind the Gas Mask*, pp. 5–6.
22. Haldane: *How to be Safe from Air Raids*, pp. 54–55.
23. 'Special A.R.P. Number,' *Left News*, no. XXVIII (September 1938), p. 962.
24. Duncan Campbell, *War Plan UK: The Truth About Civil Defence in Britain* (London, 1982).
25. Cambridge Scientists' Anti-War Group et al., *Air Display Special* (July 1935).
26. Communist Party of Great Britain: *Communist Plan for Life in Hampstead*, p. 10.
27. Haldane: *A.R.P.,* p. 129.
28. Haldane: *How to be Safe from Air Raids*, pp. 34–35.
29. Haldane: *A.R.P.*, p. 130.
30. Haldane: *How to Be Safe from Air Raids*, p. 8.
31. Mass Observation, 'Sociology of A.R.P.', *New Statesman and Nation*, XVI/402 (5 November 1938), pp. 717–719.
32. Mass Observation Digitized Archive, File Report 919, Report on Female Attitude to Compulsion, 16 October 1941, p. 2.
33. *Parliamentary Debates*, Commons, 5th series, CCCXXXIV (1939), col. 1390.
34. Robin Woolven, 'London, Munich, and ARP,' *Journal of the Royal United Services Institute*, XXXXIII (1998), p. 55.
35. Woolven: 'First in the country: Dr Richard Tee and Air Raid Precautions,' pp. 54–56.
36. Calder: *Myth of the Blitz* and Paul Addison, *The Road to 1945: British Politics and the Second World War* (London, 1975).

Chapter 8 Britishness – Civilians on the Home Front and National Identity

1. *Parliamentary Debates*, Commons, 5th series, CCCXXXVI (1938), cols. 2109–2115.
2. *Parliamentary Debates*, Commons, 5th series, CCCXXXVI (1938), col. 2113.
3. *The Times*, 10 January 1938, p. 13.
4. Louis Strauss, letter to the editor, *The Times*, 3 February, 1938, p. 8.
5. Paul Ward, *Britishness Since 1870* (London, 2004), p. 3.
6. Julia Stapleton, 'Political thought and national identity in Britain, 1850–1950,' in Stefan Collini, Richard Whatmore, Brian Young, (eds) *History, Religion, and Culture: British Intellectual History 1750–1950* (Cambridge, 2000), pp. 264–266.
7. Stapleton: 'Political thought and national identity in Britain,' pp. 263–265.
8. Ward: *Britishness Since 1870*, p. 102.
9. Gertrude Himmelfarb, *Poverty and Compassion: The Moral Imagination of the Late Victorians* (New York, 1991), pp. 4–8.
10. Stefan Collini, *Public Moralists: Political Thought and Intellectual Life in Britain 1850–1930* (Oxford, 1993), pp. 84–93.
11. Deborah Cohen, *The War Come Home: Disabled Veterans in Britain and Germany, 1914–1939* (Berkeley, 2001), p. 18.
12. James Hinton, *Women, Social Leadership, and the Second World War: Continuities of Class, and Nine Wartime Lives: Mass Observation and the Making of the Modern Self* (Oxford, 2010), and Noakes: *War and the British*.
13. *Parliamentary Debates*, Commons, 5th series, CCCXXXVI (1938), col. 2113.
14. *The Times*, 12 January 1938, p. 11.
15. O'Brien: *Civil Defence*, pp. 122–123.
16. H.A. Sisson, letter to the editor, *The Times*, 26 May 1938, p. 10.
17. *Parliamentary Debates*, Commons, 5th series, CCCXXIX (1937), col. 1915.
18. Brigadier-General H. Biddulph, letter to the editor, *The Times*, 9 September 1939, p. 6.
19. Mass Observation Digitized Archive, File Report 919, Report on Female Attitude to Compulsion, 16 October 1941, p. 1. Mass Observation's total survey on compulsion yielded these results: 52 per cent were in favour of voluntary service, 37 per cent were in favour of compulsion and 11 per cent offered no opinion.
20. Hinton: *Nine Wartime Lives*.
21. A. Susan Williams, *Ladies of Influence: Women of the Elite in Interwar Britain* (London, 2000), p. 157.
22. Ross McKibbin, *Classes and Cultures: England, 1918–1951* (Oxford, 1998), p. 529.
23. David Gloster, *Architecture and the Air Raid: Shelter Technologies and the British Government 1938–44* (London, 1997), p. 50.

24. Stapleton: 'Political thought and national identity in Britain,' p. 264.

25. Sonya Rose highlights the extent to which depictions of rural England were prominent during the war itself, despite the fact that most British people lived in urban areas, Rose, *Whose People's War?*, pp. 197–238. Also see Ward: *Britishness Since 1870*, pp. 54–66; Alun Howkins, *Reshaping Rural England: A Social History 1850–1925*, (London, 1991); and David Matless, *Landscape and Englishness* (London, 1998), pp. 195–198. Angus Calder demonstrates the extent to which the idiom of rural England, or Deep England, pervaded the literature and film of World War II. Calder: *The Myth of the Blitz*. For a counterview on the overemphasis of rural nostalgia in British historiography see Peter Mandler, 'Against "Englishness": English culture and the limits to rural nostalgia, 1850–1940' *Transactions of the Royal Historical Society*, 6th series, VII (1997), pp. 155–175.

26. Papers of Sir Ove Arup, ARUP 2/11, Ove Arup, 'London's Shelter Problem,' (Consulting Engineer on A.R.P. Shelters to the Finsbury Borough Council), 15 October 1940, p. 10.

27. Mass Observation Digitized Archive, File Report 436, Shelter in London, 3 October 1940, pp. 4–10.

28. Mass Observation Digitized Archive, File Report A14, Air Raid Shelters, March 1939, p. 5.

29. Mass Observation Digitized Archive, File Report A14, Air Raid Shelters, March 1939, pp. 1, 19.

30. Viscount Rothermere of the *Daily Mail*, also a onetime supporter of the British Union of Fascists, self-importantly publicized his calls for armament throughout the 1930s in his book *Warnings and Predictions* (London, 1939).

31. *The Economist*, 28 January 1939, p. 173. See also *The Economist*, 24 July 1937, p. 175, 11 February 1939, p. 291, 22 April 1939, p. 189, and 17 June 1939, p. 653.

32. *Daily Herald*, 19 May 1938, p. 11. The leading national newspapers from the 1931–2 period were the *Daily Express*, *Daily Herald*, *Daily Mail*, *News Chronicle*, *Daily Mirror*, *Daily Sketch*, *Daily Telegraph*, *The Times*, and the *Morning Post*. Listed in McKibbin: *Classes and Cultures*, p. 504.

33. *The Times*, 10 January 1938, p. 13, 11 January 1938, p. 13, and 12 January 1938, p. 11.

34. D.C. Burn, 'Shelter From High Explosive,' *The Times*, 25 February 1938, p. 12. The paper also published letters to the editor on a wide variety of subjects dealing with ARP. Many were of a basic informative nature, advising the public of the training courses or new Home Office circulars. The letters that were critical of ARP tended to focus on specific areas of implementation, or were critical of public response.

35. Richard Titmuss noted that Home Office files suggested that virtually no substantial preparation for the evacuation of East London had been undertaken

until 1937. Richard Titmuss Papers, Titmuss_Add1 7/44, File 1, undated notes.

36. Wheeler-Bennett: *John Anderson: Viscount Waverly*, p. 202.
37. Titmuss: *Problems of Social Policy*, p. 28.
38. *Parliamentary Debates*, Commons, 5th series, CCCXXXI (1938), col. 361.
39. 'The Organization of A.R.P. in Germany,' *Journal of the Air Raid Protection Institute*, I/4 (June 1939), p. 267.
40. Jones: *Ove Arup*, p. 73.
41. *The Times*, 25 January 1938, p. 11.
42. *Parliamentary Debates*, Commons, 5th series, CCCXXXVI (1938), cols. 2119–2120.
43. *Parliamentary Debates*, Commons, 5th series, CCCXXXIII (1938), col. 1357.
44. *Journal of the Air Raid Protection Institute*, I/3 (April 1939), pp. 140–164.
45. Jones: *Ove Arup*, p. 67.
46. *New Statesman and Nation*, XVI/402 (5 November 1938), p. 347.
47. Cambridge Scientists' Anti-War Group: *Air Raid Protection*, p. 66. In fact, a total of 7 million French people took to the roads during the civilian exodus of 1940. Given this scale, it is not surprising that evacuation turned out to be less orderly and formulaic than imagined. Julia Torrie, *For Their Own Good: Civilian Evacuations in France and Germany* (New York, 2010), p. 39.
48. Cambridge Scientists' Anti-War Group, 'Air Raid Precautions,' *Nature*, CXXXIX/239, no. 239 (1 May 1937), p. 760 and Cambridge Scientists' Anti-War Group: *Air Raid Protection*, p. 74.
49. Torrie: *For Their Own Good*, pp. 20–26.
50. Torrie: *For Their Own Good*, pp. 34–37.
51. Communist Party of Great Britain: *A.R.P. for Hampstead*, p. 9.
52. Haldane: *How to Be Safe from Air Raids*, pp. 6, 8.
53. J.D. Bernal et al., letter to the editor, *The Times*, 11 February 1938, p. 10.
54. Needham Papers, K.33, *Cambridge ARP Exhibition* (c. 1941). The Group promoted improved ARP for Cambridge, also publishing a pamphlet, 'Memorandum on Air Raid Precautions for the Town of Cambridge'.
55. *Parliamentary Debates*, Commons, 5th series, CCCXXXVI (1938), col. 2105.

Chapter 9   Architecture and Idealism – The Finsbury Deep Shelter Project

1. Chermayeff: *Plan for A.R.P.*, pp. 5–6. The Tecton plan dovetailed with a separate survey of ARP policy undertaken by Chermayeff, which he published in 1939. His report was 'an attempt to draw together in a systematic form all that has so far been established *scientifically and technically* about the subject of air-raid protection'. He had similarly drawn on studies by Haldane and the

Association of Architects, Surveyors and Technical Assistants (AASTA), *A Report on the Design, Equipment and Cost of Air-Raid Shelters* (London, 1938).

2. Meisel: 'Air raid shelter policy and its critics in Britain before the Second World War,' pp. 300–319.

3. Meisel: 'Air raid shelter policy and its critics in Britain before the Second World War,' p. 315. Christopher Lawrence and Anna-K. Mayer also identify the persistence of the 'amateur' and voluntary tradition into the 1930s. Christopher Lawrence and Anna-K. Mayer, *Regenerating England: Science, Medicine and Culture in Inter-War Britain* (Amsterdam, 2000), p. 2. The prominent counterview is that of David Edgerton in *Warfare State* and *Britain's War Machine*.

4. David L. Pike, *Subterranean Cities: The World Beneath Paris and London, 1800–1945* (Ithaca, 2005), p. 281.

5. Robert Fishman, *Urban Utopias in the Twentieth Century: Ebenezer Howard, Frank Lloyd Wright, and Le Corbusier* (New York, 1977), p. 10.

6. Gavin Stamp, 'Introduction – Britain in the Thirties,' *Architectural Digest, Profile 24* (1980), pp. 2–25.

7. Anthony Jackson, 'The politics of architecture: English architecture 1929–1951,' *The Journal of the Society of Architectural Historians*, XXIX/1 (March 1965), p. 103.

8. Jones: *Ove* Arup, p. 56.

9. Alan Powers, *Serge Chermayeff: Designer, Architect, Teacher* (London, 2001), p. 97.

10. Jones: *Ove Arup*, pp. 56–71. Jones alleges that Arup could not abide the 'blind faith in Communism' of Haldane, p. 68.

11. David Dean, *The Thirties: Recalling the English Architectural Scene* (London, 1983), p. 86.

12. University College London, J.B.S. Haldane Papers, Box 30, File 1/a, F. Skinner to Haldane, 18 October 1938.

13. RIBA British Architectural Library, Papers of Sir Ove Arup, ARO/1/1, April 1934 statement. A predecessor group to Modern Architectural Research Group (MARS) had been the Twentieth Century Group, of which Serge Chermayeff and the prominent architect Wells Coates had been members. Dean: *The Thirties*, p. 112.

14. Andrew Jackson, *The Politics of Architecture: A History of Modern Architecture in Britain* (London, 1970), p. 76. In 1942 the Royal Academy Plan for London advocated much the same 'rationalized' measures to reorder London. Stamp: 'Introduction – Britain in the Thirties,' p. 5.

15. MARS was never a well-financed organization. It was funded mainly through individual subscriptions of £2 2.5, and in 1937 had a credit balance of £35 12.7. Papers of Sir Ove Arup, ARO 1/1, financial statement.

16. MARS had contact with groups as diverse as the New Homes for Old Committee, the Westminster Housing Group, the Socialist Medical Council, the Royal Institute of British Architects (RIBA), the Ministry of Heath, and British universities. Papers of Sir Ove Arup, ARO 1/5, assorted letters.

17. John Allan's biography of Berthold Luketkin notes that he remained a 'fully paid up' member of MARS until the end of 1938, but a shift in his allegiance occurred four years earlier. John Allan, *Berthold Lubetkin: Architecture and the Tradition of Progress* (London, 1992), p. 322.

18. Malcolm Reading and Peter Coe, *Lubetkin & Tecton: An Architectural Study* (London, 1992), pp. 18–19.

19. Allan: *Berthold Lubetkin*, pp. 322–323.

20. Jackson: *The Politics of Architecture*, p. 76.

21. Arts Council of Great Britain, *Thirties: British Art and Design Before the War* (London, 1980), p. 60.

22. Bill Luckin, *Questions of Power: Electricity and Environment in Inter-war Britain* (Manchester, 1990), p. 2.

23. Fishman: *Urban Utopias in the Twentieth Century*, p. xii.

24. Berthold Lubetkin Papers, LUB 3/5, copy of the Press Release by Alderman Harold Riley, Chairman of the Finsbury Borough ARP Committee, February 1939, p. 1.

25. Berthold Lubetkin Papers, LUB 3/5, copy of the Press Release by Alderman Harold Riley.

26. Allan: *Berthold Lubetkin: Architecture and the Tradition of Progress*, p. 353.

27. House of Commons Parliamentary Papers, 1937–8, Cmd. 5596, Statement showing Classification of Local Authorities for purposes of calculating Exchequer Grant, pp. 3–4.

28. Finsbury Reference Library, ARP Committee, Finsbury Borough Council Minutes, XXXIX (4 October 1938), p. 417.

29. Robin Woolven, 'Playing Hitler's game from Fitzroy Road NW1: JBS Haldane, the St Pancras Branch of the Communist Party, and deep-shelter agitation,' *Camden History Review*, XXIII (1999), p. 24.

30. *The Times*, 23 February 1938, p. 20.

31. Woolven: 'First in the country: Dr Richard Tee and air raid precautions,' p. 53.

32. Special ARP Committee Meeting, Finsbury Borough Council Minutes, XXXIX (1 February 1939), pp. 802, 849.

33. *Finsbury Citizen*, February 1939, p. 1.

34. Allan: *Berthold Lubetkin*, p. 354.

35. Chermayeff: *Plan for A.R.P: A Practical Policy for Air-raid Precautions*, p. 14.

36. Tecton Architects, *Planned A.R.P.: Based on the Investigation of Structural Protection Against Air Attack in the Metropolitan Borough of Finsbury* (London, 1939), pp. 31–71. The architects assigned a 'danger coefficient' to specific areas, with the largest such coefficient being given to the basement shelters in a block of offices in Pentonville Road, due to their poor, shallow construction. The area was also in close proximity to the King's Cross and St Pancras railway yards, likely to be a target of enemy bombers.

37. Chermayeff: *Plan for A.R.P.*, p. 16.

38. Home Office, *Air Raid Precautions for Government Contractors* (London, 1934).

39. Tecton Architects: *Planned A.R.P.*, pp. 113–125.

40. *Finsbury Citizen*, February 1939, p. 1.
41. Tecton Architects: *Planned A.R.P.*, pp. 38–41.
42. Tecton Architects: *Planned A.R.P.*, pp. 95–96.
43. Allan: *Berthold Lubetkin*, p. 358.
44. Tecton Architects: *Planned A.R.P.*, p. 3.
45. Jones: *Ove Arup*, p. 72.
46. *Daily Worker*, 7 February 1939, p. 3.
47. *Finsbury Citizen*, February 1939, p. 1.
48. *News Chronicle*, 7 February 1939, p. 10.
49. *News Chronicle*, 22 March 1939, p. 10.
50. *Manchester Guardian*, 17 January 1939, p. 10.
51. *Daily Telegraph*, 7 February 1939, p. 15.
52. *Evening Standard*, 8 February 1939, p. 6.
53. *Architects' Journal*, 4 May 1939, pp. 722–724.
54. 'Report on the Conference of Structural ARP held at RIBA, 13–15 June, 1938,' *Journal of the Royal Institute of British Architects*, XXXXV/16 (27 June 1938), pp. 779–832.
55. *Journal of the Air Raid Protection Institute*, I/2 (February 1939), p. 59.
56. David Gloster: 'Architecture and the Air Raid,' p. 23.
57. The lack of 'authoritative standards' was lamented in the forward to the 'Special ARP Supplement,' *Architectural Design and Construction* (May 1939), p. 2.
58. *Architect and Building News*, 21 October 1938, pp. 57–58.
59. *Architect and Building News*, 10 February 1939, p. 179.
60. 'Special ARP supplement,' *Architectural Design and Construction*, p. 23.
61. The *Architects' Journal*, 7 July 1939, p. 17.
62. Institution of Structural Engineers, *Report on Air Raid Precautions* (London, 1939).
63. *Architects' Journal*, 13 October 1938, p. 596.
64. *Architect and Building News*, 17 February 1939, p. 209.
65. Jackson: *The Politics of Architecture*, p. 76.
66. Dean: *The Thirties*, p. 140.
67. J.B.S. Haldane Papers, Box 30, File 1/a, F. Skinner to Haldane, 18 October 1938.

Chapter 10   Dissent, Patriotism and the Final Showdown over Deep Shelter Policy

1. *New Statesman and Nation*, XVII/420 (11 March 1939), p. 347.
2. NA, CAB 16/197 CID Civil Defence (Policy) Sub-Committee, Minutes of the third meeting, p. 53.
3. *The Economist*, 11 February 1939, p. 291.
4. *The Times*, 10 January 1939, p. 9.
5. O'Brien: *Civil Defence*, pp. 190–191.

6. *Daily Worker*, 7 February 1939, p. 3.
7. *Parliamentary Debates*, Commons, 5th series, CCCXXXXV (1939), col. 1709, 1710 and vol. CCCXXXXVII (1939), col. 2486–7.
8. NA, CAB 16/197, CID Civil Defence (Policy) Sub-Committee, Minutes of the third meeting, 25 January 1939, p. 47.
9. NA, CAB 16/197, CID, Civil Defence (Policy) Sub-Committee, Minutes of the fifth meeting, 14 April 1939, p. 92.
10. NA, CAB 16/197, Memo by the Lord Privy Seal, 24 January 1939, p. 153.
11. NA, CAB 16/197, draft of the Hailey report, p. 237.
12. Letter from O. Harrington, Winston Churchill's private secretary at Chartwell, 20 March 1939, cited in Allan: *Berthold Lubetkin*, p. 361.
13. NA, CAB 16/197, Memo by the Lord Privy Seal, 24 January 1939, p. 153.
14. *Time and Tide*, XIX/46 (12 November 1939).
15. Office of the Lord Privy Seal, *Air Raid Shelters: Report of the Lord Privy Seal's Conference* (London, 1939), p. 6. The official historian Terence O'Brien endorsed this opinion about the primary concerns of the Commission. O'Brien: *Civil Defence*, p. 192.
16. NA, CAB 16/197, CID Civil Defence (Policy) Sub-Committee, Minutes of the fifth meeting, p. 91.
17. Sir John Anderson quoted in *The Architect and Building News*, 24 February 1939, p. 240.
18. O'Brien: *Civil Defence*, p. 192.
19. Woolven: 'Playing Hitler's game from Fitzroy Road NW1,' p. 25.
20. Office of the Lord Privy Seal: *Air Raid Shelters*, p. 17.
21. Office of the Lord Privy Seal: *Air Raid Shelters*, pp. 19, 20–22.
22. NA, CAB 16/197, CID Civil Defence (Policy) Sub-Committee, Minutes of the fifth Meeting, p. 90.
23. Gloster: 'Architecture and the Air Raid,' p. 50.
24. Office of the Lord Privy Seal: *Air Raid Shelters*, p. 20.
25. *Finsbury Citizen*, April 1939, p. 1.
26. Mass Observation Digitized Archive, File Report A14, Air Raid Shelters, March 1939, pp. 2–13.
27. Hinton: *Nine Wartime Lives*, pp. 178–179.
28. Mass Observation Digitized Archive, File Report 291, 20 July 1940, p. 2.
29. Mass Observation Digitized Archive, File Report 291, 20 July 1940, p. 7.
30. Mass Observation Digitized Archive, File Report A14, Air Raid Shelters, March 1939, p. 18.
31. NA, CAB 16/197, CID Civil Defence (Policy) Sub-Committee, Minutes of the fifth meeting, pp. 89–91, 103. A memo by the Lord Privy Seal, 24 January 1939, p. 155, emphasized the need to give the press a 'carefully worded statement' on shelter policy.
32. NA, CAB 16/197, draft of the Hailey Report, p. 239.
33. NA, CAB 16/197, CID Civil Defence (Policy) Sub-Committee, Minutes of the third meeting, p. 52.

34. NA, CAB 16/197, CID Civil Defence (Policy) Sub-Committee, Minutes of the third meeting, p. 55.

35. Finsbury Borough Council Minutes, vol. XXXX (25 April 1939), pp. 74–82.

36. Finsbury Council Special Meeting, Finsbury Borough Council Minutes, vol. XXXIX (25 April 1939), pp. 74–82.

37. Berthold Lubetkin, letter to the editor, *The Times*, 24 April 1939, p. 8.

38. Finsbury Borough Council Minutes, vol. 40 (25 April 1939), p. 82.

39. Berthold Lubetkin Papers, LUB 3/5, Copy of the Press Release by Alderman Harold Riley.

40. Tecton Architects: *Planned A.R.P.*, p. 135.

41. Finsbury Borough Council Minutes, vol. XXXX (25 April 1939), pp. 76–77.

42. Allan, *Berthold Lubetkin*, p. 361.

43. For example, AASTA, 'What is wrong with official shelter policy?' *Municipal Journal*, April 1940, cited in Allan: *Berthold Lubetkin*, p. 361.

44. Cyril Helsby, letter to the editor, *The Times*, 2 January 1939, p. 10.

45. *Finsbury Citizen*, July 1939, p. 1.

46. *Finsbury Citizen*, May 1939, p. 1.

47. *Daily Express*, 18 July 1939, p. 1. The *Manchester Guardian* also commentated favourably on the plan, 18 July 1939, p. 12.

48. Finsbury Borough Council Minutes, vol. 40 (17 July 1939), pp. 311–313, and vol. 40 (25 July 1939), p. 329 and vol. 40 (11 August 1939), p. 340.

49. Office of the Lord Privy Seal: *Air Raid Shelters*, pp. 18–19.

50. Both quotations, *Finsbury Citizen*, August 1939, p. 1.

51. Allan: *Berthold Lubetkin*, p. 362.

52. Allan: *Berthold Lubetkin*, p. 360.

53. Finsbury Borough Council Minutes, vol. XXXX (6 September 1939), p. 366.

54. Berthold Lubetkin Papers, LUB 3/7, Pre-report of the 'Report on the design, cost, and relative safety of air raid shelters,' presented to the Finsbury Council 6 February 1939, pp. 33–40.

55. O'Brien: *Civil Defence*, p. 195.

56. *The Architect and Building News*, 10 March 1939, p. 291.

57. Woolven: 'First in the country,' pp. 54–55.

58. *The Economist*, 17 June 1939, p. 653.

59. Meisel: 'Air raid shelter policy,' p. 313.

60. Lord John Baker, *Enterprise Versus Bureaucracy: The Development of Structural Air-Raid Precautions During the Second World War* (Oxford, 1978), p. ix.

Conclusions

1. Herbert Morrison, *Herbert Morrison: An Autobiography by Lord Morrison of Lambeth* (London, 1960), p. 206.

2. University College London, George Orwell Papers, Item E/2, Diary Entry, 3 September 1939. It is unclear precisely what type of shelters he is referring to,

perhaps trenches, converted basements, or sandbagged cellars which, as in September 1938, were once again hastily constructed.

3. Harrisson and Madge: *War Begins at Home*, pp. 49–55.
4. Bell: 'Landscapes of fear,' pp. 165–168.
5. Jones: *British Civilians in the Front Line*, pp. 29–30.
6. Bell: 'Landscapes of fear,' p. 163.
7. Gardiner, *Wartime Britain 1939–1945* (London, 2004), p. 640.
8. Powers: *Strategy Without Slide-Rule*, pp. 158–160.
9. A.C. Grayling, *Among the Dead Cities: Was the Allied Bombing of Civilians in WWII a Necessity or a Crime?* (London, 2006) and Jörg Friedrich, *The Fire: The Bombing of Germany, 1940–1945* (New York, 2008).
10. *New Statesman and Nation*, XVI, no. 402 (5 November 1938), pp. 717–719.
11. Mass Observation Digitized Archive, File Report 919, Report on Female Attitude to Compulsion, 16 October 1941.
12. Fears over the subversive possibilities of underground worlds had been prominent since the late nineteenth century with the advent of underground transport. Pike: *Subterranean Cities: The World Beneath Paris and London, 1800–1945*.
13. Home Office, *Fire Precautions in War Time* (London, 1939).
14. *Parliamentary Debates*, Commons, 5th series, CCCCLXXVIII (1950), col. 43.
15. Calder: *The Myth of the Blitz*, pp. 60–64.
16. Richard Titmuss Papers, Titmuss_Add1/7/44, 17 March 1949, Memo, Sir Keith Hancock to Richard Titmuss.
17. Gloster: 'Architecture and the air raid,' p. 16.
18. Wheeler-Bennett: *John Anderson*, p. 223.
19. Meisel: 'Air raid shelter policy and its critics,' p. 317.
20. Mass Observation Digitized Archive, File Report A14, Air Raid Shelters, March 1939, p. 18.
21. NA, CAB 16/197, CID Civil Defence (Policy) Sub-Committee, Minutes of the fifth meeting, p. 102.
22. Jones: *Ove Arup*, pp. 78–79, and Wheeler-Bennett: *John Anderson*, pp. 253–255.
23. Harrisson and Madge: *War Begins at Home*, p. 119.
24. Jones: *British Civilians in the Front Line*, p. 49.
25. Donoughue and Jones: *Herbert Morrison*, p. 268.
26. Donoughue and Jones: *Herbert Morrison*, pp. 267–289.
27. Chermayeff: *Plan for A.R.P*, pp. 50–51.
28. Harrisson and Madge: *War Begins at Home*, pp. 119–120.
29. Angus Calder and Dorothy Sheridan, eds. *Speak for Yourself: A Mass-Observation Anthology, 1937–1949* (Oxford, 1985), pp. 101–118.
30. Cambridge University Library, Joseph Needham Papers, K.31, clipping from *News Chronicle*, 12 February 1937.
31. Serge Chermayeff, letter to the editor, The *Architect and Building News*, 24 February 1939, p. 240.

32. Clark: *J.B.S.*, p. 127.
33. Dean: *The Thirties*, p. 139.
34. Papers of Sir Ove Arup, ARUP 2/11, Arup: 'London's shelter problem,' p. 1 and Berthold Lubetkin Papers, LUB 3/8, Ove Arup letter to Berthold Lubetkin, 6 November 1940.
35. Jones: *Ove Arup*, pp. 84–86.
36. Cambridge University Library, Needham Papers, K 33, *Cambridge ARP Exhibition* (c. 1941).
37. Liddell Hart Military Archives, Liddell Hart Papers, LH 1/65/3, memorandum from J.D. Bernal to Basil Liddell Hart, c. October 1938.
38. Edgerton: *Britain's War Machine*, p. 291.
39. Brown: *J.D. Bernal*, pp. 134–135.
40. Werskey: *The Visible College*, p. 233.
41. George Orwell, *The Lion and the Unicorn: Socialism and the English Genius* (London, 1941). See *Michael Shelden, Orwell: The Authorized Biography* (New York, 1991).
42. University College London, George Orwell Papers, File G, George Orwell to Victor Gollancz, 8 January 1940.
43. Chris Waters, 'J.B. Priestley 1894–1984, Englishness and the politics of nostalgia,' in Susan Pedersen and Peter Mandler, (eds), *After the Victorians: Private Conscience and Public Duty in Modern Britain* (London, 1994).
44. J.B. Priestley, *Postscripts* (London, 1940).
45. Grayzel: *At Home and Under Fire*, p. 318.
46. Bourke: *Fear*, p. 242.
47. Peter Mandler, *The English National Character: The History of an Idea from Edmund Burke to Tony Blair* (New Haven, 2006), p. 192.
48. Angus Calder: *The Myth of the Blitz*, p. 2.
49. T.H. Wintringham, *Armies of Freemen* (London, 1940), p. viii.
50. Noakes: *War and the British*, p. 78.
51. Harrisson and Madge: *War Begins at Home*, p. 106.
52. NA, HO 199/434 'Air raids memorandum on the preservation of civilian morale,' 1939 memorandum, pp. 1–8. Haldane was a participant, along with other physicians and scientists.

BIBLIOGRAPHY

Archival Sources

British Architectural Library, Victoria and Albert Museum, London:
Berthold Lubetkin Papers
Material Relating to Tecton Architectural Firm and the Modern Architectural
    Research Group (MARS)
Papers of Sir Ove Arup

Cambridge University Library:
J.D. Bernal Papers
Joseph Needham Papers (including Cambridge Scientists' Anti-War Group)

Centre for Military Archives, King's College, London:
Basil Liddell Hart Papers
C.H. Foulkes Papers
P.R.C. Groves Papers

Islington Local History Centre, Finsbury, London:
Archives of the Borough of Finsbury, Finsbury Borough Council Minutes
    (1938–40)

London School of Economics:
Richard Titmuss Papers
Fabian Society Papers

Mass Observation Digitized Archive:
File Reports

National Archives, Kew:
AIR Series, Air Ministry Documents
CAB 16 Series, Cabinet Papers

HO 45 Series, Civil Defence
WO33 Series, Chemical Defence Committee

Royal Aeronautical Society (National Aerospace Library)
C.G. Grey Papers

University College, London:
George Orwell Papers
J.B.S. Haldane Papers related to ARP

British Government Sources:

House of Commons Parliamentary Papers:
Sessions 1937–8, 1938–9
Parliamentary Debates, Commons, 5th Series

Newspapers and Periodicals

Aeroplane
Architect and Building News
Architects' Journal
Architectural Design and Construction
Architectural Digest
The Builder
Building
Finsbury Citizen
Daily Express
Daily Herald
Daily Mail
Daily Telegraph
Daily Worker
Eastern Evening News
The Economist
Evening Express (Aberdeen)
Evening Standard
The Financial Times
Flight
Hampstead and Highgate Express
Journal of the Air Raid Protection Institute
Journal of the Royal Institute of British Architects
Labour Monthly
Left News
Left Review
Manchester Guardian
Nature

New Statesman and Nation
News Chronicle
Popular Flying
Reynold's News
The Times
Time and Tide
Yorkshire Observer
Yorkshire Observer Budget

Contemporary Sources

Association of Architects, Surveyors and Technical Assistants. *A Report on the Design, Equipment and Cost of Air-Raid Shelters.* (London, 1938).

Angell, Norman. *The Meance to Our National Defence.* (London, 1934).

Aragon, Louis. *Authors Take Sides on the Spanish War.* (London, Left Review, 1937).

Duchess of Atholl. *Searchlight on Spain.* (London, 1938).

Beaton, Cecil. *Winged Squadrons.* (London, 1942).

Bernal, J.D. *The Social Function of Science.* (London, 1939).

Blythe, Henry. *Spain Over Britain: A Study of the Strategical Effect of Italian Intervention on the Defence of the British Empire.* (London, 1937).

Borkenau, Franz. *The Spanish Cockpit.* (London, 1937).

British Movement Against War and Fascism. *Behind the Gas Mask: An Exposure of the Proposed Air Defence Measures.* (London, c. 1935).

Brockway, Fenner. *The Truth About Barcelona.* (London, 1937).

Brooksbank, Alan. *Traps for Young Soldiers and Civilians in Chemical (Gas) Warfare.* (Sydney, 1937).

Campbell, Malcolm. *The Peril From the Air.* London: Hutchinson and Co, c. 1937.

Capper-Johnson, Karlin. *Air Raid Precautions: An Appeal – And an Alternative.* London: Friends' Peace Literature Committee, [n.d.].

The Cambridge Scientists' Anti-War Group. *The Protection of the Public From Aerial Attack: Being a Critical Examination of the Recommendations put Forward by the Air Raid Precautions Department of the Home Office.* London: Victor Gollancz, 1937.

———. *Air Raid Protection: The Facts.* London: Fact, no. 13, 1938.

———. *Cambridge ARP Exhibition.* Cambridge, c. 1941.

———. *Memorandum on Air Raid Precautions for the Town of Cambridge.* Cambridge: [n.d.].

Cambridge Scientists' Anti-War Group, the Fellowship of Reconciliation, Womens' International League and the Cambridge Anti-War Council. *Air Display Special.* (Cambridge, July 1935).

Cambridge Socialist League and the Cambridge Scientists Anti-War Group. *Why Are They Fighting in Spain?* Cambridge: c. 1937.

Christopher, Caudwell. *Studies in a Dying Culture; with an Introduction by John Strachey.* London: Lane, 1938.

Central Office of Information, *The Aircraft Builders: An Account of British Aircraft Production 1935–1945.* London: HMSO, 1947.

Charlton, L.E.O. *War Over England.* London: Longmans Green, 1936.

———. *The Menace of the Clouds.* London: William Hodge, 1937.

234   THE COMING OF THE AERIAL WAR

Chermayeff, Serge. *Plan for A.R.P: A Practical Policy for Air-Raid Precautions*. London: Frederick Muller, 1939.

Communist Party of Great Britain. *Save Peace! Aid Spain*. (London, 1937).

———. *Communist Plan for Life in Hampstead*. (London, c. 1937).

———. *A.R.P. Act Now!* (London, c. 1938).

———. *A.R.P. for Hampstead*. (London, 1938).

———. *A.R.P.: The Practical Air Raid Protection Britain Needs*. (London, 1938).

———. *London District Congress 1938 Discussion Statement*. (London, 1938).

———. *A.R.P. Safety Now*. (London, 1939).

———. *Defence of the People*. (London, 1939).

Communist Party of Great Britain, London District Committee. *A.R.P. for Londoners: In the Opinion of the Experts only the Tunnel Scheme Can Give Real Protection*. (London, 1938).

Communist Party of Great Britain, Sheffield Branch. *A.R.P.: A complete plan for the safety of the people of Sheffield*. (Sheffield, 1938).

Davison, Peter, (ed) *Orwell in Spain: The Full Text of Homage to Catalonia with Associated Articles, Reviews and Letters from The Complete Works of George Orwell. With an introduction by Christopher Hitchens*. London: Penguin Books, 2001.

Deedes, William F. *A.R.P.: A Complete Guide to Civil Defence Measures*. London: St Clement's Press Ltd, 1939.

Dening, B.C. *Modern War: Armies, not Air Forces, Decide Wars*. Hampshire: North Hants Printing Co. Ltd, 1937.

Engelbrecht, H.C. and Hanighen, F.C. *Merchants of Death: A Study of the International Armaments Industry*. London: George Routledge and Sons, 1934.

Geneva Inter-Parliamentary Union. *What Would Be the Character of a New War?* London: Victor Gollancz, 1933.

Foulkes, C.H. *'Gas!' The Story of the Special Brigade*. London: W. Blackword and Sons, 1934.

———. *Commonsense and ARP: A Practical Guide for Householders and Business Managers*. London: C. Arthur Pearson, 1939.

Fuller, J.F.C. *The Reformation of Warfare*. New York, NY: E. P. Dutton, 1923.

———. *The Foundations of the Science of War*. London: Hutchinson, 1926.

Gannes, Harry. *Spain in Revolt*. London: Victor Gollancz, 1936.

Graves, Robert and Alan Hodge. *The Long Weekend: A Social History of Great Britain*. London: Abacus, 1995 [1940].

Greaves, H.R.G. *The Truth About Spain*. London: Victor Gollancz, 1938.

Grey, C.G. *A History of the Air Ministry*. London: Allen and Unwin, 1940.

———. *British Fighter Planes*. London: Faber and Faber, 1941.

Groves, P.R.C. *Behind the Smoke-Screen*. London: Faber and Faber Ltd., 1934.

Guest, Carmel Haden, (ed) *David Guest: A Scientist Fights for Freedom (1911–1938)*. London: Lawrence and Wishart, 1938.

Guest, L. Haden. *If Air War Comes: A Guide to Air Raid Precautions and Anti-Gas Treatment*. London: Eyre and Spottiswoode, 1937.

Earl Halsbury. *1944*. London: Thorton Butterworth, Ltd., 1926.

Haldane, J.B.S. *Callinicus: A Defence of Chemical Warfare*. London: Keegan Paul, 1925.

———. *A.R.P.* London: Victor Gollancz, 1938.

———. *How to Be Safe From Air Raids*. London: Victor Gollancz, 1938.

Hamilton, Donald. *The Civil Defence Act 1939 as it Affects Employers and Property Owners*. London: Jordan and Sons Ltd., 1939.

Hammer, Norman. *A Catechism of Air Raid Precautions*. 5th edn. London: John Bale, Sons and Curnow Ltd, 1939.

Harrisson, Tom and Charles Madge, eds. *War Begins at Home by Mass Observation*. London: Chatto & Windus, 1940.

Holborn's People's Air Raid Protection Committee. *A.R.P. – A Plan for Holborn*. London, 1938.

Home Office. *Air Raid Precautions for Government Contractors*. London, HMSO, 1934.

———. *ARP Handbook (No. 2), 1ˢᵗ ed.: Anti-Gas Precautions and First Aid for Air Raid Casualties*. London: HMSO, 1935.

———. *ARP Handbook (No. 1): Personal Protection against Gas*. London: HMSO, 1937.

———. *ARP Handbook (No. 5) Structural Precautions against Bombs and Gas*. London: HMSO, 1938.

———. *ARP Handbook (No. 8): The Duties of the Air Raid Wardens*. London: HMSO, 1938.

———. *The Protection of Foodstuffs Against Poison Gas*. London: HMSO, 1938.

———. *The Protection of Your Home Against Air Raids*. London: HMSO, 1938.

———. *Training of Air Raid Wardens*. London: HMSO, 1939.

Huxley, Aldous, (ed) *An Encyclopaedia of Pacifism*. London: Chatto & Windus, 1937.

Hyde, H. Montgomery and Falkiner Nuttall, G.R. *Air Defence and the Civil Population*. London: The Crescent Press Ltd., 1937.

Institution of Structural Engineers. *Report on Air Raid Precautions*. London, 1939.

International Brigade Association. *British Battalion XV International Brigade: Memorial Souvenir*. London: Marston Printing Company, 1939.

Jameson, Storm, (ed) *Challenge to Death*. With a forward by Viscount Cecil. London: Constable and Co, Ltd, 1934.

Jameson, Storm. *In the Second Year*. London: Cassell, 1936.

Kendall, James. *Breathe Freely! The Truth About Poison Gas*. London: G. Bell and Sons Ltd, 1938.

Koestler, Arthur. *Spanish Testament*. London: Victor Gollancz, 1937.

Labour Party. *The Sky's The Limit! Plain Words on Plane Profits*. London, c. 1934.

———. *Who's Who in Arms*. London, 1935.

Langdon-Davies, John. *Air Raid: The Technique of Silent Approach, High Explosive, Panic*. London: George Routledge and Sons, 1938.

Laski, Harold J. *The Labour Party, The War and the Future*. London: Labour Party Publications, 1939.

Le Corbusier. *Aircraft*. London: The Studio Ltd., 1935.

Leavis, F.R. *Mass Civilization and Minority Culture (Minority Pamphlets no. 1)*. Cambridge, 1930.

Left Book Club. *This Month's Book A.R.P.* London: Victor Gollancz, 1938.

Lehmann, John, Jackson, T.A. and Day Lewis, C. (eds). *Ralph Fox: A Writer In Arms*. London: Lawrence and Wishart, 1937.

Lehmann-Russbuett, Otto. *Germany's Air Force (With an Introduction by Wickham Steed and an Appendix)*. London: Allen and Unwin, 1935.

Liddell Hart, B.H. *Paris or the Future of War*. New York, NY. E.P. Dutton and Company, 1925.

————. *When Britain Goes to War: Adaptability and Mobility.* 2nd edn. London: Faber and Faber, 1935.

Liepmann, Heinz. *Death From the Skies: A Study of Gas and Microbial Warfare.* London: Martin Secker and Warburg, Ltd., 1937.

Lindsay, Jack. *England, My England.* London: Fore Publications, 1939.

Lindsay, Jack and Edgell Rickword. *A Handbook of Freedom: A Record of English Democracy Through Twelve Centuries.* London: Lawrence and Wishart, 1939.

Marquess of Londonderry. *Wings of Destiny.* London: MacMillan, 1943.

'Martian.' *A.R.P.: A Reply to Professor J.B.S. Haldane, F.R.S., The Royal Institute of British Architects and Some Others, Including the British Government.* London: John Bale, Sons and Curnow, Ltd, 1938.

Morison, Frank. *War on Great Cities: A Study of the Facts.* London: Faber and Faber Ltd., c. 1937.

Morton, A.L. *A People's History of England.* London: Victor Gollancz, 1938.

Noel-Baker, Philip. *Hawkers of Death: The Private Manufacture and Trade in Arms.* London, 1935.

Office of the Lord Privy Seal, *Air Raid Shelters: Report of the Lord Privy Seal's Conference.* London: HMSO, 1939.

O'Dell Pierce, W. *Air War: Its Technical and Social Aspects.* London: Watts and Co, 1937.

Orwell, George. *Keep the Aspidistra Flying.* London: Victor Gollancz, 1936.

————. *Homage to Catalonia.* London: Secker and Warburg, 1938.

————. *Coming up for Air.* London: Victor Gollancz, 1939.

————. *The Lion and the Unicorn: Socialism and the English Genius.* London: Secker and Warburg, 1941.

Orwell, George. Peter Davison, (ed) *Orwell in Spain: The Full Text of Homage to Catalonia with Associated Articles, Reviews and Letters from the Complete Works of George Orwell.* London: Penguin, 2001.

Peace Pledge Union. *Are You Prepared to Support or Sanction Another War?* London, 1937.

Pickett, F.N. *Don't Be Afraid of Poison Gas: Hints for Civilians in the event of a Poison Gas Attack.* London: Simpkin Marshall Ltd., 1934.

Pollitt, Harry. *I Accuse Baldwin.* London, c. 1938.

Pratt, J. Davidson. *Gas Defence.* London: British Science Guild, 1935.

Prentiss, Augustin M. *Chemicals in War: A Treatise on Chemical Warfare.* New York, NY: McGraw-Hill, 1937.

Priestley, J.B. *Postscripts.* London: William Heinemann, 1940.

De Purton MacRoberts, Noel. *ARP Lessons from Barcelona – Some Hints for Local Authorities and for the Private Citizen.* London: Eyre and Spottiswoode, 1938.

Rickword, Edgell. *War and Culture: The Decline of Culture Under Capitalism.* London, [n.d.].

————. *A Handbook of Freedom: A Record of English Democracy through Twelve Centuries.* London: Lawrence and Wishart, 1939.

Romilly, Esmond. *Boadilla.* London: Hamish Hamilton, 1937.

Viscount Rothermere. *Warnings and Predictions.* London: Eyre and Spottiswoode, 1939.

Rust, Bill. *Britons in Spain: The History of the XVth International Brigade.* London: Lawrence and Wishart, 1939.

Samuely, Felix James, et al. *Civil Protection: The Application of the Civil Defence Act and Other Government Requirements for Air Raid Shelters Etc.* London: Architectural Press, 1939.

Shirlaw, G.B. *Casualty: Training, Organisation and Administration of Civil Defence Casualty Services.* London: Secker and Warburg, 1940.

Simey, T.S. and Williams, Mary L. *The Civil Defence Acts, 1937 & 1939.* London: Charles Knight and Co. Ltd., 1939.

Sloan, Pat. *John Cornford: A Memoir.* London: Jonathan Cape, 1938.

Socialist Medical Association. *Gas Attacks: Is There any Protection?* London: Lawrence and Wishart, 1936.

Sommerfield, John. *Volunteer in Spain.* London: Lawrence and Wishart, 1937.

Spaight, J.M. *Air Power and the Cities.* London: Longmans Green, 1930.

———. *Air Power and the Next War.* London: Bles, 1938.

Steer, G.L. *The Tree of Gernika: A Field Study of Modern War.* London: Hodder and Stoughton Ltd, 1938.

Tecton Architects. *Planned ARP: Based on the Investigation of Structural Protection Against Air Attack in the Metropolitan Borough of Finsbury.* London: The Architectural Press, 1939.

Thuillier, Henry. *Gas in the Next War.* London: Geoffrey Bles, 1939.

Trustees of the British Museum. *Air Raid Precautions in Museums, Picture Galleries and Libraries.* London: British Museum, 1939.

Turner, C.C. *Britain's Air Peril: The Danger of Neglect, Together with Considerations on the Role of An Air Force.* London: Sir Isaac Pitman and Sons Ltd, [n.d.].

Waugh, Evelyn. *Put Out More Flags.* London: Chapman and Hall, 1942.

Wherry Anderson, B. *The Romance of Air-Fighting.* London: Cassel, 1917.

Wintringham, T.H. *Air Raid Warning! Why the Royal Air Force is to be Doubled.* London: The Workers' Bookshop, 1934.

———. *War! – And the Way to Fight Against It.* London: CPGB, [n.d. c. 1934].

———. *The Coming World War.* New York, NY: Thomas Seltzer, 1935.

———. *Armies of Freemen.* London: George Routledge and Sons, 1940.

———. *English Captain.* New York, NY: Harmondsworth, 1941.

Union of Democratic Control. *The Secret International: Armament Firms at Work.* London, 1932.

———. *An Exposure of the War Machine.* London, 1933.

———. *Poison Gas.* London, 1935.

Von Richthofen, Manfred Freiherr. *The Red Air Fighter: With Preface and Explanatory Notes by C.G. Grey.* London: The 'Aeroplane' and General Publishing Co., 1918.

Yates, E. Leighton. *A Christian Attitude Towards Air-Raid Precautions.* London: The Fellowship of Reconciliation, 1938.

Secondary Bibliography

Addison, Paul. *The Road to 1945: British Politics and the Second World War.* London: Cape, 1975.

Alexander, Bill. *British Volunteers for Liberty: Spain 1936–1939.* London: Lawrence and Wishart, 1982.

Allan, John. *Berthold Lubetkin: Architecture and the Tradition of Progress*. London: Royal Institute of British Architects, 1992.

Andrew, Christopher. *The Defence of the Realm: The Authorized History of MI5*. London: Allen Lane, 2009.

Arts Council of Great Britain. *Thirties: British Art and Design before the War*. London: Victoria and Albert Museum Committee, 1980.

Baker, John. *Enterprise Versus Bureaucracy: The Development of Structural Air-Raid Precautions During the Second World War*. Oxford: Pergamon, 1978.

Barnett, Correlli. *Britain and Her Army: A Military, Political and Social History of the British Army 1509–1970*. London: Cassell and Co., 1970.

———. *The Collapse of British Power*. London: Eyre Methuen, 1972.

———. *The Audit of War*. London: MacMillan, 1986.

Baxendale, John. *Priestley's England: J.B. Priestley and English Culture*. Manchester: Manchester University Press, 2007.

Baxendale, John and Christopher Pawling. *Narrating the Thirties: A Decade in the Making: 1930 to the Present*. London: MacMillan Press Limited, 1996.

Beevor, Anthony. *The Battle for Spain: The Spanish Civil War 1936–1939*. London: Weidenfeld and Nicolson, 2006.

Bell, Amy. 'Landscapes of fear: wartime London, 1939–1945.' *Journal of British Studies* IIL (January 2009), pp. 153–175.

Benewick, Robert. *The Fascist Movement in Britain*. London: Allen Lane, 1972 [1969].

Benson, Frederick R. *Writers in Arms: The Literary Impact of the Spanish Civil War*. New York, NY: New York University Press, 1967.

Bergonzi, Bernard. *Reading the Thirties: Texts and Contexts*. London: MacMillan Press, Ltd., 1978.

Peter Berresford, Ellis and Schofield, Jennifer. *Biggles! The Life Story of Captain W.E. Johns, Creator of Biggles, Worruls, Gimlet and Steeley*. London: Velcoe Publishing, 1993.

Bialer, Uri. *The Shadow of the Bomber: The Fear of Air Attack and British Politics, 1932–1939*. London: Royal Historical Society, 1980.

Biddle, Tami Davis. *Rhetoric and Reality in Air Warfare: The Evolution of British and American Ideas about Strategic Bombing, 1914–1945*. Princeton, NJ: Princeton University Press, 2002.

Blythe, Ronald. *The Age of Illusion: England in the Twenties and Thirties, 1919–1940*. London: Phoenix Press, 1963.

Bond, Brian. *British Military Policy Between the Two Wars*. Oxford: Oxford University Press, 1980.

Bourke, Joanna. *Fear: A Cultural History*. London: Virago, 2005.

———. 'Fear and anxiety: writing about emotion in history.' *History Workshop Journal* LV (Spring, 2003), pp. 111–133.

Boyle, Andrew. *Trenchard: Man of Vision*. London: Collins, 1962.

Branson, Noreen and Margot Heinemann. *Britain in the 1930s*. New York, NY: Praeger Publishers, 1971.

Brooke, Stephen. *Labour's War: The Labour Party during the Second World War*. Oxford: Clarendon Press, 1992.

Brown, Andrew. *J.D. Bernal: The Sage of Science*. Oxford: Oxford University Press, 2005.

Buchanan, Tom. *The Spanish Civil War and the British Labour Movement*. Cambridge: Cambridge University Press, 1991.
———. *Britain and the Spanish Civil War*. Cambridge: Cambridge University Press, 1997.
———. *The Impact of the Spanish Civil War on Britain: War, Loss and Memory*. Brighton: Sussex Academic Press, 2007.
Budiansky, Stephen. *Air Power: The Men, Machines, and Ideas that Revolutionized War, From Kitty Hawk to Gulf War II*. New York, NY: Viking, 2004.
Calder, Angus. *The People's War*. London: Cape, 1969.
———. *The Myth of the Blitz*. London: Pimlico, 1992.
Calder, Angus and Sheridan, Dorothy (eds) *Speak for Yourself: A Mass-Observation Anthology, 1937–1949*. Oxford: Oxford University Press, 1985.
Camden Arts Group. *Hampstead in the Thirties: A Committed Decade*. London: Camden Arts Council, 1974.
Carroll, Stuart (ed). *Cultures of Violence: Interpersonal Violence in Historical Perspective*. London: Palgrave Macmillan, 2007.
Cavarero, Adriana and McCuaig, William (trans) *Horrorism: Naming Contemporary Violence*. New York, NY: Columbia University Press, 2009.
Ceadel, Martin. *Pacifism in Britain 1914–1945: The Defining of a Faith*. Oxford: Clarendon Press, 1980.
———. *Semi-Detached Idealists: The British Peace Movement and International Relations, 1854–1945*. Oxford: Oxford University Press, 2000.
Clark, Jon, Heinemann, Margot, Margolies, David and Snee, Carole (eds) *Culture and Crisis in Britain in the Thirties*. London: Lawrence and Wishart, 1979.
Clark, Ronald. *J.B.S.: The Life and Work of J.B.S. Haldane*. Oxford: Oxford University Press, 1984.
Clarke, I.F. *Voices Prophesying War 1763–1984*. Oxford: Oxford University Press, 1966.
Cohen, Deborah. *The War Come Home: Disabled Veterans in Britain and Germany, 1914–1939*. Berkeley, CA: University of California Press, 2001.
Colley, Linda. *Britons: Forging the Nation, 1707–1837*. New Haven, CT: Yale University Press, 1992.
Collini, Stefan. *Public Moralists: Political Thought and Intellectual Life in Britain 1850–1930*. Oxford: Oxford University Press, 1993.
Collini, Stefan, Whatmore, Richard and Young, Brian (eds) *History, Religion, and Culture: British Intellectual History 1750–1950*. Cambridge: Cambridge University Press, 2000.
Colls, Robert and Dodd, Philip (eds) *Englishness: Politics and Culture 1880–1920*. London: Croom Helm, 1986.
Connelly, Mark. *Reaching for the Stars: A New History of Bomber Command in WWII*. London: IB Tauris, 2001.
Cook, Colin. 'A Fascist memory: Oswald Mosley and the myth of the airman.' *European Review of History*, IV, no. 2 (1997): 147–162.
Coombes, John E. *Writing from the Left: Socialism, Liberalism and the Popular Front*. New York, NY: Harvester Wheatsheaf, 1989.
Copsey, Nigel. *Anti-Fascism in Britain*. London: MacMillian Press, Ltd., 2000.
Cunningham, Hugh. 'The language of patriotism? 1750–1914.' *History Workshop Journal* XII (1981): 8–33.

Cunningham, Valentine, ed. *Spanish Front: Writers on the Civil War*. Oxford: Oxford University Press, 1986.

————. *British Writers of the Thirties*. Oxford: Oxford University Press, 1989.

Dean, David. *The Thirties: Recalling the English Architectural Scene*. London: RIBA Drawings Series, 1983.

Deane, Patrick (ed) *History in Our Hands: A Critical Anthology of Writings on Literature, Culture and Politics from the 1930s*. London: Leicester University Press, 1998.

Donoughue, Bernard and Jones, G.W. *Herbert Morrison: Portrait of a Politician*. London: Weidenfeld and Nicolson, 1973.

Duncan, Campbell. *War Plan UK: The Truth About Civil Defence in Britain*. London: Burnett Books, 1982.

Edgerton, David. *England and the Aeroplane: An Essay on a Militant and Technological Nation*. London: MacMillan, 1991.

————. 'Science and the nation: Towards new histories of twentieth-century Britain.' *Historical Research*, LXXVIII, no. 199 (February 2005): 96–112.

————. *Warfare State: Britain, 1920–1970*. Cambridge: Cambridge University Press, 2006.

————. *Britain's War Machine: Weapons, Resources and Experts in the Second World War*. London: Allen Lane, 2011.

Faulks, Sebastian. *The Fatal Englishman: Three Short Lives*. London: Hutchinson, 1996.

Fernbach, David. 'Tom Wintringham and socialist defense strategy.' *History Workshop Journal*, XIV (1982): 63–91.

Fielding, Steven. 'What did 'The People' want?: The meaning of the 1945 general election.' *The Historical Journal*, XXXV, no. 3 (1992): 623–639.

Fielding, Steven, Peter Thompson and Nick Tiratsoo. *'England Arise!': The Labour Party and Popular Politics in 1940s Britain*. Manchester: Manchester University Press, 1995.

Fishman, Robert. *Urban Utopias in the Twentieth Century: Ebenezer Howard, Frank Lloyd Wright, and Le Corbusier*. New York, NY: Basic Books, Inc., 1977.

Ford, Hugh. *A Poets' War: British Poets and the Spanish Civil War*. Philadelphia, IL: University of Pennsylvania Press, 1965.

Francis, Martin. *The Flyer: British Culture and the Royal Air Force, 1939–1945*. Oxford: Oxford University Press, 2008.

————. 'Tears, tantrums, and bared teeth: The emotional economy of three Conservative prime ministers, 1951–1963.' *Journal of British Studies* XXXXI, no. 3 (2002): 354–387.

French, David. *The British Way in Warfare, 1688–2000*. London: Unwin Hyman, 1990.

Friedrich, Jörg. *The Fire: The Bombing of Germany, 1940–1945*. New York, NY: Columbia University Press, 2008.

Fritzsche, Peter. *A Nation of Fliers: German Aviation and the Popular Imagination*. Cambridge, MS: Harvard University Press, 1994.

Fussell, Paul. *The Great War in Modern Memory*. Oxford: Oxford University Press, 1975.

————. *Abroad: British Literary Travelling Between the Wars*. Oxford: Oxford University Press, 1980.

Fyrth, Jim (ed). *Britain, Fascism and the Popular Front.* London: Lawrence and Wishart, 1985.

Gardiner, Juliet. *Wartime Britain: 1939–1945.* London: Headline Book Publishing, 2004.

———. *The Blitz: The British Under Attack.* London: HarperPress, 2010.

———. *The Thirties: An Intimate History.* London: HarperPress, 2010.

Gardner, Dan. *Risk: The Science and Politics of Fear.* Toronto: McClelland and Stewart, 2008.

Gat, Azar. *Fascist and Liberal Visions of War: Fuller, Liddell Hart, Douhet, and Other Modernists.* Oxford: Clarendon Press, 1998.

Girard, Marion. *A Strange and Formidable Weapon: British Responses to World War I Poison Gas.* Lincoln, Nebraska, NE: University of Nebraska Press, 2008.

Gloster, David. 'Architecture and the air raid: Shelter technologies and the British government 1938–44.' MsC. Imperial College, London, 1997.

Gloversmith, Frank (ed). *Class, Culture and Social Change: A New View of the 1930s.* Sussex: The Harvester Press, 1980.

Goldsmith, Maurice. *Sage: A Life of J.D. Bernal.* London: Hutchinson, 1980.

Goldstein, Laurence. *The Flying Machine and Modern Literature.* London: MacMillan, 1986.

Gooch, John. *The Prospect of War; Studies in British Defence Policy, 1847–1942.* London: Frank Cass, 1981.

Grainger, J.H. *Patriotisms: Britain 1900–1939.* London: Routledge and Keegan Paul, 1986.

Grayling, A.C. *Among the Dead Cities: Was the Allied Bombing of Civilians in WWII a Necessity or a Crime?* London: Bloomsbury, 2006.

Grayzel, Susan. *At Home and Under Fire: Air Raids and Culture in Britain from the Great War to the Blitz.* Cambridge: Cambridge University Press, 2012.

Gregg, John. *The Shelter of The Tubes: Tube Sheltering in London.* Harrow Weald: Capital Transport Publishing, 2001.

Griffiths, Richard. *Fellow Travelers of the Right: British Enthusiasts for Nazi Germany, 1933–9.* London: Constable, 1980.

Haapamaki, Michele. 'Writers in arms and the Just War: The Spanish Civil War, literary activism, and Leftist masculinity.' *Left History* X/2 (Fall 2005): 33–52.

Haber, F.L. *The Poisonous Cloud: Chemical Warfare in the First World War.* Oxford: Clarendon Press, 1986.

Hammond, James W., Jr. *Poison Gas: The Myth Versus Reality.* Westport, Connecticut: Greenwood Press, 1999.

Harris, Robert and Jeremy Paxman. *A Higher Form of Killing: The Secret Story of Gas and Germ Warfare.* London: Chatto and Windus, 1982.

Harrison, Mark (ed). *The Economics of WWII: Six Powers in International Comparison.* Cambridge: Cambridge University Press, 1998.

Hattersley, Roy. *The Edwardians.* London: Little, Brown, 2004.

———. *Borrowed Time: The Story of Britain Between the Wars.* London: Little, Brown, 2007.

Heater, Derek. *Citizenship: The Civic Ideal in World History, Politics and Education.* 3rd edn. Manchester: University of Manchester Press, 2004.

Himmelfarb, Gertrude. *Poverty and Compassion: The Moral Imagination of the Late Victorians.* New York, NY: Knopf, 1991.

Hinton, James. *Protests and Visions: Peace Politics in 20ᵗʰ Century Britain*. London: Hutchinson Radius, 1989.

———. 'Voluntarism versus Jacobinism; labor, nation, and citizenship in Britain, 1850–1950.' *International Labour and Working-Class History* IIL (Fall 1995): 68–90.

———. *Women, Social Leadership, and the Second World War: Continuities of Class*. Oxford: Oxford University Press, 2002.

———. *Nine Wartime Lives: Mass Observation and the Making of the Modern Self*. Oxford: Oxford University Press, 2010.

Hoare, Samuel. *Nine Troubled Years*. London: Collins, 1954.

Hodges, Sheila. *Gollancz: The Story of a Publishing House 1928–1978*. London: Victor Gollancz, 1978.

Holman, Brett. 'World Police for World Peace: British Internationalism and the Threat of a Knock-Out Blow from the Air, 1919–1945.' *War in History* XVII/3 (2010): 313–332.

Hopkins, James K. *Into the Heart of the Fire: The British in the Spanish Civil War*. Stanford, CA: Stanford University Press, 1998.

Howkins, Alun. *Reshaping Rural England: A Social History 1850–1925*. London: Routledge, 1991.

Hyde, H. Montgomery. *British Air Policy Between the Wars 1918–1939*. London: Heinemann, 1976.

Hynes, Samuel. *A War Imagined: the First World War and English Culture*. London: The Bodley Head, 1990.

Imperial War Museum. *The Spanish Civil War Collection: Sound Archive Oral History Recordings*. London: Trustees of the Imperial War Museum, 1996.

Jackson, Andrew. 'The politics of architecture: English architecture 1929–1951.' *The Journal of the Society of Architectural Historians* XXIV/1 (March 1965): 97–107.

———. *The Politics of Architecture: A History of Modern Architecture in Britain*. London: The Architectural Press, 1970.

Jackson, Angela. *British Women and the Spanish Civil War*. London and New York, NY: Routledge, 2002.

James, Thurston. 'Charles Grey and his pungent pen: personal recollections of a great aeronautical journalist.' *Journal of the Royal Aeronautical Society* LXXIII/706 (October 1969): 839–52.

Jones, Helen. *British Civilians in the Front Line: Air Raids, Productivity and Wartime Culture, 1939–45*. Manchester: Manchester University Press, 2006.

Jones, Neville. *The Beginnings of Strategic Air Power: A History of the British Bomber Force 1923–1939*. London: Frank Cass, 1987.

Jones, Peter. *Ove Arup: Masterbuilder of the Twentieth Century*. New Haven, CT: Yale University Press, 2006.

Kershaw, Ian. *Making Friends with Hitler: Lord Londonderry, the Nazis and the Road to World War II*. New York, NY: The Penguin Press, 2004.

Kier, Elizabeth. *Imagining War: French and British Military Doctrine Between the Wars*. Princeton, NJ: Princeton University Press, 1997.

Kumar, Krishan. *The Making of English National Identity*. Cambridge: Cambridge University Press, 2003.

Laity, Paul (ed). *Left Book Club Anthology*. London: Victor Gollancz, 2001.

Larios, Jose. *Combat Over Spain: Memoirs of a Nationalist Fighter Pilot, 1936–1939*. London: Neville Spearman, 1968.
Larrazábal, Jesús Salas. (M.A. Kelley, trans, D. Mondey, ed). *Air War Over Spain*. London: Ian Allen Ltd., 1969.
Lawrence, Christopher and Mayer, Anna K., eds. *Regenerating England: Science, Medicine and Culture in Inter-war Britain*. Amsterdam: Rodopi, 2000.
Lawrence, T.E. (D. Garnett, ed). *Letters of T.E. Lawrence*. London: World Books, 1938.
Laybourn, Keith. *The Rise of Socialism in Britain: c. 1881–1951*. Phoenix Mill: Sutton Publishing, 1997.
Lehmann, John. *Whispering Gallery: Autobiography I*. London: Longmans Green, 1955.
Light, Alison. *Femininity, Literature and Conservatism between the Wars*. London and New York, NY: Routledge, 1991.
Lowry, Bernard. *British Home Defences, 1940–1945*. Oxford: Osprey, 2004.
Lucas, John. *The Radical Twenties: Writing, Politics and Culture*. New Brunswick, NJ: Rutgers University Press, 1999.
Luckin, Bill. *Questions of Power: Electricity and Environment in Inter-War Britain*. Manchester: Manchester University Press, 1990.
Lutman, Stephen. 'Orwell's patriotism.' *Journal of Contemporary History* II/2 (1967): 149–58.
MacDougall, Ian (ed). *Voices from the Spanish Civil War: Personal Recollections of Scottish Volunteers in Republican Spain 1936–9*. Edinburgh: Polygon, 1986.
MacNeice, Louis. *The Strings are False: An Unfinished Autobiography*. London: Faber and Faber, 1965.
McKibbin, Ross. *Classes and Cultures: England, 1918–1951*. Oxford: Oxford University Press, 1998.
Mackay, Robert. *Half the Battle: Civilian Morale in Britain during the Second World War*. Manchester: Manchester University Press, 2001.
Mandler, Peter. 'Against 'Englishness': English culture and the limits to rural nostalgia, 1850–1940.' *Transactions of the Royal Historical Society*. 6th Series, VII (1997): 155–175.
———. *The English National Character: The History of an Idea from Edmund Burke to Tony Blair*. New Haven, CT: Yale University Press, 2006.
Matless, David. *Landscape and Englishness*. London: Reaktion Books Ltd., 1998.
Matthew, H.C.G. and Harrison, B. (eds) *Oxford Dictionary of National Biography*. Oxford: Oxford University Press, 2004. Online ed., edited by Lawrence Goldman, May 2006.
Meisel, Joseph S. 'Air Raid shelter policy and its critics in Britain before the Second World War.' *Twentieth Century British History*, V/3 (1994): 300–319.
Middelboe, Penelope, Fry, Donald and Grace, Christopher (eds) *We Shall Never Surrender: Wartime Diaries 1939–1945*. London: MacMillan, 2011.
Miles, Peter and Malcolm Smith. *Cinema, Literature and Society: Elite and Mass Culture in Interwar Britain*. London: Croom Helm, 1987.
Miles, Wyndham D. 'The idea of chemical warfare in modern times.' *Journal of the History of Ideas*, XXXI/2 (April–June 1970): 297–304.
Millman, Brock. 'British home defence planning and civil dissent, 1917–1918.' *War in History*, V/2 (April 1998): 204–232.
Mitchinson, Naomi. *You May Well Ask: A Memoir*. London: Flamingo, 1979.

Mitford, Deborah, Duchess of Devonshire. *Wait for Me! Memoirs*. New York, NY: Farra, Straus and Giroux, 2010.

Morgan, Kevin. *Against Fascism and War: Raptures and Continuities in Britain Communist Politics 1935–41*. Manchester: Manchester University Press, 1989.

Morgan, Marjorie. *National Identities and Travel in Victorian Britain*. New York, NY: Palgrave, 2001.

Morris, A.J.A. *The Scaremongers: The Advocacy of War and Rearmament 1896–1914*. London: Routledge and Keegan Paul, 1984.

Morrison, Herbert. *Herbert Morrison: An Autobiography by Lord Morrison of Lambeth*. London: Odhams Press, 1960.

Morrow, John H. *The Great War in the Air*. Washington, WA: Smithsonian Institution Press, 1993.

Neillands, Robin. *The Bomber War: Arthur Harris and the Allied Bomber Offensive 1939–1945*. London: John Murray, 2001.

Newbery, Charles Allen (ed) F. Peter Woodford, transcribed and annotated by Robin Woolven. *Wartime St. Pancras: A London Borough Defends Itself*. Camden: Camden History Society, 2006.

Noakes, Lucy. *War and the British: Gender, Memory and National Identity*. London: I.B. Tauris, 1998.

O'Brien, Terence. *Civil Defence*. London: HMSO, 1955.

Omissi, David E. *Air Power and Colonial Control, The Royal Air Force, 1919–1939*. Manchester: University of Manchester Press, 1990.

Overy, Richard. *The Morbid Age: Britain Between the Wars*. London: Allen Lane, 2009.

Panchasi, Roxanne. *Future Tense: The Culture of Anticipation in France Between the Wars*. Ithaca, NY: Cornell University Press, 2009.

Paris, Michael. *Winged Warfare: The Literature and Theory of Aerial Warfare in Britain, 1857–1917*. Manchester: Manchester University Press, 1992.

———. *Warrior Nation: Images of War in British Popular Culture*. London: Reaktion Books, 1999.

Patterson, Ian. *Guernica and Total War*. Cambridge, MS: Harvard University, 2007.

Peattie, Mark, Drea, Edward J. and van de Ven, Hans (eds) *The Battle for China: Essays on the Military History of the Sino-Japanese War of 1937–1945*. Stanford, CA: Stanford University Press, 2011.

Pedersen, Susan. *Family, Dependence, and the Origins of the Welfare State in Britain and France, 1914–1945*. Cambridge: Cambridge University Press, 1993.

Pedersen, Susan and Mandler, Peter (eds) *After the Victorians: Private Conscience and Public Duty in Modern Britain: Essays in Memory of John Clive*. London: Routledge, 1994.

Penrose, Harald. *British Aviation: The Adventuring Years 1920–1929*. London: Putnam, 1973.

———. *British Aviation: The Ominous Skies 1935–1939*. London: HMSO, 1980.

Pick, Daniel. *War Machine: The Rationalization of Slaughter in the Modern Age*. New Haven, CT: Yale University Press, 1993.

Pidgeon, Nick, Kasperson, Roger E. and Slovic, Paul (eds). *The Social Amplification of Risk*. Cambridge: Cambridge University Press, 2003.

Pike, David L. *Subterranean Cities: The World Beneath Paris and London, 1800–1945*. Ithaca, NY: Cornell University Press, 2005.

Pimlott, Ben. *Labour and the Left in the 1930s*. Cambridge: Cambridge University Press, 1977.

Plamper, Jan. 'The History of Emotions: An Interview with William Reddy, Barbara Rosenwein, and Peter Stearns.' *History and Theory* IL (May 2010): 237–265.

Powers, Alan. *Serge Chermayeff: Designer, Architect, Teacher*. London: RIBA Publications, 2001.

Powers, Barry D. *Strategy Without Slide-Rule: British Air Strategy 1914–1939*. London: Croom Helm, 1976.

Preston, Paul. *The Spanish Civil War: Reaction, Revolution and Revenge*. New York, NY: W.W. Norton and Co, 2007.

Price, Richard M. *The Chemical Weapons Taboo*. Ithaca, NY: Cornell University Press, 1997.

Pugh, Martin. *'Hurrah for the Blackshirts!': Fascists and Fascism in Britain Between the Wars*. London: Jonathan Cape, 2005.

———. *'We Danced All Night': A Social History of Britain Between the Wars*. London: The Bodley Head, 2008.

Rattigan, Neil. *This is England: British Film and the People's War, 1939–1945*. London: Associated University Press, 2001.

Reading, Malcolm and Peter Coe. *Lubetkin & Tecton: An Architectural Study*. London: Triangle Architectural Publishing, 1992.

Reddy, William. *The Navigation of Feeling: A Framework for the History of Emotions*. Cambridge: Cambridge University Press, 2001.

Reid, Brian Holden. *J.F.C. Fuller: Military Thinker*. London: MacMillan, 1987.

Richter, Donald. *Chemical Soldiers: British Gas Warfare in World War I*. Lawrence, Kansas, KS: University Press of Kansas, 1992.

Roberts, Edwin A. *The Anglo-Marxists: A Study in Ideology and Culture*. Lanham, MD: Rowan and Littlefield, 1997.

Robertson, Linda R. *The Dream of Civilized Warfare: World War I Flying Aces and the American Imagination*. Minneapolis, MN: University of Minnesota Press, 2003.

Robertson, Scot. *The Development of RAF Strategic Bombing Doctrine, 1919–1939*. London: Praeger, 1995.

Robin, Corey. *Fear: The History of a Political Idea*. Oxford: Oxford University Press, 2004.

Romani, Robert. *National Character and Public Spirit in Britain and France, 1750–1914*. Cambridge: Cambridge University Press, 2002.

Roper, Michael. 'Between Manliness and Masculinity: The 'War Generation' and the Psychology of Fear in Britain, 1914–1950.' *Journal of British Studies* XXXXIV (April 2006): 343–362.

Rose, Alexander. 'Radar and air defence in the 1930s.' *Twentieth Century British History*, IX/2 (1998): 219–245.

Rose, Sonya O. *Which People's War? National Identity and Citizenship in Britain 1939 1945*. Oxford: Oxford University Press, 2003.

Satia, Priya. 'The defense of inhumanity: Air control and the British idea of Arabia.' *American Historical Review*, III (2006): 16–51.

———. *Spies in Arabia: The Great War and the Cultural Foundations of Britain's Covert Empire in the Middle East*. Oxford: Oxford University Press, 2008.

Shelmerdine, Brian. *British Representations of the Spanish Civil War*. Manchester: Manchester University Press, 2006.

Sherry, Michael S. *The Rise of American Air Power: The Creation of Armageddon.* New Haven, CT: Yale University Press, 1987.

Singer, P.W. *Wired for War: The Robotics Revolution and Conflict in the Twenty-first Century.* New York, NY: The Penguin Press, 2009.

Simer, Christopher Joel. 'Apocalyptic visions: Fear of aerial attack in Britain, 1920– 1938', PhD diss., University of Minnesota, 1999.

Skidelsky, Robert. *Oswald Mosley.* New York, NY: Holt Rinehart and Winston, 1975.

Smith, Malcolm. "A matter of faith': British strategic air doctrine before 1939.' *Journal of Contemporary History,* XV (1980): 423–442.

———. *British Air Strategy Between the Wars.* Oxford: Clarendon, 1984.

Spiers, Edward M. *Chemical Warfare.* Urbana and Chicago, IL: University of Illinois Press, 1986.

Stansky, Peter and William Abrahams. *Journey to the Frontier: Julian Bell and John Cornford: Their Lives and the 1930s.* London: Constable, 1966.

Stapleton, Julia. 'Citizenship versus patriotism in twentieth-century England.' *The Historical Journal* IIL/1 (2005): 151–178.

Stradling, Robert. *History and Legend: Writing the International Brigades.* Cardiff: University of Wales Press, 2003.

Swann, Brenda and Francis Aprahamian, eds. *J.D. Bernal: A Life in Science and Politics.* London: Verso, 1999.

Taylor, Miles. 'Patriotism, history, and the Left in twentieth-century Britain.' *The Historical Journal,* XXXIII/4 (1990): 971–987.

Thompson, E.P. *Customs in Common.* New York, NY: The New Press, 1993.

Thorpe, Andrew. *Britain in the 1930s: The Deceptive Decade.* Oxford: Blackwell, 1992.

Terraine, John. *The Right of the Line: The Royal Air Force in the European War 1939 1945.* London: Hodder and Stoughton, 1985.

Titmuss, Richard. *Problems of Social Policy.* London: HMSO, 1950.

Torrie, Julia. *For Their Own Good: Civilian Evacuations in France and Germany.* New York, NY: Berghahn Books, 2010.

Vilensky, Joel A. *Dew of Death: The Story of Lewisite, America's World War I Weapon of Mass Destruction.* Bloomington and Indianapolis, IN: Indiana University Press, 2005.

Ward, Paul. *Red Flag and Union Jack: Englishness, Patriotism and the British Left, 1881–1924.* Suffolk: The Boydell Press, 1998.

———. Paul Ward, *Britishness Since 1870.* London: Routledge, 2004.

Werskey, Gary. *The Visible College.* London: Allen Lane, 1978.

———. 'The Visible College Revisited: Second Opinions on the Red Scientists of the 1930s.' *Minerva* VL (2007): 305–319.

Weintraub, Stanley. *The Last Great Cause: The Intellectuals and the Spanish Civil War.* New York, NY: Weybright and Talley, 1968.

Wheeler-Bennett, John W. *John Anderson: Viscount Waverly.* London: MacMillan and Co. Ltd, 1962.

Williams, A. Susan. *Ladies of Influence: Women of the Elite in Interwar Britain.* London: Allen Lane, 2000.

Williams, Rosalind. *Notes on the Underground: An Essay on Technology, Society, and the Imagination.* Cambridge, MA: The MIT Press, 1990.

Wilson, Jeremy. *Lawrence of Arabia.* London: Heinemann, 1989.

Wohl, Robert. *The Spectacle of Flight: Aviation and the Western Imagination: 1920 1950*. New Haven, CT: Yale University Press, 2005.

Wood, Neal. *Communism and British Intellectuals*. New York, NY: Columbia University Press, 1959.

Woolven, Robin. 'Air Raid Precautions in St. Pancras, 1935–45: The Borough against the German Air Force.' *Camden History Review*, XVI (1989): 20–5.

———. 'London, Munich, and ARP.' *Journal of the Royal United Services Institute*, XXXXIII (1998): 54–8.

———. 'Playing Hitler's game from Fitzroy Road NW1: JBS Haldane, the St Pancras Branch of the Communist Party, and deep-shelter agitation.' *Camden History Review*, XXIII (1999): 22–5.

———. 'First in the country: Dr Richard Tee and Air Raid Precautions.' *Hackney History*, VI (2000): 50–8.

———. 'Civil defence in London 1935–1945: The formation and implementation of the policy for, and the performance of, the A.R.P. (later C.D.) services in London', PhD diss., University of London, 2002.

Ziegler, Philip. *London at War, 1939–1945*. London: Sinclair-Stevenson, 1995.

INDEX